5th Workshop on Narrative Understanding (wnu2023)

Toronto, Canada
14 July 2023

ISBN: 978-1-7138-8238-1

Printed from e-media with permission by:

Curran Associates, Inc.
57 Morehouse Lane
Red Hook, NY 12571

Some format issues inherent in the e-media version may also appear in this print version.

Printed with permission by Curran Associates, Inc. (2024)

Association for Computational Linguistics
209 N. Eighth Street
Stroudsburg, Pennsylvania 18360

Phone: 1-570-476-8006
Fax: 1-570-476-0860

acl@aclweb.org

Additional copies of this publication are available from:

Curran Associates, Inc.
57 Morehouse Lane
Red Hook, NY 12571 USA
Phone: 845-758-0400
Fax: 845-758-2633
Email: curran@proceedings.com
Web: www.proceedings.com

wnu2023 2023

The 5th Workshop on Narrative Understanding

Proceedings of the Workshop

July 14, 2023

Order copies of this and other ACL proceedings from:

Association for Computational Linguistics (ACL)
209 N. Eighth Street
Stroudsburg, PA 18360
USA
Tel: +1-570-476-8006
Fax: +1-570-476-0860
acl@aclweb.org

Introduction

Welcome to the 5th Workshop on Narrative Understanding!
This is the 5th iteration of the workshop, which brings together an interdisciplinary group of researchers from AI, ML, NLP, Computer Vision and other related fields, as well as scholars from the humanities to discuss methods to improve automatic narrative understanding capabilities. We are happy to present 13 papers on this topic (along with 6 non-archival papers to be presented only at the workshop). These papers explore and address a variety of challenges in the narrative understanding space. We would like to thank everyone who submitted their work to this workshop and the program committee for their helpful feedback. We would also like to thank our invited speakers for their participation in this workshop.
-Faeze, Elizabeth, Khyathi, Nader, Mohit, and Snigdha

Organizing Committee

Organizer

Nader Akoury
Elizabeth Clark
Mohit Iyyer
Snigdha Chaturvedi
Faeze Brahman
Khyathi Chandu

Program Committee

Chairs

Nader Akoury, University of Massachusetts Amherst
Faeze Brahman, Allen Institute for AI
Khyathi Raghavi Chandu, Allen Institute of AI
Snigdha Chaturvedi, University of North Carolina, Chapel Hill
Elizabeth Clark, Google Research
Mohit Iyyer, University of Massachusetts Amherst

Program Committee

Maria Antoniak, Allen Institute for Artificial Intelligence
Anneliese Brei, University of North Carolina at Chapel Hill
Marzena Karpinska, University of Massachusetts Amherst
Siyan Li, Stanford University
Vishakh Padmakumar, New York University
Rudolf Rosa, Charles University, Faculty of Mathematics and Physics, Institute of Formal and Applied Linguistics
Melanie Sclar, Paul G. Allen School of Computer Science & Engineering, University of Washington
Katherine Thai, University of Massachusetts Amherst
Bram Van Dijk, Leiden University
Anvesh Rao Vijjini, UNC Chapel Hill
Bingsheng Yao, Rensselaer Polytechnic Institute
Chao Zhao, University of North Carolina at Chapel Hill

Table of Contents

What's New?
Identifying the Unfolding of New Events in a Narrative

Seyed Mahed Mousavi[*], **Shohei Tanaka**[†,‡], **Gabriel Roccabruna**[*],
Koichiro Yoshino[†,‡], **Satoshi Nakamura**[‡], **Giuseppe Riccardi**[*]
[†]Guardian Robot Project, RIKEN, Japan
[‡]Nara Institute of Science and Technology, Japan
[*]Signals and Interactive Systems Lab, University of Trento, Italy
mahed.mousavi@unitn.it, giuseppe.riccardi@unitn.it

Abstract

Narratives include a rich source of events unfolding over time and context. Automatic understanding of these events provides a summarised comprehension of the narrative for further computation (such as reasoning). In this paper, we study the Information Status (IS) of the events and propose a novel challenging task: the automatic identification of *new* events in a narrative. We define an event as a triplet of subject, predicate, and object. The event is categorized as new with respect to the discourse context and whether it can be inferred through commonsense reasoning. We annotated a publicly available corpus of narratives with the new events at sentence level using human annotators. We present the annotation protocol and study the quality of the annotation and the difficulty of the task. We publish the annotated dataset, annotation materials, and machine learning baseline models for the task of new event extraction for narrative understanding.

1 Introduction

The task of narrative understanding is a challenging topic of research and has been studied in numerous domains (Piper et al., 2021; Sang et al., 2022). Recent studies include important applications of this task in supporting professionals in mental health. (Tammewar et al., 2020; Adler et al., 2016; Danieli et al., 2022). Automatic narrative understanding may provide a summarized comprehension of the users' recollections that can be used to engage in personal and grounded dialogues with the narrator. Narrative understanding has been approached in different ways (Kronenfeld, 1978; Chambers and Jurafsky, 2008; Kim and Klinger, 2018). A research direction in this field focuses on extracting the sequence of events that are mentioned in the narrative to obtain a summarized understanding of the whole narrative and its characters (Chen et al., 2021; Mousavi et al., 2021). In these works, the event is mostly represented by a predicate along with its corresponding subject and object dependencies. This definition relies on two assumptions a) the predicate represents an action/occurrence relation between the subject and the object dependencies; b) reoccurring characters across different events are the protagonists of the narrative.

There have been interesting studies on different aspects of events in a narrative such as linking the correlated events as a chain (Chambers and Jurafsky, 2008), learning semantic roles of participants (Chambers and Jurafsky, 2009), commonsense inference (Rashkin et al., 2018), and temporal common-sense reasoning (Zhou et al., 2019).

In order to obtain a concise and salient understanding of the narrative through the events, it is necessary to identify and select the events that relate to a new happening/participant in the narrative and have novel contributions. The process of recognizing a new event implicitly involves the event coreference resolution task, which consists of detecting the mentions of the same event throughout the content (Zeng et al., 2020). Essentially, an event that is referring to a previous event is not considered new. Nevertheless, even if an event appears in the narrative for the first time it might be part of commonsense knowledge, and thus not provide any new information.

In this paper, we address the problem of identifying new events as they unfold in the narrative. This task is inspired and motivated by the need to a) extract salient information in the narrative and position them with respect to the rest of the discourse events and relations, and b) acquire new events from a sequence of sentential units of narratives. This task can facilitate higher levels of computation and interaction such as reasoning, summarization, and human-machine dialogue. Last but not least, we believe this task is a novel and very challenging machine learning task to include in natural language understanding benchmarks.

Proceedings of the The 5th Workshop on Narrative Understanding, pages 1–10

We assess whether an event is new in a narrative according to their Information Status (IS) (Prince, 1988; Mann and Thompson, 1992). IS refers to whether a piece of information, which can be represented as an entity or other linguistic forms, is new or old. We consider an event new if it has not been previously observed in the context and provides novel information to the reader; that is, its information (the event and/or participants) is not presented priorly in the discourse stretch, and it can not be inferred through commonsense. For instance, *Bob **saw** Alice* is a new event if it is the first time that Alice is introduced in the narrative or the first time Bob saw her. However, once this event is selected as new, *Bob **looked at** Alice* will not be a new event anymore. Furthermore, if *Bob **married** Alice* is considered as a new event, *Alice **is** Bob's wife* can be inferred through commonsense and thus is not a new event. An example of new and old events is presented in Figure 1. While there are eight events in the narrative sentences, two of them do not represent any novel information and thus are not new.

For this purpose, we developed an unsupervised model to extract markable event candidates from the narratives. We parsed a publicly available dataset of narratives, SEND (Ong et al., 2021), and using the developed model, extracted all the markable events for each sentence. In the next step, we designed and conducted an annotation task using five human annotators to select the events in each sentence that are discourse-new with respect to the narrative context. In order to validate the annotation protocol and evaluate the results, we developed several neural and non-neural baselines for the task of new event extraction in both candidate-selection and sequence-tagging settings.

The contributions of this paper can be summarized as follows:

- We present the novel task of new event detection for narrative understanding along with its annotation methodology and evaluation.
- We present the annotated version of a public corpus of emotional narratives for the task of automatic detection of new events in a narrative.
  [1].
- We introduce several baseline benchmarks for the task of new event detection based on discourse heuristics and deep neural networks, in two different settings of candidate selection and sequence tagging.

[1]Link to our Repository

So uh during my childhood **I had two dogs;** **one was named Flash**, **one was named Fluff.**

I got them when I was three and around the age of eight, **we were moving to the US** from Guyana.

When we were living in the US, **we rented a house** for a short time and **my father bought a big sofa.**

Figure 1: An example of a narrative and the corresponding events. There are eight events in the sentences (highlighted), while six of them are presenting new information (bold) and the remaining two are referring to the already-mentioned events in the context (not bold).

2 Literature Review

Event Extraction The definition of the event concept has been the topic of study in different disciplines, originating in philosophy (Mourelatos, 1978). Early attempts to understand the semantics and structures of events in the text used hand-coded scripts with predefined slot frames to be filled by the values extracted from the text (Kronenfeld, 1978). This approach was later adopted by other works (Kim and Klinger, 2018; Ebner et al., 2020). Kim and Klinger (2018) consider the activation of emotions as an event and study such events through different properties such as cause, experiencer, target, etc. In this definition, not only verb phrases but also noun phrases and prepositional phrases that manifest an emotion in a narrative participant can represent events. (Ebner et al., 2020) studied the events and their participants by the verb-specific roles the participants can have (the arguments of the event "attack" are of types "attacker" and "target"). In this work, the authors formalized the event understanding as an argument-linking task.

To address the expensive nature of designing domain-specific frames, Chambers and Jurafsky (2008) proposed an unsupervised approach to extract the event chains in a narrative according to the linguistic structures of the narrative sentences. Based on the assumption that reoccurring participants among different events are the protagonists of the narrative, the authors defined an event in a sentence as a predicate (verb) and the verb dependencies including the protagonist. This work was complemented further by considering the role of the protagonists in each event and the neighboring events in order to obtain a schema (Chambers and Jurafsky, 2009).

Event-Centric Understanding There have been several studies on the application of event-centric narrative understanding. Mostafazadeh et al. (2016) studied the understanding of commonsense stories via event chain extraction model (Chambers and Jurafsky, 2008). Rashkin et al. (2018) conducted a task on inferring the next possible intents and reactions of the participants in a narrative based on the observed events through commonsense. Zhou et al. (2019) studied the application of temporal reasoning such as order/frequency of events in the narrative for the question-answering setting. Mousavi et al. (2021) extracted events in a personal narrative to construct the personal space of events and participants in the user's life as a graph.

Event Co-reference Resolution The event coreference resolution task is focused on identifying the events that refer to previously mentioned events in a context. Two events are considered identical if they share the same spatiotemporal location (Quine, 1985). Bejan and Harabagiu (2010) studied the detection of coreferential events by measuring the similarity among two events using lexical and semantic features. Zeng et al. (2020) proposed a model based on BERT pre-trained model (Devlin et al., 2019) to integrate event-specific paraphrases and argument-aware semantic embeddings for this task.

3 Definition of New Event

We introduce the task of identifying the new events in a narrative to obtain a distilled and concise representation of the whole narrative and its characters. We follow the definition of an event that was used by Chambers and Jurafsky (2008) based on the verb and its dependencies. That is, a verb is a core element of an event and supports the relation among its dependencies such as subject, object/oblique nominals which are considered as the participants of the event (Mousavi et al., 2021).

Prince (1988) defined the notion of old or new Information Status (IS) with respect to two aspects of the hearer's beliefs and the discourse model. New information according to the hearer's belief is the one that is assumed not to be already known for the hearer, while discourse-new information is the one that has not been mentioned or has not occurred priorly in the discourse-stretch (Prince, 1988). Nissim et al. (2004) adopts the IS concept and defines three categories of old, new, and mediated for the status of entities in a dialogue. The notion of old follows the definition provided by Prince (1988) closely. However, the authors define mediated as entities that have not been introduced directly in the context but are inferrable or generally known to the hearer; while the new category spans over entities that are not introduced priorly in the dialogue context, nor can they be inferred from the previously mentioned entities.

	Value
#Narratives (Train:Valid:Test)	193 (114:40:39)
#Subject (# female)	49 (30)
Avg. Narrative Len.	28.10 utterances
Avg. Utterance Len.	15.44 tokens
#Vocabulary	4,416 unique tokens

Table 1: The statistics of SEND dataset (Ong et al., 2021). The dataset is provided with official train, valid and test sets. The majority of narrators are female and each narrative consists of approximately 430 tokens on average.

We extend the definition of the new category in entities (Nissim et al., 2004) to events. We define new events as those that are not mentioned in the narrative context and can not be inferred through commonsense by the reader. In this work, we do not consider further distinctions such as old or mediated.

4 Annotation of New Event

4.1 Annotation Task Description

Narrative Dataset We conducted an annotation task for identifying the new events in narratives at the sentence level. The corpus used in this study is the SEND dataset (Ong et al., 2021), which is a collection of emotional narratives. The dataset consists of 193 narratives from 49 subjects, collected by asking each narrator to recount 3 most positive and 3 most negative experiences of her/his life. The statistics of the SEND dataset are presented in Table 1 (the train, valid, and test sets are the official splits).

Task Design To reduce the annotators' workload, we developed a baseline model inspired by Mousavi et al. (2021) to automatically parse and extract all event candidates for each sentence in the narrative as the triplets of (subject, predicate, object). In the cases where more than 5 candidates were extracted for a sentence, we created 5 clus-

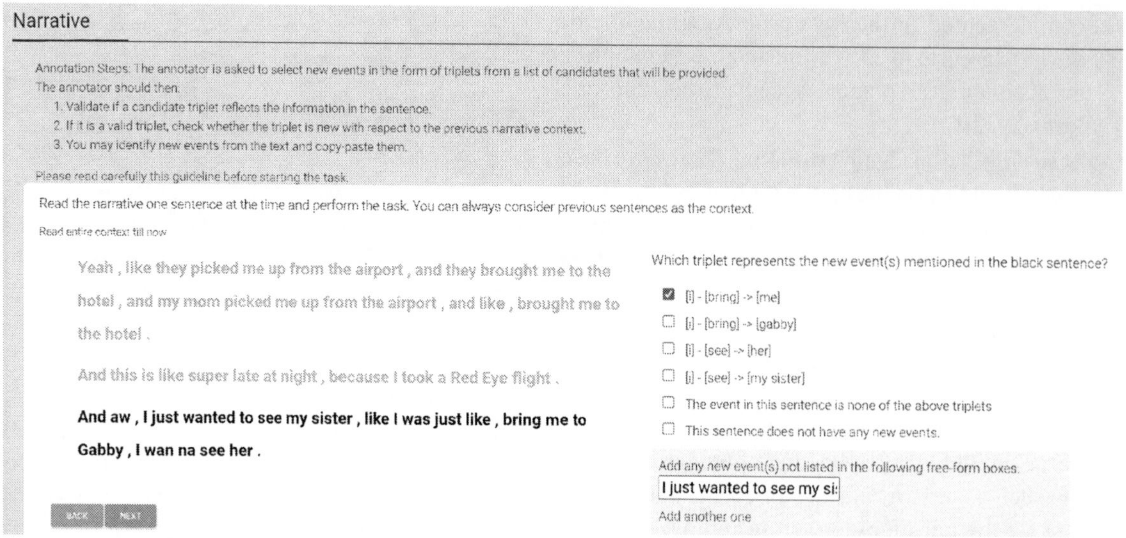

Figure 2: The user interface of the annotation platform. The annotator is presented with the narrative one sentence at a time on the left side of the screen. The event candidates and the option to add new events as free-from text are located on the right side of the interface. Moreover, a short version of the guidelines and the previous context of the narrative are shown to the annotator throughout the annotation.

ters using Levenshtein distance (Yujian and Bo, 2007) (hierarchical clustering) and the candidate with the most number of tokens in each cluster was selected to be presented to the annotator. We randomly sampled 21 narratives from the SEND dataset and reserved them as backup data (13 narratives from the train set, 4 from the valid set, and 4 from the test set). Using the extraction pipeline, we extracted all subject-predicate-object triplets as event candidates in the remaining 172 narratives at the sentence level.

Annotation UI The user interface (UI) of the annotation platform is presented in Figure 2. Throughout the task, the annotator is presented with a brief version of the task guidelines on the top of the display (with access to the complete version). The narrative is presented on the left side of the screen with the current sentence in black and the context in grey. The narrative is updated progressively sentence-by-sentence while the annotator has access to the previous sentences of the context. For each sentence, the annotation question, the list of the triplet candidates and the possibility to select and add continuous span from the text are presented on the right side.

Annotation Task During the task, the annotators were presented with a narrative one sentence at a time and the corresponding list of candidates. They were asked to control if any of the candidate triplets in the list is valid (i.e. it reflects the information in the sentence correctly); and whether it provides new information with respect to the previous narrative context, that can not be inferred through commonsense. In the case of valid and new information, the annotators were asked to select that candidate as a new event. Furthermore, if there were no candidates extracted for a sentence or the new information in a sentence was not presented as a valid candidate, the annotator was asked to add the new information by simply copying the segment that conveys it from the sentence and adding it as continuous span text.

Task Execution We recruited five annotators for the task of new event annotation. The annotators were non-native English speakers with certified English proficiency. After an introductory meeting with the annotators, they were asked to carry out the first qualification task which consisted of annotating one narrative, sampled from the valid set. The result of the first qualification batch was checked manually and a few refinements were made with the annotators. The annotators were then asked to perform a second qualification task using another narrative randomly sampled from the valid set. The Inter-Annotator Agreement (IAA) level during the two qualification tasks, which is presented in Table 2, indicates the improvement in the annotators' performance from one qualification batch to the other. The IAA for the event candidates is calculated using Krippendoff's α (Krippendorff,

Annotation Format	Qualifications First	Qualifications Second	Overall IAA
Selected Candidates	0.22	0.55	0.54
Added Spans	0.32	0.60	0.66

Table 2: Inter-Annotator Agreement (IAA) during the qualification tasks and over the whole annotation task. The results indicate an improvement in the performance of annotators from one qualification batch to the other. The IAA is computed for candidate selection and continuous span selection annotation using Krippendoff's α and the extension of Cohen's κ for segmentation agreement, respectively.

Sentence 1: So uh during my childhood I had two dogs; one was named Flash, one was named Fluff.

Candidates:
a. [i] - [had] -> [my childhood]
b. **[i] - [had] -> [two dogs]** ✔
c. **[one] - [was named] -> [fluff]** ✔
d. [i] - [so had] -> [two dogs]
e. **[one] - [was named] -> [flash]** ✔

Sentence 2: I got them when I was three and around the age of eight we were moving to the US from Guyana.

Candidates:
a. [i] - [got] -> [them]
b. **[we] - [were moving to] -> [the us]** ✔
c. [we] - [were moving to] -> [guyana]

Sentence 3: When we were living in the US, we rented a house for a short time and my father bought a big sofa.

Candidates:
a. [we] - [were living in] -> [the us]
b. **[we] - [rented] -> [a house]** ✔

Added Spans: ***my father bought a big sofa***

Figure 3: An example of sentences in a narrative and the corresponding events; while the baseline model has extracted various event candidates, only a few of them are valid and new events (bold). Furthermore, the baseline model has missed an event in the third sentence which is added as a span from the sentence.

Selected New Events as Candidates	
#Candidates selected	1536
Avg. candidates selected:	
per Sentence	0.57
per Narrative	9.0
per Narrator	31.4
%Candidates selected in:	
1st half of the Sentence	43%
2nd half of the Sentence	57%
1st half of the Narrative	55%
2nd half of the Narrative	45%
Added New Events as Continuous Spans	
#Spans added	2254
Avg. spans added:	
per Sentence	0.8
per Narrative	13.3
per Narrator	46.0
%Spans added in:	
1st half of the Sentence	38.1%
2nd half of the Sentence	61.9%
1st half of the Narrative	96.9%
2nd half of the Narrative	3.1%

Table 3: The statistics of the annotated dataset. While only 1536 extracted candidates (out of 6938, thus 22%) were selected as new events, 2254 new events were added by the annotators as continuous span text. Moreover, almost all of the continuous span events appear in the first half of the narrative, while event candidates have a quite normal distribution.

2011), while the IAA for the continuous span text is calculated by the extension of Cohen's κ for segmentation agreement (Fournier and Inkpen, 2012), averaged among all annotators. The remaining 170 narratives were divided into 11 batches. In each batch, one narrative was annotated by all annotators for the purpose of continuous quality control of the results, while the rest was equally divided among the annotators. To prevent unreliable and biased agreements, all 11 overlapping narratives were from different narrators.

4.2 Annotation Result Evaluation

We annotated the dataset of personal narratives, SEND (Ong et al., 2021), with new events in the sentence level by five human judges. An example of the annotation results is presented in Figure 3. While the baseline model has extracted various possible event candidates from the sentence, only a few of them are **valid** events that are representing ***new*** information. Moreover, the model has failed to extract an event in the third sentence which is added as a span from the text.

Throughout the task, the IAA level on the overlapping narratives was computed to ensure a consistent annotation quality. We observed negligible fluctuations in the IAA level during the task (<0.9 for Krippendoff's α), except for one batch; for which the low-quality contributions were detected and refinements were made with one annotator. The overall IAA level of the annotated dataset is presented in Table 2. The results are close to the level obtained in the second qualification batch.

The statistics of the annotated dataset, presented in Table 3, indicate that the majority of the annotated events were added as continuous span text and were not extracted by the baseline model. Moreover, while the event candidates appear in the nar-

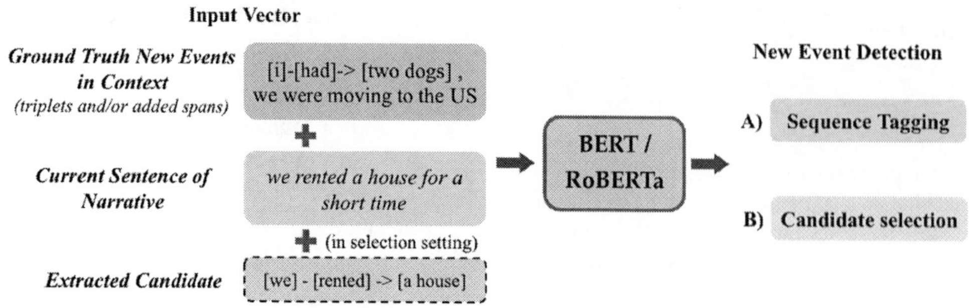

Figure 4: The neural baselines for the task of new event detection. The input vector consists of the new events in the context (ground truth) and the current sentence. In the candidate selection setting, the input vector includes the extracted candidate as an additional segment as well. The model encodes the input vector and outputs either a) a sequence of tags, corresponding to the tokens in the sentence; or b) a binary decision to categorize the candidate as new or not.

	Prec.	Rec.	F1
Random	24.0	29.2	26.3
Binary	22.8	49.4	31.2
First Candidate	27.7	33.7	30.4
Last Candidate	30.1	36.7	33.1
New Subject	24.6	28.6	26.5
New Entity	25.1	88.9	39.1
BERT	35.6	51.1	41.6
RoBERTa	40.4	83.1	**54.3**

Table 4: The results of the new event candidate selection baselines. The performance of the neural models is averaged over 10 runs.

rative with an approximately uniform distribution, almost all of the continuous span events are located in the first half of the narrative. This result is in line with the definition of new events since the events mentioned before in the context are "old" events. Nevertheless, in both cases of candidate events and continuous span events, we observe that the second halves of the sentences contain more information than the other half, indicating that the narrators tend to mention the new events at the end of the sentence.

5 Baselines for New Event Detection

We developed neural and non-neural baselines to validate the outcome of the annotation task, and, as baselines for the novel task of new event detection in a narrative. Considering the two annotation formats of selecting candidates and adding continuous spans, we formalize the task using two settings of candidate selection and sequence tagging.

5.1 Candidate Selection Baselines

The first group of models is tasked to select the new events from the candidates extracted by our baseline model. The rule-based models are:

- **Random Selector**: for each sentence and its event candidates, it randomly picks one candidate as the new event in the sentence.
- **Binary Selector**: for each of the event candidates of a sentence, it randomly decides whether it is a new event or not. Thus, each candidate has a 50% chance of being selected as a new event.
- **First Candidate Selector**: that selects the first event candidate that is extracted for a sentence as the new event.
- **Last Candidate Selector**: which selects the last event candidate that is extracted for a sentence as the new event for the sentence.
- **New Subject Selector**: which selects the first candidate that contains a new (unseen) subject in the list of candidates as the new event. In other words, the number of selected candidates is equal to the number of non-repetitive subjects in the candidate list of the narrative.
- **New Entity Selector**: which selects all the event candidates that include new subjects or new objects at the narrative level. Thus, it selects all candidates unless they differ in the verb only. In that case, it selects one of them as the new event.

Neural Network Models In addition to the rule-based models, we developed neural models based on Pre-trained Language Models (PLMs) as baselines for the task of new event candidate selection presented in Figure 4. For this purpose, we model the input vector with three elements as event candidate, current sentence, and context new events. The context new events denote the new events (ground truth) in the narrative context up to the current sentence. In cases where the size of the input vector exceeds the model limits (for instance 512 tokens per BERT-based models), the model trims the former part of the context new events. The model encodes this vector and outputs the classification decision of whether the event candidate (triplet) is a new event or not. The PLMs we fine-tuned for this purpose are BERT (Devlin et al., 2019), and RoBERTa (Liu et al., 2019).

The results of the candidate selection baselines are presented in Table 4. We observe that *Last Candidate Selector* has achieved the highest precision level among rule-based models. This is in line with the annotation result analysis, indicating the percentage of selected new event candidates to be slightly higher at the end of sentences. On the other hand, *New Entity Selector* achieves the highest level of recall while having a very low level of precision, as it selects all candidates unless the variation is only in the verb predicate. Moreover, the F1 scores of all the rule-based models are less than 40.0%. This indicates that features such as the novelty in elements or occurrence position are not enough to achieve high performance on the task of new event selection. While both neural models outperform the rule-based ones, RoBERTa outperforms all the baselines in this task by having the highest level of precision while maintaining a high recall.

5.2 Sequence Tagging Baselines

The second group of the models is developed for the task of new event detection in a sequence tagging setting. That is, the models tag the sequence of tokens (chunks) which are representing a new event in the sentence. The analysis performed on the continuous span events selected by the human judges indicated that several events can share the same tag spans such as subject or object. Therefore, we formalize this task as a binary tagging task rather than IOB tagging task and leave the development of the models for IOB tagging of multiple spans with overlap as future work. Similar to the previous task, we developed rule-based and neural baselines for new event sequence tagging. The developed rule-based baselines are:

- **Random Tagger**: which randomly tags tokens in a sentence as the new event tokens.
- **Early Tagger**: which tags the tokens in the first 30% of a sentence as the new event tokens.
- **Late Tagger**: which tags the tokens in the last 30% of a sentence as the new event tokens.

Neural Network Models Using BERT (Devlin et al., 2019), and RoBERTa (Liu et al., 2019) PLMs, we developed two neural baselines for this task. The models take as input the current sentence and the context new events which are the sequences of new events in the narrative context up to the current sentence. Similarly to the previous neural baselines, if the input vector exceeds the size limits of the models the former part of the context new events is trimmed. The model encodes this vector and outputs a tag sequence consisting of $\mathbf{E}_{(\text{vent})}$

	Prec. (%)	Rec. (%)	F1 (%)
Random	18.8	49.7	27.3
Early	17.4	29.5	21.9
Late	20.2	34.0	25.4
BERT	33.2	82.2	47.3
RoBERTa	34.3	81.3	**48.3**

Table 5: The results of the new event sequence tagging baselines. The models are trained and tested on continuous span events annotated by the human judges only. The performance of the neural models is averaged over 10 runs.

	Prec. (%)	Rec. (%)	F1 (%)
Random	31.1	49.6	38.2
Early	30.8	31.6	31.2
Late	29.9	30.4	30.2
BERT	54.9	84.3	66.5
RoBERTa	55.5	84.8	**67.1**

Table 6: The results of the new event sequence tagging baselines. Compared to Table 5, in this setting, the models are trained and tested on both selected candidates and continuous span events annotated by the human judges. The performance of the neural models is averaged over 10 runs.

or **O**, corresponding to the tokens in the sentence, indicating whether or not they describe a new event.

We initially trained the sequence tagging baselines using the annotated continuous span events. The results of this experiment are presented in Table 5. We observed that precision scores and consequently F1 scores are not significantly different among rule-based models. This indicates that the position of the tokens in the sentence is not the most contributing factor to the prediction accuracy. Similar to the previous task, the neural models have the highest performance among the baselines. However, their precision is considerably lower than the recall.

Similar to the previous task, the neural models have the highest performance among the baselines. However, their performance can be further improved by increasing the precision since it is considerably lower than the recall. The agreement level of the rule-based models is significantly small since the metric takes into consideration the beginning and the end of the tag spans. This is in contrast with the precision and recall metrics which focus on only binary values of each tag.

In the next step, we evaluated the same baseline models using both the selected event candidates and the continuous span annotations as the train and test sets. The results of this experiment, presented in Table 6, show a boost in the performance of all models using the mentioned train and test sets. Nevertheless, the same performance trends among models can be observed in this experiment as well.

6 Conclusions

In this work, we study the events in narratives according to their Information Status. We introduce the new task of identifying new events as they unfold in the narrative. In our definition of the event, the verb is the central element that represents a relation/happening that engages its dependencies such as subject, object, or oblique nominals. Meanwhile, we define an event as new if it provides novel information to the reader with respect to the discourse (discourse-new) and if such information can not be inferred through commonsense. We annotated a complete dataset of personal narratives with new events at the sentence level using human annotators. We then developed several neural and non-neural baselines for the task of new event detection in both settings of candidate selection and sequence tagging. We share the annotated dataset and the baselines with the community. We believe this task can be a novel and challenging task in narrative understanding and can facilitate and support other tasks in natural language understanding, human-machine dialogue, and natural language generation.

7 Limitations

The dataset used in this work is a personal narrative corpus in English collected in-vitro (e.g. subjects in a lab setting). Further work will be needed to extend it to other languages, genres, and naturalistic conditions. The reproducibility of the annotation task may be subject to variability due to the fact that the task is done by five internal annotators and not through crowd-sourcing techniques.

Acknowledgements

The authors would like to thank Desmond C. Ong for providing the dataset and useful discussions about the annotation task.
We acknowledge the support of the MUR PNRR project FAIR - Future AI Research (PE00000013) funded by the NextGenerationEU.

References

Jonathan M Adler, Jennifer Lodi-Smith, Frederick L Philippe, and Iliane Houle. 2016. The incremental validity of narrative identity in predicting well-being: A review of the field and recommendations for the future. *Personality and Social Psychology Review*, 20(2):142–175.

Cosmin Bejan and Sanda Harabagiu. 2010. Unsupervised event coreference resolution with rich linguistic features. In *Proceedings of the 48th Annual Meeting of the Association for Computational Linguistics*, pages 1412–1422, Uppsala, Sweden. Association for Computational Linguistics.

Nathanael Chambers and Dan Jurafsky. 2008. Unsupervised learning of narrative event chains. In *Proceedings of ACL-08: HLT*, pages 789–797, Columbus, Ohio. Association for Computational Linguistics.

Nathanael Chambers and Dan Jurafsky. 2009. Unsupervised learning of narrative schemas and their participants. In *Proceedings of the Joint Conference of the 47th Annual Meeting of the ACL and the 4th International Joint Conference on Natural Language Processing of the AFNLP*, pages 602–610, Suntec, Singapore. Association for Computational Linguistics.

Muhao Chen, Hongming Zhang, Qiang Ning, Manling Li, Heng Ji, Kathleen McKeown, and Dan Roth. 2021.

Event-centric natural language processing. In *Proceedings of the 59th Annual Meeting of the Association for Computational Linguistics and the 11th International Joint Conference on Natural Language Processing: Tutorial Abstracts*, pages 6–14, Online. Association for Computational Linguistics.

Morena Danieli, Tommaso Ciulli, Seyed Mahed Mousavi, Giorgia Silvestri, Simone Barbato, Lorenzo Di Natale, Giuseppe Riccardi, et al. 2022. Assessing the impact of conversational artificial intelligence in the treatment of stress and anxiety in aging adults: Randomized controlled trial. *JMIR mental health*, 9(9):e38067.

Jacob Devlin, Ming-Wei Chang, Kenton Lee, and Kristina Toutanova. 2019. BERT: Pre-training of deep bidirectional transformers for language understanding. In *Proceedings of the 2019 Conference of the North American Chapter of the Association for Computational Linguistics: Human Language Technologies, Volume 1 (Long and Short Papers)*, pages 4171–4186, Minneapolis, Minnesota. Association for Computational Linguistics.

Seth Ebner, Patrick Xia, Ryan Culkin, Kyle Rawlins, and Benjamin Van Durme. 2020. Multi-sentence argument linking. In *Proceedings of the 58th Annual Meeting of the Association for Computational Linguistics*, pages 8057–8077, Online. Association for Computational Linguistics.

Chris Fournier and Diana Inkpen. 2012. Segmentation similarity and agreement. In *Proceedings of the 2012 Conference of the North American Chapter of the Association for Computational Linguistics: Human Language Technologies*, pages 152–161.

Evgeny Kim and Roman Klinger. 2018. Who feels what and why? annotation of a literature corpus with semantic roles of emotions. In *Proceedings of the 27th International Conference on Computational Linguistics*, pages 1345–1359, Santa Fe, New Mexico, USA. Association for Computational Linguistics.

Klaus Krippendorff. 2011. Computing krippendorff's alpha-reliability.

David B Kronenfeld. 1978. Scripts, plans, goals, and understanding: an inquiry into human knowledge structures by roger c. schank and robert p. abelson. *Language*, 54(3):779–779.

Yinhan Liu, Myle Ott, Naman Goyal, Jingfei Du, Mandar Joshi, Danqi Chen, Omer Levy, Mike Lewis, Luke Zettlemoyer, and Veselin Stoyanov. 2019. Roberta: A robustly optimized bert pretraining approach.

William C Mann and Sandra A Thompson. 1992. *Discourse description: Diverse linguistic analyses of a fund-raising text*, volume 16. John Benjamins Publishing.

Nasrin Mostafazadeh, Nathanael Chambers, Xiaodong He, Devi Parikh, Dhruv Batra, Lucy Vanderwende, Pushmeet Kohli, and James Allen. 2016. A corpus and cloze evaluation for deeper understanding of commonsense stories. In *Proceedings of the 2016 Conference of the North American Chapter of the Association for Computational Linguistics: Human Language Technologies*, pages 839–849, San Diego, California. Association for Computational Linguistics.

Alexander P. D. Mourelatos. 1978. Events, processes, and states by alexander p. d. mourelatos. *Linguistics and Philosophy*, 2(3):415–434.

Seyed Mahed Mousavi, Roberto Negro, and Giuseppe Riccardi. 2021. An unsupervised approach to extract life-events from personal narratives in the mental health domain. In *Italian Conference on Computational Linguistics 2021 (CLiC-it)*, Milan, Italy.

Malvina Nissim, Shipra Dingare, Jean Carletta, and Mark Steedman. 2004. An annotation scheme for information status in dialogue. In *Proceedings of the Fourth International Conference on Language Resources and Evaluation (LREC'04)*, Lisbon, Portugal. European Language Resources Association (ELRA).

Desmond C. Ong, Zhengxuan Wu, Zhi-Xuan Tan, Marianne Reddan, Isabella Kahhale, Alison Mattek, and Jamil Zaki. 2021. Modeling emotion in complex stories: The stanford emotional narratives dataset. *IEEE Transactions on Affective Computing*, 12(3):579–594.

Andrew Piper, Richard Jean So, and David Bamman. 2021. Narrative theory for computational narrative understanding. In *Proceedings of the 2021 Conference on Empirical Methods in Natural Language Processing*, pages 298–311.

Ellen F. Prince. 1988. The zpg letter: Subjects, definiteness, and information-status. pages 295–325. John Benjamins.

Willard Van Orman Quine. 1985. Events and reification. *Actions and events: Perspectives on the philosophy of Donald Davidson*, pages 162–171.

Hannah Rashkin, Maarten Sap, Emily Allaway, Noah A. Smith, and Yejin Choi. 2018. Event2Mind: Commonsense inference on events, intents, and reactions. In *Proceedings of the 56th Annual Meeting of the Association for Computational Linguistics (Volume 1: Long Papers)*, pages 463–473, Melbourne, Australia. Association for Computational Linguistics.

Yisi Sang, Xiangyang Mou, Jing Li, Jeffrey Stanton, and Mo Yu. 2022. A survey of machine narrative reading comprehension assessments. *arXiv preprint arXiv:2205.00299*.

Aniruddha Tammewar, Alessandra Cervone, Eva-Maria Messner, and Giuseppe Riccardi. 2020. Annotation of emotion carriers in personal narratives. In *Proceedings of the Twelfth Language Resources and*

Evaluation Conference, pages 1517–1525, Marseille, France. European Language Resources Association.

Li Yujian and Liu Bo. 2007. A normalized levenshtein distance metric. *IEEE transactions on pattern analysis and machine intelligence*, 29(6):1091–1095.

Yutao Zeng, Xiaolong Jin, Saiping Guan, Jiafeng Guo, and Xueqi Cheng. 2020. Event coreference resolution with their paraphrases and argument-aware embeddings. In *Proceedings of the 28th International Conference on Computational Linguistics*, pages 3084–3094, Barcelona, Spain (Online). International Committee on Computational Linguistics.

Ben Zhou, Daniel Khashabi, Qiang Ning, and Dan Roth. 2019. "going on a vacation" takes longer than "going for a walk": A study of temporal commonsense understanding. In *Proceedings of the 2019 Conference on Empirical Methods in Natural Language Processing and the 9th International Joint Conference on Natural Language Processing (EMNLP-IJCNLP)*, pages 3363–3369, Hong Kong, China. Association for Computational Linguistics.

Emotion and Modifier in Henry Rider Haggard's Novels

Salim Sazzed
Department of Computer Science
Old Dominion University
Norfolk, VA, 23529
salim.sazzed@gmail.com

Abstract

In recent years, there has been a growing scholarly interest in employing quantitative methods to analyze literary texts, as they offer unique insights, theories, and interpretations. In light of this, the current study employs quantitative analysis to examine the fiction written by the renowned British adventure novelist Sir Henry Rider Haggard. Specifically, the study aims to investigate the affective content and prevalence of distinctive linguistic features in six of Haggard's most distinguished works. We evaluate dominant emotional states at the sentence level as well as investigate the deployment of specific linguistic features such as modifiers and deontic modals, and collocated terms. Through sentence-level emotion analysis, the findings reveal a notable prevalence of *joy*-related emotions across the novels. Furthermore, the study observes that intensifiers are employed more commonly than the mitigators as modifiers and the collocated terms of modifiers exhibit high similarity across the novels. By integrating quantitative analyses with qualitative assessments, this study presents a novel perspective on the patterns of emotion and specialized grammatical features in some of Haggard's most celebrated literary works.

1 Introduction

Henry Rider Haggard (1856-1925) was a prominent British novelist and acclaimed adventure fiction writer known for his captivating tales set in exotic locations, particularly Africa. He is considered a pioneer in the lost world genre, characterized by thrilling narratives of exploration and discovery in remote and enigmatic places. One of his most famous series of novels features the adventures of Allan Quatermain, a white hunter. Haggard's works are notable for their vivid descriptions of African landscapes, depictions of African culture, and imaginative portrayals of ancient civilizations. In addition to the Allan Quatermain series, Haggard's novels *She* and its sequel, *The Return of She*, have gained widespread recognition as seminal examples of imperialistic fiction, showcasing a fusion of adventure, romanticism, and supernatural elements.

Digital humanities is an interdisciplinary field that combines humanities disciplines such as history, literature, and philosophy with computer science and technology to study and create new forms of digital culture (Burdick et al., 2016). In recent years, interest in quantitative analysis of digital humanities has been on the rise with the help of accessible tools and methodologies that encompass a range of approaches, including natural language processing (NLP) and text mining, network analysis, data visualization, statistical analysis, and machine learning (Sazzed, 2022; Levine, 2022). More researchers and professionals in this field are becoming interested in using numerical and statistical methods to study various cultural and humanistic phenomena. Researchers have been using NLP and text mining techniques to analyze text depicting literary works, historical documents, or online archives for diverse purposes (Samothrakis and Fasli, 2015; Simonton, 1990; Dinu and Uban, 2017; San Segundo, 2017; Stockwell and Mahlberg, 2015).

In this study, we focus on analyzing the emotional and specific linguistic features of six of Henry Rider Haggard's most celebrated novels, employing a variety of natural language processing (NLP) techniques. In particular, we aim to explore the following research aspects-

RQ1: How emotional tones are illustrated in Henry Rider Haggard's most popular classics?

RQ2: Whether the usage of two linguist features: modifiers and deontic modals vary across Haggard's popular novels?

We first analyze the presence of various forms of emotions across the six novels by scrutinizing the distribution of emotions at the sentence level. We find similar patterns of emotions at the sentence

Proceedings of the The 5th Workshop on Narrative Understanding, pages 11–15
July 14, 2023

level in all six novels, with *joy* being the most frequently occurring emotion. In addition, we conduct a linguistic analysis to identify the occurrence of specific linguistic phenomena, such as the usage of mitigators, intensifiers, and deontic modals. Our results indicate that although the comparative presence of intensifiers and modifiers varies across the novels a bit, in general, the percentages are similar, within the range of 0.2%- 0.3% for intensifiers and 0.19%-0.25% for mitigators. Overall, our findings indicate substantial degrees of consistency in all the attributes studied across all six novels.

2 Dataset

The six literary works, namely *King Solomon's Mines* (KSM), *Allan Quatermain* (AQ), *The Holy Flower* (HF), *The Ivory Child* (IC), *She* (SHE), and *Ayesha, the Return of She* (ARS), are obtained from the Project Gutenberg[1] library as UTF-8 formatted text files. To ensure only literary content is analyzed, we manually remove the metadata present in the text file of each novel. The NLTK tokenizer (Bird et al., 2009) is employed to segment the text of each novel into sentences. Very short sentences containing fewer than three words are excluded from the analysis. The resulting dataset is summarized in Table 1.

Novel	#Sentence	#Words	#Words/Sent.
KSM	3251	81078	24.93
AQ	3801	104942	27.61
HF	4995	119918	24.00
IC	4190	111884	26.70
SHE	3977	111192	27.95
ARS	4504	116175	25.79

Table 1: Length related statistics of six novels

3 Emotion Analysis

Emotion analysis in literature is the study of emotions and sentiments expressed in written works, such as novels, poems, and short stories employing computational and linguistic methods. Emotion analysis can recognize emotional words and phrases, identify patterns of emotion over time, and categorize emotions into broad categories, such as joy, anger, or sadness. Here, we explore the distributions of prevalent emotions at the sentence-level.

[1]https://www.gutenberg.org

We utilize the EmoNet emotion recognition framework (Abdul-Mageed and Ungar, 2017) to ascertain the prevailing emotions at the sentence level. The EmoNet framework can identify eight primary categories of emotions (Plutchik, 1980), namely *joy* (JOY), *anticipation* (ANT), *surprise* (SUR), *trust* (TRU), *anger* (ANG), *disgust* (DIS), *fear* (FEA), and *sadness* (SAD) in text. We compute the relative frequencies of each primary emotion category in each of the novels and report their respective distributions. It should be noted that according to the authors of EmoNet, each primary emotion category in EmoNet encompasses three related types (i.e., subcategories) of emotions, as defined by Plutchik (1980). For example, *joy* encompasses the following three types of emotions- *ecstasy*, *joy*, and *serenity*. Therefore, overall, 24 types of emotions are considered in this study.

4 Specialized Modifiers

We analyze the presence of three specific types of linguistic feature, intensifier, mitigator and deontic modal, which can be grouped under a broader category of modifiers. Intensifiers and mitigators allow the precise representation of attitudes and opinions by adapting the strength or weakness of the language to correspond to the circumstance. On the other hand, the deontic modal expresses obligations, permissions, or requirements in relation to actions or events.

4.1 Intensifier

An intensifier is a word or phrase employed to strengthen or increase the impact of an adjective, adverb, or verb in a sentence. Intensifiers are used to express degree or emphasis and can help to convey the speaker's attitude or level of certainty about the information being communicated. Some common intensifiers include- *very*, *quite*, *absolutely*, *totally*, *completely*, and *utterly*. In addition, we examine which words are collocated with the top intensifiers.

4.2 Mitigator

A mitigator is a word or phrase used to soften or lessen the impact of an adjective, adverb, or verb in a sentence. Similar to intensifiers, mitigators are used to articulate degree or emphasis; however, they have the opposite effect of the intensifier. Instead of strengthening the impact of a word, mitigators weaken it. Some common mitigators include

Figure 1: Terms emphasized by the intensifier *very* in six novels

a little, *somewhat*, *kind of*, *rather*, and *slightly*. In addition to identifying top mitigators, we investigate the words associated (i.e., co-occurring) with them.

4.3 Deontic Modals

Deontic modals refer to a category of modal verbs that express obligation, permission, or necessity. They are typically used to denote what is required, permitted, or prohibited by some rule or principle. In this study, we consider the following deontic modals: *must*, *have to*, *should*, *ought to*, *may*, *might*, *could*, and *can*. We investigate the occurrence of deontic modals in all six novels.

5 Results and Discussion

Table 1 highlights that out of the six analyzed novels, HF is the longest, encompassing nearly 5000 sentences. Examining diverse statistics, we observe that the sentence length, measured in words, exhibits minimal variation across all six novels, with average sentence length ranging from 24.0 (HF) to 27.95 (SHE). Additionally, we do not notice any relation between the word count of the novels and their average sentence length.

Table 2 presents the distributions of emotions at the sentence level across all six novels. The results indicate that, among the eight emotion categories considered, the most prominent emotion in all the novels is *joy*, with 46%-49% of sentences exhibiting the highest values for this emotion type. This finding aligns with the expectations, given the tendency of Haggard's adventure novels to feature exhilarating and exciting storylines while also exploring the calm and reflective thoughts of human consciousness. The subsequent most dominant emotions are related to *fear*, *anger*, and *sadness*, having a range of 10%-13%. However, their frequency is considerably lower compared to the *joy* category, which stands at close to 50% as the dominant emotion. It is important to note that each sentence may contain multiple emotions, and the "dominant emotion category" refers to the emotion with the highest value, which may have a varying distance from the second most prominent emotion, ranging from nearly equal values to quite a large difference.

Table 3 shows the presence of two types of modifiers: intensifiers and modifiers, in all six novels. except for KSM and ARS, the other four novels show very similar occurrences of intensifiers, around 0.3%; in KSM and ARS, the presence is much lower, around 0.2%. Nevertheless, when we consider the most occurring intensifiers, we find they are similar in all books, *very, really, utterly, absolutely* are four common intensifiers among the top five. We further analyze collocated words of the most frequently occurring intensifier. For the most occurring intensifier *very*, we find top collocated words are similar. For example, in all novels, *well*, *good*, and *much* are observed 3-5 times with it (Figure 1)

Analogously, we notice frequently occurring mitigators are very similar in all novels, with *quite*, *rather*, and *almost* being the top three mitigators in all six books. However, in contrast to the intensifiers, where *very* is the most frequently used intensifier, with a significantly higher occurrence rate than other top intensifiers, no such preeminence is observed in the realm of mitigators, as the comparable prevalence of the aforementioned mitigators, namely, *quite*, *rather*, and *almost*, is noted. We also examine the co-occurring words that accompany these mitigators. However, we notice the co-occurring words are very distinct and appear in conjunction with the top mitigators at most twice.

Novel	Emotion type							
	ANG (%)	ANT (%)	DIS(%)	FEA(%)	JOY (%)	SAD (%)	SUR (%)	TRU (%)
KSM	10.24	3.51	7.35	13.32	46.94	11.17	5.97	1.51
AQ	11.52	1.74	7.71	12.71	47.75	11.89	5.34	1.34
HF	11.93	2.36	10.01	13.23	41.70	13.85	5.51	1.4
IC	12.67	1.62	8.57	12.96	42.89	13.6	6.35	1.34
SHE	12.79	1.77	7.25	11.29	48.45	11.49	5.55	1.4
ARS	10.52	1.87	7.17	12.21	48.51	12.46	5.77	1.49

Table 2: Distributions of dominant emotions (%) at sentence level in six novels

Novel	Intensifier (%)	Top intensifiers (with frequency)
KSM	0.202 (%)	very: 122, really: 14, utterly: 12, absolutely: 4
AQ	0.322 (%)	very: 248, really: 36, utterly: 16, absolutely': 10, particularly: 6
HF	0.299 (%)	very: 275, really: 53, extremely: 9, particularly: 4, absolutely: 4
IC	0.302 (%)	very: 280, really: 29, absolutely: 6, utterly: 6, extremely: 4
SHE	0.299 (%)	very: 244, absolutely: 29, utterly: 20, really: 14, particularly: 7
ARS	0.182 (%)	very: 187, really: 7, utterly: 7, absolutely: 3, extraordinarily: 3
Novel	**Mitigator (%)**	**Top mitigators (with frequency)**
KSM	0.192 (%)	quite: 52, rather: 45, almost: 32, pretty: 10, somewhat: 9
AQ	0.215 (%)	quite: 75, almost: 58, rather: 52, pretty: 17, somewhat: 8
IC	0.278 (%)	quite: 151, rather: 81, almost: 51, somewhat': 17, pretty: 6
HF	0.248 (%)	quite: 118, rather: 95, almost: 45, somewhat: 14, pretty: 13
SHE	0.207 (%)	quite: 61, rather: 61, almost: 57, fairly: 13, somewhat: 12
ARS	0.139 (%)	quite: 51, rather: 46, almost: 28, somewhat: 27, faintly: 5

Table 3: Percentage of intensifiers and mitigators in six novels along with the frequency of top intensifiers and mitigators

Novel	Deontic modal (%)
KSM	0.61% (could:161, should:108, must:95)
AQ	0.56% (could:241, should:123, may:68)
HF	0.77% (could:259, should:223, must:160)
IC	0.78% (could:276, should:184, might:132)
SHE	0.65% (could:244, should:144, must:129)
ARS	0.80% (could:293, must:188, should:170)

Table 4: Percentages and occurrences of deontic modals in all six novels

As Table 4 depicts, the prevalent deontic modals exhibit a similar distribution across all novels. *Could* is the most frequently occurring deontic modal in all six novels, followed by *should* in all cases, except the SHE. We observe a consistent presence of the deontic modals in all novels, ranging from 0.61% to 0.80%.

6 Summary and Future Work

As a preliminary study, here, we scrutinize the emotional and specific linguistic aspects of six celebrated works of Henry Rider Haggard leveraging various NLP techniques. The emotion recognition framework reveals similar patterns of emotions in all six novels, with *joy* being the most dominant. The linguistic analysis uncovers the frequency and presence of modifiers, intensifiers, and deontic modals and the collocated words and phrases. Overall, this research observes uniformity in the examined features across all six novels. The findings of this preliminary study reveal emotional and specific linguistic aspects of some of Haggard's most celebrated works.

Some possible future works will focus on a fine-grained analysis of emotion, such as identifying sub-categories of primary emotions and understanding the changes of emotions throughout the story, and finding how it is related to plot twists and other narrative elements. Besides, we will encompass an augmented set of linguistic features to conduct a more exhaustive analysis. Furthermore, additional novels authored by Henry Rider Haggard from multiple genres will be explored to find the consistency and divergence of linguistic and psychological patterns.

References

Muhammad Abdul-Mageed and Lyle Ungar. 2017. EmoNet: Fine-grained emotion detection with gated recurrent neural networks. In *Proceedings of the 55th Annual Meeting of the Association for Computational Linguistics (Volume 1: Long Papers)*, pages 718–728, Vancouver, Canada. Association for Computational Linguistics.

Steven Bird, Ewan Klein, and Edward Loper. 2009. *Natural language processing with Python: analyzing text with the natural language toolkit.* " O'Reilly Media, Inc.".

Anne Burdick, Johanna Drucker, Peter Lunenfeld, Todd Presner, and Jeffrey Schnapp. 2016. *Digital_Humanities*. Mit Press.

Liviu P Dinu and Ana Sabina Uban. 2017. Finding a character's voice: Stylome classification on literary characters. In *Proceedings of the Joint SIGHUM Workshop on Computational Linguistics for Cultural Heritage, Social Sciences, Humanities and Literature*, pages 78–82.

Lauren Levine. 2022. The distribution of deontic modals in jane austen's mature novels. In *Proceedings of the 6th Joint SIGHUM Workshop on Computational Linguistics for Cultural Heritage, Social Sciences, Humanities and Literature*, pages 70–74.

Robert Plutchik. 1980. A general psychoevolutionary theory of emotion. In *Theories of emotion*, pages 3–33. Elsevier.

Spyridon Samothrakis and Maria Fasli. 2015. Emotional sentence annotation helps predict fiction genre. *PloS one*, 10(11):e0141922.

Pablo Ruano San Segundo. 2017. Reporting verbs as a stylistic device in the creation of fictional personalities in literary texts. *Atlantis*, pages 105–124.

Salim Sazzed. 2022. An annotated dataset and automatic approaches for discourse mode identification in low-resource bengali language. In *Proceedings of the Workshop on Multilingual Information Access (MIA)*, pages 9–15.

Dean Keith Simonton. 1990. Lexical choices and aesthetic success: A computer content analysis of 154 shakespeare sonnets. *Computers and the Humanities*, 24:251–264.

Peter Stockwell and Michaela Mahlberg. 2015. Mindmodelling with corpus stylistics in david copperfield. *Language and Literature*, 24(2):129–147.

Evaluation Metrics for Depth and Flow of Knowledge in Non-fiction Narrative Texts

Sachin Pawar, Girish K. Palshikar, Ankita Jain, Mahesh Singh
Mahesh Rangarajan, Aman Agarwal, Vishal Kumar*, **Karan Singh***
TCS Research, Tata Consultancy Services Limited, India.
{sachin7.p,gk.palshikar,ankita7.j,mahesh.psingh,mahesh.rangarajan,aman.agarwal6}@tcs.com
{vtkumar022,karanfru627}@gmail.com

Abstract

In this paper, we describe the problem of automatically evaluating quality of knowledge expressed in a non-fiction narrative text. We focus on a specific type of documents where each document describes a certain technical problem and its solution. The goal is not only to evaluate the quality of knowledge in such a document, but also to automatically suggest possible improvements to the writer so that a better knowledge-rich document is produced. We propose new evaluation metrics to evaluate quality of knowledge contents as well as flow of different types of sentences. The suggestions for improvement are generated based on these metrics. The proposed metrics are completely unsupervised in nature and they are derived from a set of simple corpus statistics. We demonstrate the effectiveness of the proposed metrics as compared to other existing baseline metrics in our experiments.

1 Introduction

Documents containing non-fiction narrative text occur in many practical applications; e.g., essays, news, emails, safety or security incident reports, insurance claims, medico-legal reports, troubleshooting guides, user manuals etc. It is important to ensure that each such document is of high quality, for which purpose we need metrics that measure their quality. While metrics for readability (or comprehensibility) are obviously usable, we need specialized metrics that attempt to measure quality of non-fiction narrative text in terms of the specific characteristics. Fictional narratives are characterized in terms of structural elements such as conflicts, plot points, dialogues, characters, character arcs, focus, etc.; there is extensive literature about their linguistic analysis. However, non-fiction narrative texts are comparatively less studied in linguistics; e.g., (Sorock et al., 1996; Bunn et al., 2008; McKenzie et al., 2010; PBG, 2014). In this paper, we identify following characteristics of non-fiction narrative texts: (i) depth and variety of factual and conceptual knowledge elements present; (ii) distribution of different classes of sentences that represent essential aspects of information content; and (iii) flow and coherence of different types of sentences. We also propose novel quantitative metrics for measuring the quality of non-fiction narrative texts in terms of these characteristics.

In this paper, we focus on a specific type of non-fiction narrative text documents – *Contextual Master (CM) stories.* Contextual Master^{TM} is a registered trademark of TCS[1], which refers to an associate who has over the time gained a significant contextual knowledge or understanding of a business domain or a particular client's business. An *CM story* is a short narrative text that a CM writes to describe a particular instance where he/she has used the expert-level knowledge to solve a specific problem or to address a specific challenge. Each such CM story generally consists of 25-30 sentences (details in Section 7.1). A typical process of writing these stories is that a CM first writes some initial version which is reviewed by reviewers for knowledge contents, readability, narration flow and other aspects like grammar. Over a few iterations of incorporating reviewers' suggestions, a story is accepted to be published internally and for marketing purposes. In this paper, our goal is to develop a system for – (i) automatic evaluation of a CM story for its knowledge contents and narration flow quality, and (ii) automatic generation of suggestions for improvement so that the time needed to produce a publishable final version of a story from its initial version is reduced. The main motivations for building this system are as follows:

- Because of the automatically generated suggestions, a CM can produce a better initial

*Work done while working at TCS Research

[1] https://www.tcs.com/tcs-way/contextual-knowledge-mastery-tcs-client-growth

Proceedings of the The 5th Workshop on Narrative Understanding, pages 16–24
July 14, 2023 ©2023 Association for Computational Linguistics

version of a story, requiring lesser time to be invested by human reviewers. This would lead to faster publication of more such stories.

- Because of the automatic evaluation, the existing CM stories can be compared with each other or ranked as per the quality of their knowledge contents. This would be helpful to search, analyze, or refer to a few top quality CM stories in a particular business area of interest.

Automatic essay scoring or grading (Ke and Ng, 2019) is a related problem but it differs from our problem in some key aspects. Essay grading is a task of automatically scoring essays based on multiple dimensions like grammar, word usage, style, relevance to the essay topic (prompt), cohesion, coherence, persuasiveness etc. On the other hand, evaluation of non-fiction narrative texts like CM stories emphasizes more on the depth of the knowledge contents which are often not explicitly evaluated by the most essay grading techniques. To some extent, *cohesion* and *coherence* are common desirable aspects for essays as well as non-fiction narrative texts like CM stories. However, cohesion and coherence of *ideas* or *topics* is expected in essays whereas in CM stories, cohesion and coherence of certain *types of sentences* is expected. Therefore, in this paper, we propose new metrics to specifically evaluate the knowledge depth and the narration quality in terms of flow of sentence types. Here, it is important to note that we refer to *knowledge* as a more conceptual and abstract notion as compared to factual and data-oriented *information*. For example, we consider *task* as one of the knowledge markers (Section 3) which is defined as a volitional activity which needs expert knowledge to carry out (Pawar et al., 2021). A task such as "`analysed the configuration of the security protocol`" clearly represents an aspect of knowledge of a CM rather than mere factual information. Similarly, we consider specialized sentence categories (such as Solution, Benefit) introduced in Section 4 as another aspects of knowledge and hence considered as part of knowledge quality metrics.

All the proposed metrics are unsupervised in nature, i.e., they do not need any set of stories which are explicitly annotated for knowledge quality by human reviewers. The specific contributions of this paper are:

- Identifying knowledge markers (Section 3) & sentence categories (Section 4)
- Evaluation metrics for knowledge quality (Section 5) and narration flow quality (Section 6)
- Statistical analysis of effectiveness of the evaluation metrics (Section 7)

2 Problem Definition

Our goal is to determine the quality of *knowledge* and *narration flow* of a CM story with respect to a set of *knowledge quality* and *narration flow quality metrics*. Each metric is designed to capture and evaluate a certain aspect of the story, as described in detail in later sections. The problem can be specifically defined in terms of input, output and training requirements as follows:
• **Input**: A text document describing a CM story s
• **Output**: (i) An evaluation score for each of the knowledge and flow metrics for the CM story s and an aggregated score combining the individual scores. (ii) A set of suggestions for improving the CM story s.
• **Training Regime**: We assume that a set D^{train} of *final* CM stories is available which have been revised and improved by taking into consideration the suggestions from human reviewers.
Summary of the Proposed Solution: We propose a two-phase solution to this problem which is depicted in Figure 1.
• **Learning Phase**: In this phase, we use the set of *final* CM stories (D^{train}) to calculate certain corpus statistics of the proposed knowledge and flow quality metrics. As this set consists of all the stories which are already revised and improved as per human reviewers' suggestions, we assume that the corpus statistics learned from this set characterize a set of *ideal* values for these metrics.
• **Operating Phase**: In this phase, given a new CM story, we evaluate its knowledge and flow metrics with respect to the corpus statistics learned using D^{train}. We also generate a set of specific suggestions for improvement.

3 Knowledge Markers

We hypothesize that the knowledge needed for solving a particular domain or technical problem is expressed in terms of certain *knowledge markers*. These knowledge markers are mentions of some key entity types as follows:
• Skills: Names of tools, technologies, or technical

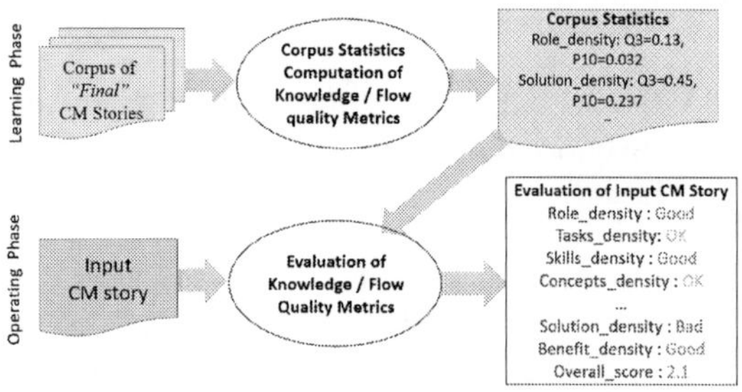

Figure 1: Architecture of the proposed solution

concepts such as SAP S4 HANA, shell scripting, data warehousing, SolarWinds.

• Tasks: A task is a volitional and knowledge-based activity carried out by a person, a group of persons, or a system (Pawar et al., 2021). Some examples of Tasks are as follows: analysed the configuration of the security protocol, integrated SolarWinds with XYZ tool, development of several innovative solutions using S4 HANA processes.

• Roles: A specific role performed by any human expert such as IT Manager, Manufacturing Solution Architect.

• Concepts: Key noun phrases corresponding to certain domain-specific *concepts*. E.g., plastic manufacturing industry, legacy BI servers, unsupervised learning.

Entity Extraction Techniques: We use different techniques for the extraction of mentions of different entity types depending on their nature. For extraction of mentions of Skill, we use a large gazette of known skill names and simply look up in this gazette for identifying skill mentions. This gazette is created semi-automatically by combining several existing resources (like DBPedia) and a list created by a semi-supervised iterative algorithm similar to the one described in Pawar et al. (Pawar et al., 2012). Task mentions are extracted using the linguistic rules described in Pawar et al. (Pawar et al., 2021). For extracting Role mentions, we adopt a gazette lookup-based strategy similar to Skill. For identification of domain-specific Concepts, we compute domain relevance scores for all the noun phrases and select only those which are above a certain threshold. We follow the domain relevance calculation as proposed by Navigli and Velardi (Navigli and Velardi, 2004).

4 Sentence Categories

In addition to the knowledge markers, an ideal CM story should describe all the aspects of a certain problem being solved such as a brief background of the problem, the problem itself, the solution that was provided, and finally what were the benefits that were achieved. Therefore, it is important to identify presence of these aspects in a given story. We propose to identify these aspects in the form of the following sentence categories:

• Background: Sentences describing some background for the client for which a problem is being solved. E.g., The client is a European healthcare organization which offers a platform to manage user manuals and operator documents.

• Problem: Sentences describing the actual problem or challenge that is being addressed in the CM story. E.g., The users were not able to search for the mortgage related documents for some of the indexed mortgage deals.

• Expert_Knowledge: Sentences describing specific technical or domain knowledge of the CM in the context of the problem being solved. E.g., He has brought 25 years of a strong domain knowledge in supply chain area.

• Solution: Sentences describing the proposed solution, analysis, or actual implementation or execution of the solution. E.g., Agile approach was adopted to develop the planned functionalities in multiple sprints.

• Benefit: Sentences describing the benefits achieved from the implemented solution. E.g., Also, manufacturing solution enabled to bring the legacy system into SAP resulting into dropping additional manpower requirement.

• Client_Appreciation: Sentences describing the positive feedback or appreciations received from the client. E.g., The client was highly impressed with the reusability of the new automated solution.

We modelled the problem of identifying appropriate sentence categories as a multi-label, multi-class sentence classification problem. We used a multi-label setting because in some cases, a sentence may have more than one valid category. For example, the following sentence belongs to Solution as well as Benefit – He used his understanding of the client's applications and restructured the database accordingly to reduce recurring issues, which resulted in reduction in incidents by 70%.

We use a sentence classification model which is based on DistilBERT (Sanh et al., 2019), a lighter version of BERT (Devlin et al., 2018). DistilBERT model is 40% smaller than BERT while retaining its 97% language understanding capabilities. DistilBERT[2] is capable of producing semantically rich representations for any input text and the individual words in it. These representations are 768 dimensional dense vectors of real numbers ($\mathbb{R}^{768}$). We use these representations for building our classifier to predict appropriate sentence categories for a sentence in a CM story.

We now explain the model architecture in detail. Let the input sentence be S which is first passed through the pre-trained DistilBERT model to obtain – (i) [CLS] token encoding which provides the representation of the entire input text S, and (ii) the representations for each word in S.

$$\mathbf{x_{CLS}}, X = DistilBERT(S) \quad (1)$$

Here, $\mathbf{x_{CLS}} \in \mathbb{R}^{768}$ and $X \in \mathbb{R}^{L\times768}$ where L is the maximum number of words in any input sentence (we use $L = 128$). Let $X_i \in \mathbb{R}^{768}$ be the representation for the ith word in S. We use attention mechanism so that the contribution of each word in S is determined based on its importance for prediction of each of the sentence categories. We use 6 attention layers corresponding to the 6 sentence categories. Each attention layer is similar to the one described in Basiri et al. (2021).

$$a_i^c = \mathbf{w_a^c}^T \cdot X_i + b^c \quad (2)$$

Here, $\mathbf{w_a^c} \in \mathbb{R}^{768}$ and $b^c \in \mathbb{R}$ are the weight vector and the bias of the attention layer for category c, respectively. $a_i^c \in \mathbb{R}$ is the score for the ith word as computed by the attention layer for category c. These scores are normalized across all the words in S to obtain final attention weights (α_i^c's) which are used to obtain a weighted average of word representations.

$$\alpha_i^c = \frac{exp(a_i^c)}{\sum_{j=1}^{L} exp(a_j^c)}\ ;\ \mathbf{x_w^c} = \sum_{i=1}^{L} \alpha_i^c \cdot X_i \quad (3)$$

Finally, the overall representation ($\mathbf{x_{final}^c} \in \mathbb{R}^{1536}$) of the input sentence is obtained by concatenating representations obtained in Equations 1 and 3.

$$\mathbf{x_{final}} = [\mathbf{x_{CLS}}; \mathbf{x_w^c}] \quad (4)$$

This final representation is then passed through a linear transformation layer to obtain a hidden representation.

$$\mathbf{x_h^c} = ReLU(W_h \cdot \mathbf{x_{final}^c} + \mathbf{b_h}) \quad (5)$$

[2]We preferred DistilBERT due to its better efficiency within constraints of our deployment environment. However, without loss of generality, the proposed technique can be used with any of the encoder models from the BERT family given sufficient compute resources.

Sentence Category	Precision	Recall	F1
Background	0.787	0.808	0.797
Expert_Knowledge	0.817	0.870	0.843
Problem	0.762	0.701	0.730
Solution	0.803	0.704	0.750
Benefit	0.782	0.806	0.794
Client_Appreciation	0.875	0.854	0.864
Overall (micro avg)	0.794	0.766	**0.780**
Overall (macro avg)	0.804	0.791	**0.796**

Table 1: Sentence classifier evaluation results

Here, $W_h \in \mathbb{R}^{H\times1536}$ and $\mathbf{b_h} \in \mathbb{R}^H$ are the weight matrix and the bias vector of the hidden layer, where H is the number of units in the hidden layer (we use $H = 500$). Finally, each sentence category has its different output layer to predict a probability distribution over two labels – c and Not-c.

$$y_{pred}^c = Softmax(W_o^c \cdot \mathbf{x_h^c} + \mathbf{b_o^c}) \quad (6)$$

$$loss_c = CrossEntropyLoss(y_{gold}^c, y_{pred}^c) \quad (7)$$

$$loss = \sum_c loss_c \quad (8)$$

Here, $W_o^c \in \mathbb{R}^{2\times H}$ and $\mathbf{b_o^c} \in \mathbb{R}^2$ are the weight matrix and the bias vector of the output layer corresponding to the sentence category c. Cross entropy loss is computed using the predicted and the gold-standard label distributions which is summed over all categories to get the overall loss. The model is then trained to minimize this loss over the labelled training data. We used a training set of 1618 sentences which were labelled manually using a few active learning iterations. We evaluated the trained sentence classification model on a held out evaluation dataset of 636 sentences. Table 1 shows the classification performance of this model where the F1-score of around 80% was achieved.

5 Knowledge Quality Metrics

In this section, we describe our proposed *knowledge quality metrics* based on the knowledge markers and the sentence categories described in the previous sections. For a CM story s, for each knowledge marker and sentence category, we compute a metric which measures its density within the story as follows:

$$\text{Skills\_density}(s) = \frac{No.\ of\ Skill\ entity\ mentions\ in\ s}{No.\ of\ sentences\ in\ s}$$

$$\text{Solution\_density}(s) = \frac{No.\ of\ Solution\ sentences\ in\ s}{No.\ of\ sentences\ in\ s}$$

Here, the division by the number of sentences in s offsets the effect of the length of the story. We similarly compute such metrics for all knowledge markers as well as sentence categories – Skills_density, Tasks_density, Roles_density, Concepts_density (*based on knowledge markers*), Background_density, Problem_density, Expert_Knowledge_density, Solution_density, Benefit_density, and Client_Appreciation_density (*based on sentence categories*).

One limitation of these knowledge quality metrics is that the metrics are dependent on the density of multiple knowledge markers but do not explicitly check whether multiple such markers are relevant or pertinent to each other. We plan to handle this as a future work and currently assume that there is no malicious intent in writing the document (e.g., by adding multiple irrelevant entities in text to artificially boost the quality score).

5.1 Learning Phase

As described in Figure 1, in the learning phase, we consider a corpus of *final* accepted CM stories. As these stories have been revised in several iterations to incorporate human reviewers' suggestions, we can assume that these are *ideal* from the point of view of knowledge quality. Therefore, we compute some useful corpus statistics of the knowledge quality metrics defined above. We calculate these metrics for all the CM stories in the training corpus and then we calculate the following corpus statistics for each metric m:

- Mean and Standard Deviation (μ_m and σ_m)
- Quartiles ($q1_m$: 25th percentile, $q2_m$: 50th percentile, i.e., *median*, and $q3_m$: 75th percentile)
- Percentile ($p10_m$: 10th percentile)

We have overall 10 knowledge quality metrics – based on 4 knowledge markers and 6 sentence categories. In order to capture the inter-dependence among these metrics, we also estimate the covariance matrix Σ (of size 10×10) from the same corpus. Table 2 shows the estimated corpus statistics of the proposed knowledge quality metrics.

5.2 Operating Phase

As described in Figure 1, in this phase, a given story is evaluated with respect to the knowledge quality metrics using the corpus statistics generated from the training corpus.

Evaluation of Knowledge Quality Metrics: We evaluate each knowledge quality metric m for the given CM story s as *Good*, *OK*, or *Bad* as follows. Let v_{ms} be the value of the metric m computed for the story s.

$$\textit{Good}\ (v_{ms} \geq q3_m);\ \textit{OK}\ (q3_m > v_m \geq p10_m);\ \textit{Bad}\ (v_{ms} < p10_m)$$

Generating Suggestions for Improvement: For any of the above metrics, if a given story has a value lower than $p10_m$, a corresponding suggestion for improvement is shown to the user so that the story can be revised accordingly. For example, if Benefit_density of a story has a very low value, the corresponding suggestion would be – *Please add more details about the specific benefits achieved because of your solution.* If the metric Skills_density has a very low value, the corresponding suggestion would be – *Please mention the names of some specific tools or technologies which were employed to solve the problem.*

Aggregated Knowledge Quality Metrics: We explored the following two ways to get a single aggregate metric which captures the overall knowledge quality of a CM story by combining the individual knowledge quality metrics.

• **Distance from the mean vector** ($Dist_{mean}$): This metric is based on the mean vector ($\vec{\mu} \in \mathbb{R}^{10}$) and the co-variance matrix ($\Sigma \in \mathbb{R}^{10\times10}$) learned from the corpus of *final* accepted stories as described above. For a new story s, let $\vec{v_s}$ ($\in \mathbb{R}^{10}$) be the vector representing values of all the 10 knowledge quality metrics. Then the metric is computed as the Mahalanobis distance of $\vec{v_s}$ from $\vec{\mu}$.

$$Dist_{mean}(s) = \sqrt{(\vec{v_s} - \vec{\mu})^T \Sigma^{-1} (\vec{v_s} - \vec{\mu})} \quad (9)$$

Lower the value of $Dist_{mean}(s)$, better is the knowledge quality of s because the lower value indicates that the story s is more similar to the *ideal* stories.

• **Sum of the scaled metrics** (Z_{sum}): This metric is computed as the sum of scaled values of all the 10 knowledge quality metrics. For a new story s, let v_{ms} ($\in \mathbb{R}$) be the value of the knowledge quality metric m. This value is scaled using the mean (μ_m) and standard deviation (σ_m) of m estimated from the corpus of *final* accepted stories as described above. The metric is computed as follows:

$$Z_{sum}(s) = \sum_m \frac{v_{ms} - \mu_m}{\sigma_m} \quad (10)$$

Here, the higher values of Z_{sum} indicate better knowledge quality.

6 Narration Flow Quality Metrics

In addition to the knowledge content, it is also important to evaluate the narration quality of any narrative text such that it measures how well-structured the flow of narration is. In this section, we describe our proposed metric to evaluate the flow of different sentence categories in a CM story.

Sentence Categories Flow Metric: A good *flow* of sentence categories is that sequence of sentence categories which is generally used to describe an *ideal* story. For example, generally any story begins with some background of the problem followed by the description of the problem itself. Then the contextual knowledge of the CM is discussed followed by the proposed or implemented solution. Finally, the story concludes by discussing the benefits that were achieved by the solution and whether any appreciations were received for it. Though it is not mandatory to strictly follow this flow of narration and some sentences can be out of place, the good stories are generally structured in this way. Moreover, a good cohesive story will contain all the sentences describing a certain aspect (say Problem) in close proximity of each other and also at a proper relative position within the entire story. Hence, we propose a new metric – SCF (Sentence Categories Flow) which tries to capture these aspects of an ideal flow of sentence categories in a CM story.

First, a relative position of each sentence within the CM story is determined as follows. For any i^{th} sentence in a CM story consisting of n sentences, the relative position is $\frac{i}{n}$. For a particular sentence category (say Solution), we create a sample of relative positions of all sentences belonging to that category from all the stories in our training corpus. We compute mean (μ_{RP}) and standard deviation (σ_{RP}) of this sample (e.g., for Solution, $\mu_{RP} = 0.6$ and $\sigma_{RP} = 0.22$; this means that normally the Solution sentences occur in a story after 60% of the overall sentences are written). Now, given any new story s, the metric $SCF_{Solution}(s)$ is computed as the number of sentences of category Solution in s whose relative position is more than one standard deviation away from the mean, i.e., relative position outside the range $[\mu_{RP} - \sigma_{RP}, \mu_{RP} + \sigma_{RP}]$. Similar metrics are computed for other sentence categories in the same way (*note that μ_{RP} and σ_{RP} are specific to each sentence category*). Lower the value of this SCF metric, better is the narration flow quality, because it simply counts the number of sentences of a particular sentence category which are at *unusual* relative positions within a story. Based on this metric, suggestions for improvement are generated for those sentences in a CM story for which the relative position is outside the expected range. E.g., *Please consider re-positioning the Solution sentence [x] which is appearing too early (or late) in your story.* We also compute a single aggregate metric to combine the SCF metrics for individual sentence categories: $SCF_{all} = \sum_c SCF_c$.

7 Experimental Analysis

In this section, we describe our experiments in terms of datasets, baselines, and the evaluation strategy.

7.1 Datasets

We use the following two datasets[3] of CM stories.

- **Training corpus** (D^{train}): It is a large corpus of $53,675$ CM stories consisting of 1.4 million sentences and 28.8 million words. The median length of these CM stories is 23 sentences. This corpus contains all the *final* CM stories which have been reviewed by human reviewers and revised multiple times by the story writers (CMs) to incorporate the reviewers' suggestions. Hence, we consider D_{train} to be a set of *ideal* stories and use it to learn corpus statistics (see Table 2) of the knowledge quality metrics and flow quality metrics.
- **Evaluation dataset** (D_i^{eval}, D_f^{eval}): It consists of 67 CM stories where for each story two versions are available – (i) *initial* version ($\in D_i^{eval}$) which was written by the story writer (CM), and (ii) the corresponding *final* version ($\in D_f^{eval}$) which was prepared after a few iterations of incorporating suggestions for improvement by human reviewers. Both D_i^{eval} and D_f^{eval} consist of *paired* initial and final versions of 67 CM stories where the number of sentences are 2517 and 2010, respectively. The median lengths of these CM stories are 33 and 29 sentences for D_i^{eval} and D_f^{eval}, respectively.

7.2 Baselines

We explored 3 baseline metrics.

- **Readability Score**: We used Flesch reading-ease score (FRES) which was proposed by Flesch

[3] The datasets can not be made available publicly as they contain private and confidential information about our organization as well as its customers.

Metric	p10	q1	q2	q3	mean (μ)	st. dev. (σ)
Skills_density	0.000	0.048	0.103	0.174	0.125	0.103
Tasks_density	0.300	0.387	0.500	0.615	0.509	0.178
Roles_density	0.037	0.067	0.100	0.148	0.111	0.066
Concepts_density	0.000	0.875	1.333	1.681	1.193	0.746
Background_density	0.053	0.091	0.136	0.188	0.143	0.073
Problem_density	0.091	0.143	0.200	0.269	0.209	0.097
Expert_Knowledge_density	0.043	0.074	0.107	0.143	0.113	0.056
Solution_density	0.192	0.250	0.320	0.400	0.327	0.108
Benefit_density	0.050	0.091	0.138	0.190	0.143	0.073
Client_Appreciation_density	0.000	0.037	0.061	0.091	0.066	0.042

Table 2: Corpus statistics of the proposed knowledge quality metrics estimated from the training corpus D^{train}

(1979). It is calculated as follows:

$$FRES(s) = 206.835 - 1.015 \times \frac{\#words\ in\ s}{\#sentences\ in\ s} - 84.6 \times \frac{\#syllables\ in\ s}{\#words\ in\ s}$$

The higher values of FRES score indicate better readability. If any story has lower readability than a threshold, then a few longest sentences (in terms of #words) and a few longest words (in terms of #syllables) are suggested for potential simplification. For D^{train}, the mean FRES score is observed to be 40.2 with standard deviation of 8.4, so the threshold used is 31.8 (mean - st.dev.).

• **Perplexity**: It is generally used for evaluating the quality of language model (Jurafsky and Martin, 2021). Here, we borrow this metric to evaluate a specific sequence of sentence categories appearing in a CM story. A language model (using bigrams and trigrams of sentence categories) is learned over the sequences of sentence categories appearing in D^{train} and is used to compute perplexity of the sequences of sentence categories in D_i^{eval} and D_f^{eval}. Hence, a lower perplexity value indicates more similarity with the sequences of sentence categories observed in D^{train}.

• **Essay Grading** (EG): We trained the hierarchical neural network based model proposed by Zhang and Litman (2018) using their code[4] on the ASAP3 dataset[5] and evaluated on our datasets D_i^{eval} and D_f^{eval}.

7.3 Evaluation Strategy

We compute each evaluation metric (the proposed knowledge quality and narration flow quality metrics as well as the baseline metrics) for both the datasets – D_i^{eval} and D_f^{eval}. Next, for each metric, we determine whether it is consistently assigning a better score for a *final* version of a story as compared to its corresponding *initial* version. For this purpose, we use one-sided, two-samples, paired t-test to check whether the scores for *final* stories are significantly better than those of *initial* stories, using a specific metric. Here, the intuition behind this evaluation is – each story in D_i^{eval} is revised as per the suggestions of human reviewers to obtain the corresponding story in D_f^{eval}. If our metric consistently assigns a better value for a *final* version of a story as compared to its *initial* version, then it can be said that the metric is able to capture the same aspects of the story which human reviewers also think are important. Moreover, because the automatically generated suggestions for improvement are based on the same metrics, this evaluation strategy also implicitly measures the effectiveness of those suggestions.

We now describe the one-sided, two-samples, paired t-test for a metric m in detail. We compute the values of metric m for all 67 stories in D_i^{eval} as well as D_f^{eval}, so that we get two paired samples of size 67 each – S_i^{eval} and S_f^{eval}. The null and alternate hypotheses are as follows:

H_0: Mean of S_i^{eval} = Mean of S_f^{eval}

H_1: Mean of S_i^{eval} < Mean of S_f^{eval} (*if the metric m is such that higher values indicate better quality*); **OR**

H_1: Mean of S_i^{eval} > Mean of S_f^{eval} (*if the metric m is such that lower values indicate better quality*)

7.4 Analysis of Results

Table 3 shows the evaluation results for – (i) our proposed aggregated knowledge quality metrics (D_{mean} and Z_{sum}) and the flow quality metric (SCF_{all}), and (ii) the baseline metrics ($FRES$,

[4]https://github.com/Rokeer/co-attention

[5]https://www.kaggle.com/c/asap-aes

Metric	Mean(S_i^{eval})	Mean(S_f^{eval})	p-value
$Dist_{mean} \downarrow$	3.064	2.544	**0.00001**
$Z_{sum} \uparrow$	-0.053	0.089	**0.00043**
$SCF_{all} \downarrow$	10.443	8.015	**0.02974**
$FRES \uparrow$	36.147	35.111	0.89956
$Perplexity \downarrow$	6.486	6.178	0.08759
$EG \uparrow$	0.654	0.613	0.98258

Table 3: Evaluation results for aggregated knowledge quality metrics and narration flow quality metrics using the evaluation datasets D_i^{eval} and D_f^{eval}. (Arrows besides a metric indicate its nature - $\uparrow$ indicates higher the better and $\downarrow$ indicates lower the better; **Bold** p-values indicate the statistically significant result with $\alpha = 0.05$)

$Perplexity$, and EG). The aggregated metrics D_{mean} and Z_{sum} capture the combined effect of the proposed 10 knowledge quality metrics and both these metrics are showing statistically significant difference between S_i^{eval} and S_f^{eval}. Another proposed metric SCF_{all} for evaluating the sentence categories flow quality is also showing a statistically significant difference between S_i^{eval} and S_f^{eval}. However, for the baseline metric $Perplexity$, no statistically significant difference is observed at $\alpha = 0.05$. The other two baseline metrics $FRES$ and EG, assign better scores for initial versions as compared to the final versions, which is against our expectation that final versions should be relatively better than the corresponding initial versions.

$FRES$ is designed to measure *ease of reading* and although it is an important aspect of a narrative text, in case of CM stories, more emphasis is given to produce knowledge-rich text. Such knowledge-dense documents may become little less readable which can be observed in our experiments where the average readability of the final CM stories is little less than the initial versions. Similarly, EG is assigning higher scores for initial versions of the CM stories as compared to the final versions. This shows that the essay grading techniques give more importance to other aspects than those measuring the knowledge and flow quality in non-fiction documents like CM stories. For computing $Perplexity$, we are considering bigrams and trigrams of sentence categories. Hence, it tends to focus on small local window (of 2-3 sentences) and may not capture overall order of sentence categories in an entire CM story. On the other hand, our proposed metric SCF is able to evaluate flow of sentence categories in a better way as it is not limited within a small local window of sentences. Rather, it focuses on identifying sentences whose relative placement in a CM story is quite unusual.

7.5 Deployment

The system based on the proposed techniques is deployed for evaluating CM stories as well as for automatically generating suggestions for improvement. The initial feedback of the system is positive and we are planning to conduct detailed user-studies as a future work.

8 Conclusions and Future Work

We proposed a set of novel evaluation metrics for depth and flow of knowledge in non-fiction narrative texts that are unsupervised as well as interpretable. We focused on a specific type of documents identified as CM stories. Two different types of evaluation metrics were proposed: (i) for measuring the quality of the knowledge contents in a CM story, and (ii) for evaluating flow of different categories of sentences in a CM story. We demonstrated the effectiveness of the proposed metrics as compared to the existing metrics like perplexity, readability, and essay grading.

In future, we plan to explore how the proposed metrics can be adapted to other types of non-fiction narrative texts such as security incident reports. One interesting research direction is whether we can discover the key sentence categories automatically for a new type of documents. We also plan to develop some new narration flow quality metrics such as a metric based on sequence entropy.

9 Acknowledgements

We would like to acknowledge the support of Haridas Menon and Karthik Parvathi from TCS HR for this work. We would also like to acknowledge the contributions of TCS' Technical Communication Group for helping us identify a proper set of sentence categories and also for providing an initial set of annotated sentences.

References

2014. Understanding the social context of fatal road traffic collisions among young people: a qualitative analysis of narrative text in coroners' records. *BMC Public Health*, 14.

Mohammad Ehsan Basiri, Shahla Nemati, Moloud Abdar, Erik Cambria, and U Rajendra Acharya. 2021. Abcdm: An attention-based bidirectional cnn-rnn deep model for sentiment analysis. *Future Generation Computer Systems*, 115:279–294.

Terry L. Bunn, Svetla Slavova, and Laura Hall. 2008. Narrative text analysis of kentucky tractor fatality reports. *Accident Analysis and Prevention*, 40(2):419–425.

Jacob Devlin, Ming-Wei Chang, Kenton Lee, and Kristina Toutanova. 2018. BERT: Pre-training of deep bidirectional transformers for language understanding. *arXiv preprint arXiv:1810.04805*.

Rudolf Flesch. 1979. How to write plain english. *University of Canterbury. Available at http://www. mang. canterbury. ac. nz/writing_guide/writing/flesch. shtml.[Retrieved 5 February 2016]*.

Dan Jurafsky and James H Martin. 2021. Speech and language processing (3rd edition). `https://web.stanford.edu/~jurafsky/slp3/`.

Zixuan Ke and Vincent Ng. 2019. Automated essay scoring: A survey of the state of the art. In *IJCAI*, volume 19, pages 6300–6308.

Kirsten McKenzie, Deborah Anne Scott, Margaret Ann Campbell, and Roderick John McClure. 2010. The use of narrative text for injury surveillance research: A systematic review. *Accident Analysis and Prevention*, 42(2):354–363.

Roberto Navigli and Paola Velardi. 2004. Learning domain ontologies from document warehouses and dedicated web sites. *Computational Linguistics*, 30(2):151–179.

Sachin Pawar, Girish Palshikar, and Anindita Sinha Banerjee. 2021. Weakly supervised extraction of tasks from text. In *Proceedings of the 18th International Conference on Natural Language Processing (ICON)*.

Sachin Pawar, Rajiv Srivastava, and Girish Keshav Palshikar. 2012. Automatic gazette creation for named entity recognition and application to resume processing. In *5th ACM COMPUTE Conference: Intelligent & scalable system technologies*, pages 1–7.

Victor Sanh, Lysandre Debut, Julien Chaumond, and Thomas Wolf. 2019. Distilbert, a distilled version of bert: smaller, faster, cheaper and lighter. *arXiv preprint arXiv:1910.01108*.

Gary S. Sorock, Thomas A. Ranney, and Mark R. Lehto. 1996. Motor vehicle crashes in roadway construction workzones: An analysis using narrative text from insurance claims. *Accident Analysis and Prevention*, 28(1):131–138.

Haoran Zhang and Diane Litman. 2018. Co-attention based neural network for source-dependent essay scoring. In *Proceedings of the Thirteenth Workshop on Innovative Use of NLP for Building Educational Applications*, pages 399–409.

Modeling Readers' Appreciation of Literary Narratives Through Sentiment Arcs and Semantic Profiles

Yuri Bizzoni
Center for Humanities Computing /
Aarhus University, Denmark
yuri.bizzoni@cc.au.dk

Pascale Feldkamp Moreira
Comparative Literature,
School of Communication and Culture /
Aarhus University, Denmark
pascale.moreira@cc.au.dk

Mads Rosendahl Thomsen
Comparative Literature,
School of Communication and Culture /
Aarhus University, Denmark
madsrt@cc.au.dk

Kristoffer L. Nielbo
Center for Humanities Computing /
Aarhus University, Denmark
kln@cas.au.dk

Abstract

Predicting the perception of literary quality and reader appreciation of narrative texts are highly complex challenges in quantitative and computational literary studies due to the fluid definitions of quality and the vast feature space that can be considered when modeling a literary work. This paper investigates the potential of sentiment arcs combined with topical-semantic profiling of literary narratives as indicators for their literary quality. Our experiments focus on a large corpus of 19th and 20[the] century English language literary fiction, using GoodReads' ratings as an imperfect approximation of the diverse range of reader evaluations and preferences. By leveraging a stacked ensemble of regression models, we achieve a promising performance in predicting average readers' scores, indicating the potential of our approach in modeling perceived literary quality.

1 Introduction

Defining what contributes to the perceived literary quality of narrative texts (or lack thereof) is an ancient and highly complex challenge of quantitative literary studies. The versatility of narrative and the myriad of possible definitions of a text's quality ultimately complicate the issue. In addition, the diversity and size of the possible feature space for modeling a literary work contribute to the complexity of the matter. It can even be argued that the quality of a literary text is not systematic and that "quality" is an expression of noisy preferences, as it mostly encodes idiosyncratic tastes that depend on individual reader inclinations and capacities. However, various studies have shown that this 'literary preference as noise' position is not tenable because text-intrinsic features (e.g., text coherence, literary style) and text-extrinsic factors (e.g., reader demographics) systematically impact perceived literary quality (Mohseni et al., 2021; Koolen et al., 2020a; Bizzoni et al., 2022b). At the same time, the questions of how such features interplay and what kind of metric we should use to validate them remain open. Thus, current research on the perception of literary quality implicitly tries to answer two primary questions: 1) Is it possible to define literary quality at all, and 2) Is it possible to identify the intrinsic or extrinsic features that contribute to the perception of literary quality? While quality as a single measure may be impossible to agree on (Bizzoni et al., 2022a), it is hard to refute that reader preferences can be measured in different ways, both in terms of consistent attention given to literary works over time, and to valuations made by critics and readers. The intrinsic qualities of texts are more difficult to agree upon as the quality of a literary work consist of many elements, some that are virtually impossible to grasp by computational methods (e.g. the effect of metaphors or images). In addition, there are text-extrinsic features, such as the public image of the author or author-gender (Wang et al., 2019; Lassen et al., 2022), which influence reviews to a degree that is hard to account for. Still, as mentioned there is evidence that intrinsic models do have some predictive value when considering an array of different features , which pertain to both style and narrative. As such, the difficulty is not to only to model literary quality, as including intrinsic and extrinsic features such as genre and author-gender in a models of quality has resulted

Proceedings of the The 5th Workshop on Narrative Understanding, pages 25–35
July 14, 2023 ©2023 Association for Computational Linguistics

in good performances (Koolen et al., 2020a) – but in elucidating what to include in a feature-set and why, and in seeking a level of interpretability.

In this study, we aim to investigate the relationship between a narrative's emotional trajectory, its fine-grained semantic profile, and its perceived literary quality. Using the average of hundreds of thousands of readers' ratings, we examine how sentiment-arcs and semantic profiles of literary narratives influence their perceived quality, exploring the prediction of these factors through a machine learning model trained on multiple features, encompassing both sentiment-related aspects and their dynamic progression, as well as semantic categorization. We also claim that access to a diverse corpus of works with a significant representation of highly successful works in all genres is an essential prerequisite for developing models with a credible performance. Without the inclusion of the best regarded works, it is not possible to produce a model that relates to what is commonly understood as the highest level of literary achievement. The 9,000 novels corpus used in our study contains several of such works from 1880 to 2000, including major modernist and postmodernist writers as well as fiction from a range of popular genres.

2 Related works

Studies that predict the perception of literary quality from textual features have primarily relied on classical stylometric features, such as sentence-length or readability (Koolen et al., 2020b; Maharjan et al., 2017), the percentage of word classes, such as adverbs or nouns (Koolen et al., 2020b) or the frequencies of n-grams in the texts (van Cranenburgh and Koolen, 2020). More recent work has tested the potential of alternative text or narrative features such as sentiment analysis (Alm, 2008; Jain et al., 2017) as a proxy for meaningful aspects of the reading experience (Drobot, 2013; Cambria et al., 2017; Kim and Klinger, 2018; Brooke et al., 2015; Jockers, 2017; Reagan et al., 2016a). Such work has focused on sentiment valence, usually drawing scores from induced lexica (Islam et al., 2020) or human annotations (Mohammad and Turney, 2013), modeling, for instance, novels' sentiment arcs (Jockers, 2017), although without considering fundamental arc-dynamics (e.g., temporal structure of plot variability) or narrative progression. By simply clustering sentiment arcs, Reagan et al. (2016a) was however able to identify six fundamental narrative arcs that underly narrative construction, while more recently, Hu et al. (2021) and Bizzoni et al. (2022b) have modeled the persistence, coherence, and predictability of sentiment arcs by fractal analysis, a method to study the dynamics of complex systems (Hu et al., 2009; Gao and Xu, 2021) and to assess the predictability and self-similarity of arcs, in order to model the relation of sentiment arcs with reader evaluation (Bizzoni et al., 2021, 2022c). Similarly, Mohseni et al. (2021) conducted fractal analysis on classical stylometric and topical features to model the difference between canonical and non-canonical literary texts. Beyond sentiment analysis, the narrative content of texts has also been shown to impact perceived quality. Relying on topic modeling, Jautze et al. (2016) has shown that a higher topic diversity in texts corresponds to higher perceived literary quality, suggesting that works with a less diverse topical palette, like genre fiction, are perceived as having overall less literary quality, while van Cranenburgh et al. (2019) has claimed that words that refer to intimate and familiar relations are distinctive of lower-rated novels, which can be linked to the hypothesis that specific genres, especially those in which women authors are dominant, are perceived as less literary (Koolen, 2018). These studies suggest that the distribution of topics touched upon in texts impacts literary quality perception. Several works have widely used resources like LIWC to model such distributions (Luoto and van Cranenburgh, 2021a; Naber and Boot, 2019). However, building on the findings of Jarmasz (2012) – i.e., that Roget's thesaurus is an excellent resource for natural language processing – Jannatus Saba et al. (2021) has shown that Roget outperforms other dictionary resources (e.g., LIWC and NRC sentiment lexicons) in modeling literary quality by category frequency – which is an intriguing argument to use the Roget categories for modelling the perception of literary quality on a larger scale.

3 Quality measures

While it is clear that various studies have recently used conceptually different features as a basis for understanding or predicting perceived literary quality, reader appreciation, or success, it should be noted that each study has a slightly different take on "quality" and that terms like "prestige", "popularity", or "canonicity" are not synonymous - although they could all be argued as aspects of quality, and a more comprehensive study would benefit from taking a stronger perspectivist approach, considering multiple definitions of quality together (Bizzoni et al., 2022a). For any study trying to assess the factors contributing to the perception of literary quality, determining the quality judgments themselves is often one, if not the first, of the most challenging tasks. Computational studies assessing literary quality often use a single standard of evaluation, which may not capture the diverse preferences of various groups of readers. Various quality measures have been used, such as readers' ratings on platforms such as GoodReads (Kousha et al., 2017), or a text's presence in established literary canons (Wilkens, 2012). Despite their diversity, different conceptions of quality can display significant convergences (Walsh and Antoniak, 2021). In this work, we have employed average book-ratings on **Goodreads**, a popular online social platform for readers that allows users, among other things, to comment, recommend, and review a book on a scale. [1] This metric possesses obvious limitations: it doesn't explicitly represent "literary quality" but arguably an aspect of it, it potentially conflates genre-specific value-judgements, and it forces GoodReads' users to reduce their literary evaluations to a mono-dimensional scale. The latter issue might also obscure important differences in rating behaviour. For example, readers of Sci-fi may be inclined to give a higher average rating on GoodReads, something that we do not take into account when using average rating as a quality metric. Nevertheless, this limitation can also be an advantage: the simplicity of the GoodReads rating system offers a streamlined approach to a problem that frequently proves overly complex for quantitative analysis. The single GoodReads' rating, representing readers' impressions on a single scale, offers a practical starting point for identifying patterns or trends across a wide range of books, genres, and authors.

On the other hand, with its 90 million users, GoodReads is argued to offer a particularly valuable insight into reading culture "in the wild" (Nakamura, 2013), as it collects books from widely different genres and curricula (Walsh and Antoniak, 2021), and derives ratings from a notably heterogeneous pool of readers in regard to backgrounds, gender, age, native languages and reading preferences (Kousha et al., 2017).

[1] https://www.goodreads.com

4 Data

We have used the Chicago Corpus as a dataset, encompassing more than 9,000 English-language novels penned or translated into English between 1880 and 2000. The selection criterion for these works is based on each novel's number of libraries holdings. This results in a diverse compilation that spans various literary styles, from popular fiction genres to highly esteemed works of literature. It comprises novels written by Nobel Prize laureates (Bizzoni et al., 2022c) and recipients of other highly regarded literary awards, as well as texts featured in canonical collections such as the Norton Anthology (Shesgreen, 2009). However, it is important to acknowledge the cultural and geographical bias present in the corpus, which exhibits a significant over-representation of Anglophone authors, limiting the scope of the analysis to a predominantly English-speaking context.

	Titles	**Authors**
Number	9089	3150
Avg. rating below 2.5	140	118
Avg. ratings	3.74	3.69

Table 1: Number of titles and authors in the corpus and below the rating of 2.5, and avg. number of ratings

5 Features

We employ three types of features, representing three distinct approaches to modeling a literary narrative. See Table 1 for a summary.

5.1 Sentiment features

We perform a simple sentiment analysis of the novels, extracting the **VADER** (Hutto and Gilbert, 2014) compound sentimental score of each sentence after tokenizing the texts with nltk (Bird, 2006). We selected this model as it is based on a lexicon and set of rules, and so remains relatively transparent. Although it was developed for social media analysis, VADER is widely employed and exhibits a good performance and consistency across domains (Ribeiro et al., 2016; Reagan et al., 2016b). When dealing with narrative, this versatility is especially valuable, as considering our corpus, we are also comparing texts across widely different (literary) genres. Moreover, the sentiment arcs resulting from VADER appear comparable to those of the **Syuzet-package** (Elkins and Chun, 2019), which was developed for literary texts (Jockers, 2017). Yet, in using VADER we side-step some of the problems of the Syuzet-package, like of word-based annotation (Swafford, 2015). To ensure the validity of our annotation, we manually inspected a selection of novels both at the sentence and arc level (e.g., fig. 1). Using VADER, the result is a rather fine-grained sentiment arc that, when de-trended, roughly describes the overall evolution of the storyline, as shown in Figure 1 (also see Hu et al. (2021) and Bizzoni et al. (2021) for more details on this method).

By examining the mean sentiment and its standard deviation for an entire novel and its subsections (e.g., the first or last ten percent), we can create a coarse representation of the narrative's emotional profile. In this study, we divide each sentiment arc into 20 segments and calculate the mean sentiment for each segment. Additionally, we include the overall sentiment mean and standard deviation as features. This approach allows for a rudimentary characterization of the sentiment-profile of the novel.

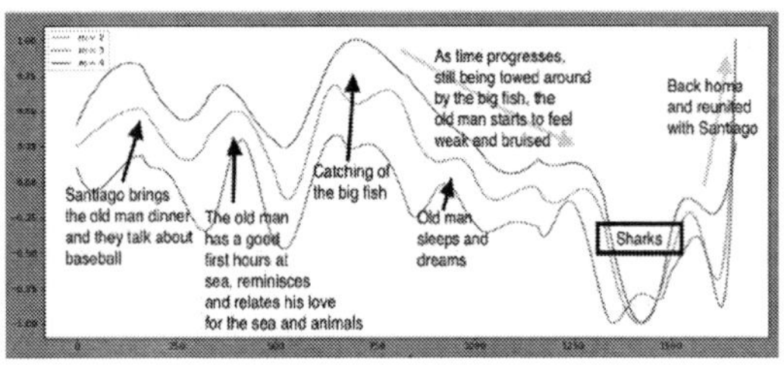

Figure 1: Sentiment arc of Hemingway's *The Old Man and the Sea* with different polynomial fits (m = polynomial degree). Values on the y-axis represent compound sentiment score as annotated with VADER, while values on the x-axis represent the narrative progression of the book by the number of sentences.

5.2 Dynamic features

As the most important aspect of a narrative arguably relies on its dynamic development rather than in its global characteristic, we relied on two measures to try and capture the high-level properties of the narratives' sentiment arcs, rather than their simple states: For each sentiment arc we computed its Hurst exponent, which represents the degree of time series persistence; and its approximate entropy, which represents the level of predictability of a series. The Hurst exponent is a measure that quantifies the persistence, or long-range dependence, of a time series, where a higher value indicates stronger trend-following behavior and a lower value represents a more anti-persistent or mean-reverting pattern. Hurst estimates of several time-dependent textual features, including narrative sentiment arcs, have been proven predictive of literary quality perception in several recent studies (Bizzoni et al., 2022b,c; Mohseni et al., 2021). Approximate entropy is a metric that evaluates the predictability of a time series by assessing the regularity and complexity of its fluctuations, with lower values indicating more predictable and repetitive patterns. In comparison, higher entropy values suggest greater randomness and unpredictability in the series. Approximate entropy has also been linked to aspects of literary quality perception (Mohseni et al., 2022).

5.3 Roget features

The aim of Roget's thesaurus was semantic classification, closely related to similar projects in areas like biology during the Victorian era, by scientists who – like Roget – were members of the Royal Society (Liddy et al., 1990). Yet the thesaurus also had an explicitly literary aim: to aid literary composition, not only as a tool to query for words and synonyms, but also as a tool for grasping "the relation which these symbols [i.e., words] bear to their corresponding ideas" (Roget, 1962). The classification scheme of the thesaurus follows six major divisions: affection, volition, intellect, abstract relations, space, and matter (Roget, 1997); each of these subdivided into three to eight subheadings, and further divided into "paragraphs". For example, "memory" with its connected words is a paragraph in the subdivision "extension of thought" within the major category of "intellect". As such, Roget-categories are semi-topical and do in a sense reflect the distribution of ideational content in literary works.

We used the Roget thesaurus of English words to construct topical representations of each narrative as the interplay of different themes with different strengths. In other words, we used the Roget thesaurus, that links each word in its collection to one or more topical-semantic categories, to derive a word-based representation of the topics "touched" by a novel (even through one single metaphoric word) and with which frequency they were mentioned. For example, the sentence

`He walked the dog`

would be linked to the categories of *Motion*

(`walked`), *Animal* (`dog`) and so forth. While the Roget thesaurus is in this respect not dissimilar from several other thesauri built to attempt a rough hyerarchization of words into concepts (see WordNet for a more modern example) we chose it due to its apparent suitability to model literary texts, as discussed in Section 2. The thesaurus was originally built around 1805 by M. R. Roget as a compilation of English language words into hyerarchical semantic clusters that would help a writer find the most apt words for their ideas. The thesaurus was partly inspired by Leibniz's symoblic languages and by Aristotle's categories, and has since its appeareance been regularly revised and increased; its most recent edition contains more than 400.000 words.

We computed how many words in a book belonged to each Roget "paragraph" (i.e., topics in each subcategory), adding the result to our feature set. While the validity of the Roget categories is questionable at linguistic and cognitive levels – like any single-handed categorization of semantics – we selected this representation due to the somewhat surprising accuracy it has demonstrated in modeling the success of literary narratives in recent studies (Saba et al., 2021; Luoto and van Cranenburgh, 2021b).

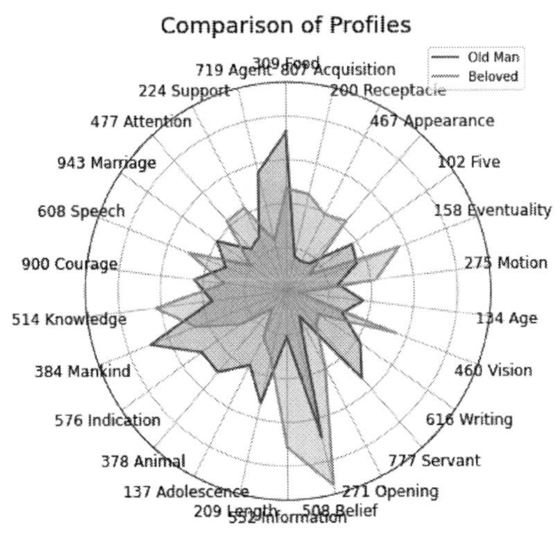

Figure 2: Profiles of Hemingway's *The Old Man and the Sea* and Morrison's *Beloved* along their most frequent categories. Hemingway's masterpiece draws on categories of food, age, animals and adolescence more than Morrison's novel, that instead peaks on speech, belief, vision and appearance.

5.4 Feature Selection

Before training a supervised prediction model on the dataset, we perform feature selection to reduce the size of the feature set and improve the interpretability of the final results. We use a filter method for feature selection (John et al., 1994), which ranks each possible feature based on a relevance weight. It then optimizes the list, shortening it to improve the model selection. The filter method of feature selection evaluates each feature independently based on a specific criterion, such as information gain or correlation with the target variable, and thus allows for the identification of the most relevant features and discarding the less important ones, ultimately leading to a reduced and more meaningful feature set for model training.

Category	Description	Number
Sentiment	mean, std SA	22
Dynamic	Hurst, AppEnt	2
Semantic	Roget categories	1044

Table 2: Feature categories and corresponding numbers.

6 Models

For our prediction task, we used a stacked ensemble model featuring a Support Vector Machine-based regressor (SVR) (Cortes and Vapnik, 1995) and a Random Forest regressor (Breiman, 2001), with a Ridge regressor as a meta-classifier (Hoerl and Kennard, 1970). The SVR is a popular choice for its ability to handle high-dimensional data and its robustness against overfitting, while the Random Forest is an ensemble method that constructs multiple decision trees to yield more accurate and stable predictions. They both outperformed other models in preliminary tests, demonstrating their promise as suitable candidates for this task. The Ridge regressor, acting as a meta-classifier in our stacked ensemble, takes the predictions from the base models as input and generates a final prediction, leveraging regularization to minimize multicollinearity issues and prevent overfitting. As we didn't find benefits in using grid search for parameter tuning, possibly due to the high computational cost and time-consuming nature of the method, we report only the results of the experiments that did not include a pre-grid search for parameter optimization, opting for a more efficient approach to model selection and training. All models were trained on

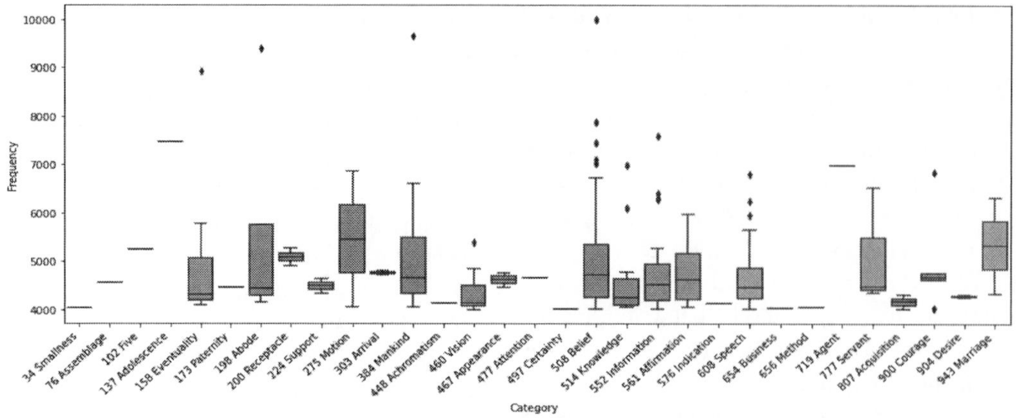

Figure 3: Raw frequencies of the most common categories in the corpus.

	Whole (9089)		score>2.5 (8949)		readers>130 (5827)	
Model	r2	MSE	r2	MSE	r2	MSE
Baseline	-1.1	0.8	-0.0041	0.11	0.0003	0.07
Sentiment Features	0.42	0.14	0.03	0.09	0.07	0.06
Roget Features	0.49	0.13	0.17	0.09	0.23	0.05
Sentiment + Roget Features	0.50	0.13	0.18	0.08	0.24	0.04
Feature selection max=500	0.41	0.14	0.16	0.09	0.22	0.06

Table 3: Model performance comparison with different features and subsets of the dataset. In parenthesis the number of titles in each subset.

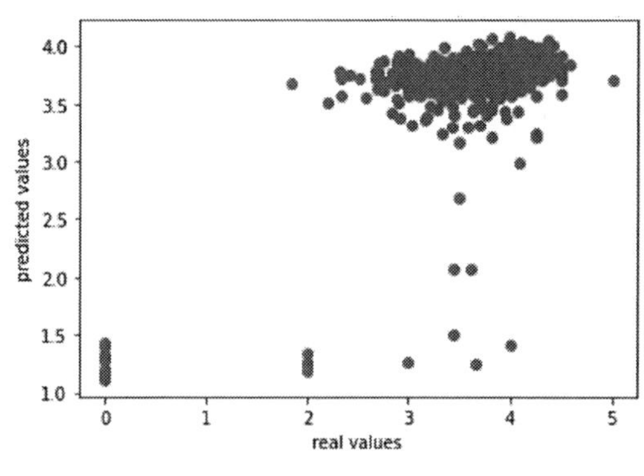

Figure 4: Distribution of real and predicted avg. rating values. Notice how ratings under 2.5 appear particularly predictable, despite their scarcity.

80% and tested on 20% of the corpus.

7 Results

7.1 Baseline

As a baseline, we used only the novels' average sentiment. This baseline relies on the intentionally simplistic idea that overall happier or sadder novels might correspond to reader-appreciation. We include this baseline to provide the reader with a comparison with a "poor model", since understanding the quality of regressor-outputs can be far from intuitive.

7.2 Using Sentiment

Using exclusively sentimental features as a basis for analysis, our model already demonstrates a notable capacity to predict GoodReaders' ratings of various literary works. However, upon closer inspection, it is evident that the high performance across the entire dataset may be somewhat misleading: a small number of exceptionally low-rated titles within the dataset exhibit a marked predictability when sentiment scores are employed as the sole predictive factor. Perhaps surprisingly, these low-rated titles seem to have overwhelmingly predictable sentimental profiles, which in turn make it relatively simple for the models to accurately predict the corresponding ratings. When we control for the low-scoring titles, sentiment analysis still appears to provide some degree of predictive power, although lower than what is achieved when bringing the Roget scores onto the scene.

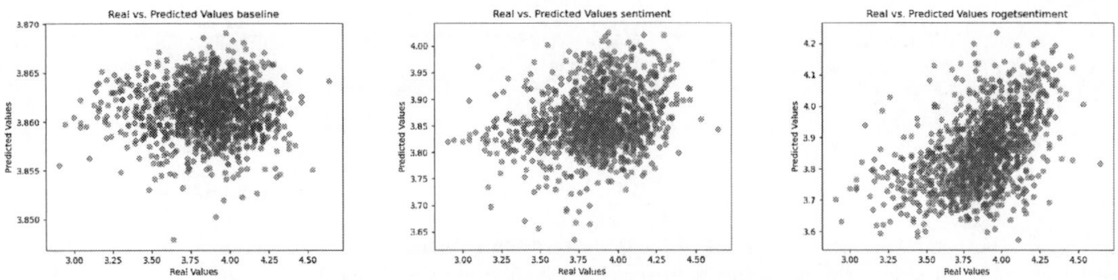

Figure 5: Distribution of real and predicted avg. rating values for all titles with more than 130 different ratings, from left to right: 1) Baseline, modelled on only one feature, the mean sentiment of arcs. 2) Using only the sentiment-arc based features. 3) Using our whole feature set: Roget features and sentiment-arc based features.

7.3 Adding Roget

Adding Roget-category frequencies in our regression model demonstrates significant improvement in predicting novels' ratings. It seems that by using these categories, we can model a broad range of linguistic and thematic elements present within the narratives, which in turn can provide valuable insights into their quality and reception. This enhancement to the model is particularly beneficial as it allows us to move beyond the limitations of relying solely on sentiment analysis. Interestingly, feature selection does not necessarily help the model. It appears that the interplay of "minor" categories maintains an important role in the overall reception of the text, and cutting the max number of features down to 500 decreases the performance of the model. On the other hand, almost halving the number of predictors reduces the r2 of "only" two points, which could be a valid tradeoff in practical applications.

7.4 Rating count thresholds

We experiment with training only the texts that have more than a given rating count (number of raters), using a threshold of 130. This represents the 0.000001 of all readers that rated books in our corpus - leaving us with 5827 titles. We find that in all cases, relying on higher scores systematically helps the models' performance. We find this particularly intriguing, as it shows that as the number of raters of a book increases, the final score may become more reliable, leading to improved predictability. This phenomenon can be likened to a larger sample size in a statistical study, where increasing the number of data points tends to produce more accurate and consistent results. The fact that our models perform better when relying on a higher number of reader scores seems to imply that there is a discernible, shared perception of literary quality among readers. This collective assessment, in turn, hints at the existence of certain objective criteria that contribute to the evaluation of a book's merit.

8 Inspecting the most rated individual titles

To better understand and analyse the strength and weakness of our model, we inspected the works that elicited its most accurate and the least predictions, considering only the "elite" of the most widely read (and often canonical) titles setting, a rating count threshold at 90,000. We provide an example of the very top and bottom of the list in Table 4. On top of the list of the **worst predicted** are both famous and infamous novels: Ayn Rand's *Atlas Shrugged*, William Gibson's *Neuromancer*, James Joyce's *Ulysses*, and Isaac Asimov's *I: Robot.* One possible explanation for this phenomenon is that these are all works that have a devoted following. As the model is solely fed with text-intrinsic features it would not be able to predict a more cult-like admiration of works that may otherwise be considered to be either very complex stylistically, like *Ulysses*, less literary, like *Atlas Shrugged*, or particularly simple in style, like *I: Robot.* Having a reputation that makes these "more than just novels", but cultural beacons of various kinds, may affect users' grading behaviour. Looking at instances with the lowest error in predicting average GoodReads rating, the **best predicted** titles in our model, it is clear that these are popular and accessible works rather than highly canonized works. Genre fiction, such as Sci-fi (Dick, Card, Butler), Fantasy (Gabaldon), and Mystery (Evanovich) dominate the list of best-predicted titles. A bit further down the list, below rank 13th, authors such as Toni Morri-

Best predicted				Worst predicted			
Error	Title	Author	Rating count	Error	Title	Author	Rating count
0,0013	*A Scanner Darkly*	Philip K. Dick	97963	0,1716	*Stoner*	John Williams	133814
0,0013	*The Big Sleep*	Raymond Chandler	144616	0,1415	*Robin*	Frances H. Burnett	1055312
0,0017	*The Color Purple*	Alice Walker	628511	0,1374	*And Then There Were None*	Agatha Christie	1124501
0,0018	*Xenocide*	Orson Scott Card	150601	0,1318	*Rebecca*	Daphne Du Maurier	557804
0,0019	*High Five*	Janet Evanovich	123615	0,1313	*Blood Meridian*	Cormac McCarthy	129364
0,002	*Kindred*	Octavia E. Butler	153340	0,128	*The Screwtape Letters*	C.S. Lewis	394394
0,0024	*Dragonfly In Amber*	Diana Gabaldon	327501	0,1193	*Atlas Shrugged*	Ayn Rand	375362
0,003	*Hatchet*	Gary Paulsen	356112	0,1102	*Ulysses*	James Joyce	120014

Table 4: Top 8 best and worst predicted titles of the best-performing model (all features), trained with a threshold of 130 readers. Error represents the difference between the real and predicted GoodReads' rating of titles.

son, Ernest Hemingway, John Steinbeck, Truman Capote, Aldous Huxley, and John Irving appear. All are known for solid craftsmanship and accessible stories.

Only conjectures can be made from inspecting these lists, but we do seem to see contours of a skewed grading that is based on more than text-intrinsic features, like a form of readerly devotion that may be playing a role in both the rating count and the average score of some titles.

Another possible interpretation of this distribution, sustained by the large amount of genre fiction among the best-predicted titles, is that the features we selected for our model, and in particular the Roget categories, behave in a characteristic way in works of genre-fiction, while more general works of literature might be distinguished better by considering stylistic features (wholly bypassed in our model). As such, Roget categories may be acting as a proxy for genre, which would be reasonable considering the ideational focus of the Roget thesaurus. The predictability of genre fiction especially may be explained if we assume that genre-fiction tends to place in a narrower grade-interval proper to their genre, while more general or "literary fiction" falls more consistently in a widert interval of ratings (from very low to very high).

An alternative hypothesis, not entirely incompatible with the above and in line with previous work (Jautze et al., 2016) , is that genre-fiction and lower-rated works tend to be more mono-topical, i.e., be less diverse in content, treating a smaller range of topics. As such, Roget categories may also to some extent be measuring topic-diversity, accurately predicting works lower that are more mono-topical. All in all, it is essential to bear in mind that our feature set does not include any stylometric features (such as word choice, sentence structure, and the use of punctuation), leaving it blind to a crucial aspect of literature – or even to "literariness" as such: stylistics contribute significantly to the experience of the uniqueness and richness of a literary work (Miall and Kuiken, 1998), and is a central part of the impact of fiction in non-genre-fiction in particular (Boot and Koolen, 2020). Since our feature-set only observes texts from the sentimental and semantic perspective, it is possible that elements central to the reading experience in some of these titles remain unobserved. Finally, the model's sensitivity to topical interplays might enable it to more accurately identify popular trends and themes and have a skewed performance towards books that follow popular topical patterns rather than those that exhibit exceptional style or depth.

9 Conclusions and future works

The present study has shown that a combination of sentiment arc features, including dynamic measures, and semantic profiling based on Roget categories enhances the predictive power of regression models for perceived literary quality – as measured through average GoodReads' scores – across thousands of novels from the 19th and 20th century. Our findings indicate that by accounting for a diverse set of psycho-semantic features in combination with measures that consider both the dynamics and valences of the novels sentiment arcs, we can obtain a performance that is better than that of any of the latter two approaches in isolation. A surprising finding was that the worst-rated titles seem to exhibit a particular predictability, possessing a more distinguishable profile in comparison to other titles, which might have contributed to an artificial inflation of our model's performance. It suggests that these particular titles may share specific sentiment or topical features that make them stand out from the rest, by which our model can identify them more easily. Our results also highlight that the sheer magnitude of readers' ratings consistently enhances model performance. This observation supports the idea that certain aspects of literary quality tap into aesthetic preferences that are shared among large numbers of readers, at least widely enough to make predictions based on text profiling more reliable with a larger pool of evaluators.

Moreover, the predictive capacity of Roget categories and sentiment arcs for literary quality perception indicate that there exists a underlying structure in how readers perceive and evaluate literary works. Roget categories enable us to capture a coarse representation of the semantic content within texts, offering insights into themes, motifs, and granular references to topics that might resonate with readers. Our related measures of sentiment arcs, in contrast, capture the emotional dynamics of the narratives, allowing us to examine the progression of feelings and the level of consistency and predictability of the story as it unfolds. This aspect is crucial because it highlights the role of sentiments in shaping the reader's engagement and overall impression of a text. By combining these two dimensions — semantic content and sentimental dynamics — we can delve deeper into the complex interplay between emotional patterns and thematic elements which impacts the perception of literary quality. This holistic approach enables us to gain a more nuanced understanding of the factors that contribute to the appreciation of literary works and the ways in which readers discern quality in literature. Additionally, this combined analysis might potentially unveil commonalities and differences among various genres, styles, and time periods, further enriching our understanding of the multifaceted nature of literary quality.

Our approach still has a large number of limitations that need to be acknowledged. First, our approach relies on a reductive representation of the narrative texts, overlooking all traditional stylometric measures. The perception of literary quality is an intricate concept that relies on numerous factors, ranging from the stylistics, characters, plot development and pace, to cultural contexts. By reducing each narrative text to a subset of chosen features, our approach inevitably discards much of the richness and subtlety of works, while the narrow range facilitated by GoodReads' scores forces the models to discern nuanced differences in perceived quality among texts that may be considered generally good by readers. This clearly limits our understanding of literary quality, especially when it comes to the more linguistically or stylistically virtuous titles. Secondly, the reliance on GoodReads scores as the sole metric of quality introduces biases, as these scores are inevitably influenced by factors such as genre preferences and reader demographics. Finally, the analysis is based on a limited sample of English-language texts from the 19th and 20th centuries, potentially limiting the generalizability of our findings to other periods, languages, or contexts. For the same reason, our study cannot consider the potential impact of translation and its effect on the reception of the texts. At the same time, given the inherent complexity of these constraints and the subjective nature of literary evaluation, the performances achieved by our models in terms of r2 scores and mean squared errors, which would be modest for easier tasks, can be considered rather promising.

Naturally, there is much that can be done from here. In the future, we intend to compile an even larger data set, in terms of both texts and features. Integrating stylometric and syntactic features, for instance, could provide additional insights into the complex nature of literary quality. Furthermore, we plan to investigate genre-specific patterns, as observing the performance of our models across different genres may reveal unique patterns and relationships that are specific to particular types of literature. Finally, we intend to use more diverse and sophisticated metrics than GoodReads: exploring alternative sources such as anthologies, awards, and canon lists. Leveraging a richer set of indicators for literary quality/qualities, we hope to gain clearer insights into the complex interplay of factors that contribute to the perception of literary quality.

References

Ebba Cecilia Ovesdotter Alm. 2008. *Affect in text and speech*. University of Illinois at Urbana-Champaign.

Steven Bird. 2006. Nltk: the natural language toolkit. In *Proceedings of the COLING/ACL 2006 Interactive Presentation Sessions*, pages 69–72.

Yuri Bizzoni, Ida Marie Lassen, Telma Peura, Mads Rosendahl Thomsen, and Kristoffer Nielbo. 2022a. Predicting Literary Quality How Perspectivist Should We Be? In *Proceedings of the 1st Workshop on Perspectivist Approaches to NLP @LREC2022*, pages 20–25, Marseille, France. European Language Resources Association.

Yuri Bizzoni, Telma Peura, Kristoffer Nielbo, and Mads Thomsen. 2022b. Fractal sentiments and fairy tales-fractal scaling of narrative arcs as predictor of the perceived quality of andersen's fairy tales. *Journal of Data Mining & Digital Humanities*.

Yuri Bizzoni, Telma Peura, Kristoffer Nielbo, and Mads Thomsen. 2022c. Fractality of sentiment arcs for literary quality assessment: The case of nobel laureates. In *Proceedings of the 2nd International Workshop on Natural Language Processing for Digital Humanities*, pages 31–41, Taipei, Taiwan. Association for Computational Linguistics.

Yuri Bizzoni, Telma Peura, Mads Rosendahl Thomsen, and Kristoffer Nielbo. 2021. Sentiment dynamics of success: Fractal scaling of story arcs predicts reader preferences. In *Proceedings of the Workshop on Natural Language Processing for Digital Humanities*, pages 1–6, NIT Silchar, India. NLP Association of India (NLPAI).

Peter Boot and Marijn Koolen. 2020. Captivating, splendid or instructive?: Assessing the impact of reading in online book reviews:. *Scientific Study of Literature*, 10(1):35–63. Publisher: John Benjamins Publishing Company.

Leo Breiman. 2001. Random forests. *Machine learning*, 45:5–32.

Julian Brooke, Adam Hammond, and Graeme Hirst. 2015. Gutentag: an nlp-driven tool for digital humanities research in the project gutenberg corpus. In *Proceedings of the Fourth Workshop on Computational Linguistics for Literature*, pages 42–47.

Erik Cambria, Dipankar Das, Sivaji Bandyopadhyay, and Antonio Feraco. 2017. Affective computing and sentiment analysis. In *A practical guide to sentiment analysis*, pages 1–10. Springer.

Corinna Cortes and Vladimir Vapnik. 1995. Support-vector networks. *Machine learning*, 20(3):273–297.

Irina-Ana Drobot. 2013. Affective narratology. the emotional structure of stories. *Philologica Jassyensia*, 9(2):338.

Katherine Elkins and Jon Chun. 2019. Can Sentiment Analysis Reveal Structure in a Plotless Novel? ArXiv:1910.01441 [cs].

Jianbo Gao and Bo Xu. 2021. Complex Systems, Emergence, and Multiscale Analysis: A Tutorial and Brief Survey. *Applied Sciences*, 11(12):5736.

Arthur E Hoerl and Robert W Kennard. 1970. Ridge regression: Biased estimation for nonorthogonal problems. *Technometrics*, 12(1):55–67.

Jing Hu, Jianbo Gao, and Xingsong Wang. 2009. Multifractal analysis of sunspot time series: the effects of the 11-year cycle and Fourier truncation. *Journal of Statistical Mechanics: Theory and Experiment*, 2009(02):P02066.

Qiyue Hu, Bin Liu, Mads Rosendahl Thomsen, Jianbo Gao, and Kristoffer L Nielbo. 2021. Dynamic evolution of sentiments in never let me go: Insights from multifractal theory and its implications for literary analysis. *Digital Scholarship in the Humanities*, 36(2):322–332.

Clayton Hutto and Eric Gilbert. 2014. Vader: A parsimonious rule-based model for sentiment analysis of social media text. In *Proceedings of the international AAAI conference on web and social media*, volume 8, pages 216–225.

SM Mazharul Islam, Xin Luna Dong, and Gerard de Melo. 2020. Domain-specific sentiment lexicons induced from labeled documents. In *Proceedings of the 28th International Conference on Computational Linguistics*, pages 6576–6587.

Swapnil Jain, Shrikant Malviya, Rohit Mishra, and Uma Shanker Tiwary. 2017. Sentiment analysis: An empirical comparative study of various machine learning approaches. In *Proceedings of the 14th International Conference on Natural Language Processing (ICON-2017)*, pages 112–121, Kolkata, India. NLP Association of India.

Syeda Jannatus Saba, Biddut Sarker Bijoy, Henry Gorelick, Sabir Ismail, Md Saiful Islam, and Mohammad Ruhul Amin. 2021. A Study on Using Semantic Word Associations to Predict the Success of a Novel. In *Proceedings of *SEM 2021: The Tenth Joint Conference on Lexical and Computational Semantics*, pages 38–51, Online. Association for Computational Linguistics.

Mario Jarmasz. 2012. Roget's thesaurus as a lexical resource for natural language processing.

Kim Jautze, Andreas van Cranenburgh, and Corina Koolen. 2016. Topic modeling literary quality. In *Digital Humanities 2016: Conference Abstracts*, pages 233–237.

Matthew Jockers. 2017. Syuzhet: Extracts sentiment and sentiment-derived plot arcs from text (version 1.0. 1).

George H John, Ron Kohavi, and Karl Pfleger. 1994. Irrelevant features and the subset selection problem. In *Machine learning proceedings 1994*, pages 121–129. Elsevier.

Evgeny Kim and Roman Klinger. 2018. A survey on sentiment and emotion analysis for computational literary studies. *arXiv preprint arXiv:1808.03137*.

Corina Koolen, Karina van Dalen-Oskam, Andreas van Cranenburgh, and Erica Nagelhout. 2020a. Literary quality in the eye of the Dutch reader: The national reader survey. *Poetics*, 79:1–13.

Corina Koolen, Karina van Dalen-Oskam, Andreas van Cranenburgh, and Erica Nagelhout. 2020b. Literary quality in the eye of the dutch reader: The national reader survey. *Poetics*, 79:101439.

Cornelia Wilhelmina Koolen. 2018. *Reading beyond the female: the relationship between perception of author gender and literary quality*. Number DS-2018-03 in ILLC dissertation series. Institute for Logic, Language and Computation, Universiteit van Amsterdam, Amsterdam.

Kayvan Kousha, Mike Thelwall, and Mahshid Abdoli. 2017. Goodreads reviews to assess the wider impacts of books. 68(8):2004–2016. _eprint: https://onlinelibrary.wiley.com/doi/pdf/10.1002/asi.23805.

Ida Marie Schytt Lassen, Yuri Bizzoni, Telma Peura, Mads Rosendahl Thomsen, and Kristoffer Laigaard Nielbo. 2022. Reviewer Preferences and Gender Disparities in Aesthetic Judgments. In *CEUR Workshop Proceedings*, pages 280–290, Antwerp, Belgium. ArXiv:2206.08697 [cs].

Elizabeth D. Liddy, Caroline A. Hert, and Philip Doty. 1990. Roget's International Thesaurus: Conceptual Issues and Potential Applications. *Advances in Classification Research Online*, pages 95–100.

Severi Luoto and Andreas van Cranenburgh. 2021a. Psycholinguistic dataset on language use in 1145 novels published in English and Dutch. *Data in Brief*, 34:106655.

Severi Luoto and Andreas van Cranenburgh. 2021b. Psycholinguistic dataset on language use in 1145 novels published in english and dutch. *Data in brief*, 34:106655.

Suraj Maharjan, John Arevalo, Manuel Montes, Fabio A. González, and Thamar Solorio. 2017. A multi-task approach to predict likability of books. In *Proceedings of the 15th Conference of the European Chapter of the Association for Computational Linguistics: Volume 1, Long Papers*, pages 1217–1227, Valencia, Spain. Association for Computational Linguistics.

David S. Miall and Don Kuiken. 1998. The form of reading: Empirical studies of literariness. *Poetics*, 25(6):327–341.

Saif Mohammad and Peter Turney. 2013. Nrc emotion lexicon. *National Research Council, Canada*, 2:1–234.

Mahdi Mohseni, Volker Gast, and Christoph Redies. 2021. Fractality and variability in canonical and non-canonical english fiction and in non-fictional texts. 12.

Mahdi Mohseni, Christoph Redies, and Volker Gast. 2022. Approximate entropy in canonical and non-canonical fiction. *Entropy*, 24(2):278.

Floor Naber and Peter Boot. 2019. Exploring the features of naturalist prose using LIWC in Nederlab. *Journal of Dutch Literature*, 10(1). Number: 1.

Lisa Nakamura. 2013. "Words with friends": Socially networked reading on Goodreads. *PMLA*, 128(1):238–243.

Andrew J Reagan, Lewis Mitchell, Dilan Kiley, Christopher M Danforth, and Peter Sheridan Dodds. 2016a. The emotional arcs of stories are dominated by six basic shapes. 5(1):1–12.

Andrew J. Reagan, Brian Tivnan, Jake Ryland Williams, Christopher M. Danforth, and Peter Sheridan Dodds. 2016b. Benchmarking sentiment analysis methods for large-scale texts: A case for using continuum-scored words and word shift graphs. ArXiv:1512.00531 [cs].

Filipe N. Ribeiro, Matheus Araújo, Pollyanna Gonçalves, Marcos André Gonçalves, and Fabrício Benevenuto. 2016. SentiBench - a benchmark comparison of state-of-the-practice sentiment analysis methods. *EPJ Data Science*, 5(1):1–29. Number: 1 Publisher: SpringerOpen.

Peter Mark Roget. 1997. *Roget's II: the new thesaurus*. Taylor & Francis.

Robert Roget. 1962. Introduction [1852]. In Peter Mark, editor, *The Original Roget's Thesaurus of English Words and Phrases.*, pages 25–43. St. Martin's Press, New York.

Syeda Jannatus Saba, Biddut Sarker Bijoy, Henry Gorelick, Sabir Ismail, Md Saiful Islam, and Mohammad Ruhul Amin. 2021. A study on using semantic word associations to predict the success of a novel. In *Proceedings of* SEM 2021: The Tenth Joint Conference on Lexical and Computational Semantics*, pages 38–51.

Sean Shesgreen. 2009. Canonizing the canonizer: A short history of the norton anthology of english literature. *Critical Inquiry*, 35(2):293–318.

Annie Swafford. 2015. Problems with the Syuzhet Package.

Andreas van Cranenburgh and Corina Koolen. 2020. Results of a single blind literary taste test with short anonymized novel fragments. *arXiv preprint arXiv:2011.01624*.

Andreas van Cranenburgh, Karina van Dalen-Oskam, and Joris van Zundert. 2019. Vector space explorations of literary language. *Language Resources and Evaluation*, 53(4):625–650.

Melanie Walsh and Maria Antoniak. 2021. The goodreads 'classics': A computational study of readers, amazon, and crowdsourced amateur criticism. *Journal of Cultural Analytics*, 4:243–287.

Xindi Wang, Burcu Yucesoy, Onur Varol, Tina Eliassi-Rad, and Albert-László Barabási. 2019. Success in books: Predicting book sales before publication. *EPJ Data Science*, 8(1):31.

Matthew Wilkens. 2012. Canons, close reading, and the evolution of method. *Debates in the digital humanities*, pages 249–58.

Word Category Arcs in Literature Across Languages and Genres

Winston Wu **Lu Wang** **Rada Mihalcea**
Computer Science and Engineering
University of Michigan
{wuws,wangluxy,mihalcea}@umich.edu

Abstract

Word category arcs measure the progression of word usage across a story. Previous work on arcs has explored structural and psycholinguistic arcs through the course of narratives, but so far it has been limited to *English* narratives and a narrow set of word categories covering binary emotions and cognitive processes. In this paper, we expand over previous work by (1) introducing a novel, general approach to quantitatively analyze word usage arcs for any word category through a combination of clustering and filtering; and (2) exploring narrative arcs in literature in eight different languages across multiple genres. Through multiple experiments and analyses, we quantify the nature of narratives across languages, corroborating existing work on monolingual narrative arcs as well as drawing new insights about the interpretation of arcs through correlation analyses.

1 Introduction

Throughout history, the narrative has been an essential medium for communicating and transferring information. The study of the structure of narratives has roots in the ancient Greek philosophers but did not gain much interest until the last few hundred years. One of the most well-known structures is Freytag's pyramid, the dramatic arc of German novelist and playwright Gustav Freytag (1894), which contains five stages: exposition, rising action, climax, falling action, and resolution. Many others have hypothesized sets of universal structures into which all narratives can be classified. For example, Foster-Harris (1959) argued that a story has three basic plots that end with a happy, unhappy, or tragic ending. Booker (2004) proposed seven basic plots: overcoming the monster, rags to riches, the quest, voyage and return, comedy, tragedy, and rebirth. Others have posited 20 plots (Tobias, 2012) and even 36 plots (Polti, 1917) that are universal across great stories.

Regardless of the actual number of different plots, one point is clear: the structures of plots naturally vary. A story's structure gives coherence to the entire plot and can be mathematically represented as a function over time, or a *narrative arc*. The American writer Kurt Vonnegut claimed in his famously rejected master's thesis (1947) that every story can be plotted as such a curve, where the x-axis is the duration of the story, and the y-axis is a character's "Ill Fortune – Great Fortune" (Vonnegut, 1999). This was a revolutionary notion at the time and only recently has been computationally investigated. Following existing computational work (Mohammad, 2011; Reagan et al., 2016; Boyd et al., 2020), we consider a *narrative arc* as a measure of word usage (count) across a story. We use the term *word category arc* to emphasize that this arc is measured by examining words that belong to certain categories. This count may be z-score standardized to better understand the relative usage of certain words across a story. Thus, an arc provides a high-level structural overview of a narrative.

All cultures tell stories, but the manner in which the stories are told differs. Narrative arcs are one method for quantifying the cultural differences in stories. We first describe a general framework for analyzing arcs in a narrative that follows closely from Vonnegut's claim. To compute arcs, we measure the usage of words in a given word category, such as positive emotion words in LIWC (Pennebaker et al., 2015), a popular dictionary of English words associated with various psychometric properties. However, LIWC is not available for many of the world's languages. Thus, we develop an automatic method to translate the English LIWC into other languages. Our automatic translations exhibit high overlap with an existing manual Chinese translation (Huang et al., 2012), indicating that machine translation is a viable alternative to human translations, which are often tedious and costly. Using our translated LIWC dictionaries,

Proceedings of the The 5th Workshop on Narrative Understanding, pages 36–47
July 14, 2023

we perform in-depth analyses of many categories of arcs, including those that represent structure and emotion, in eight different languages. Next, we investigate narrative arcs across stories in multiple languages from Project Gutenberg, a large repository of public-domain books. While different languages largely exhibit similar arcs on average, we find that different genres of stories follow diverse narrative arcs, which we concretely quantify through correlation analyses. Finally, we demonstrate how to interpret clusters of arcs, and how similar word categories can be identified by their arcs even when the categories have no words in common. Code to reproduce our experiments is available at `github.com/wswu/arcs`.

2 Related Work

Storytelling. Storytelling differences have largely been investigated in classroom settings (see McCabe (1997) for a survey). For example, the age and ethnicity of the storyteller are linked to differences in the stories' emotionality, relationality, and socialization (Pasupathi et al., 2002). However, such differences have not been investigated in novels and at the scale conducted in our work.

Narrative Arcs. The field of NLP disagrees on what exactly constitutes narrative (Piper et al., 2021). Narrative arcs are one method for studying the structure of narratives. They do not seek to capture traditional notions of narrative (e.g. sequences of events or interactions between characters) but rather measure changes in a story over time. Most previous work has focused on emotion or sentiment arcs. Mohammad (2011) study the occurrence of emotion words by applying the NRC Emotion Lexicon Mohammad and Turney (2013) to English novels and fairy tales. Reagan et al. (2016) study emotional arcs in English fiction books from Project Gutenberg using a variety of machine learning methods including principal component analysis, clustering, and self-organizing maps. Somasundaran et al. (2020) study emotional arcs in stories written by students. Boyd et al. (2020) compile a set of words associated with three narrative phases—staging, plot progression, and cognitive tension—and apply these lists to analyze a variety of texts including Project Gutenberg, self-published romance novels, sci-tech news articles, and Supreme Court opinions. Narrative arcs have also been applied to other downstream tasks, including predicting turning points in narratives (Ouyang and McKeown, 2015) and genre classification of novels (Kim et al., 2017). One common limitation in these works is their focus on English text, which we seek to remedy in our work.

LIWC Dictionaries. LIWC consists of a lexicon of word patterns associated with various psycholinguistic categories. Many previous efforts have translated earlier versions of LIWC into languages including (among others) Dutch (Boot et al., 2017; Van Wissen and Boot, 2017), German (Meier et al., 2019), and Romanian (Dudău and Sava, 2020). However, the process of translation often requires years of intensive manual effort. Computational approaches to LIWC translation are usually based on existing translation dictionaries, possibly with techniques such as triangulating through a third language (Massó et al., 2013). Van Wissen and Boot (2017) showed that using Google Translate to translate the LIWC dictionary word for word into Dutch is a viable solution. However, as of this writing, Google Translate supports only 113 languages. We develop a simple but effective automatic translation method using Wiktionary that can be applied to over 4,000 languages, and we show its effectiveness by comparing translations using this method with an existing Chinese LIWC dictionary (Huang et al., 2012).

3 Data and Dictionaries

Our analysis requires two main resources: a collection of narratives in multiple languages, and dictionaries with relevant word categories for the same set of languages.

3.1 Narratives

We utilize Project Gutenberg, a repository of over 60K public-domain books in many languages. We download the plaintext versions of books from Project Gutenberg, then remove Project Gutenberg headers and footers, lowercase, tokenize, and perform dependency parsing using spaCy.[1] Following existing work, we analyze novels within the Fiction genre, focusing on languages with the most number of books in Project Gutenberg (Figure 1) that also cover a wide range of cultures. Not shown in Figure 1 is the full English set of 13,656 fiction books. Given the uneven distribution of books across the languages, for our analyses described in Section 4.2, we downsample the set of English

[1] https://spacy.io

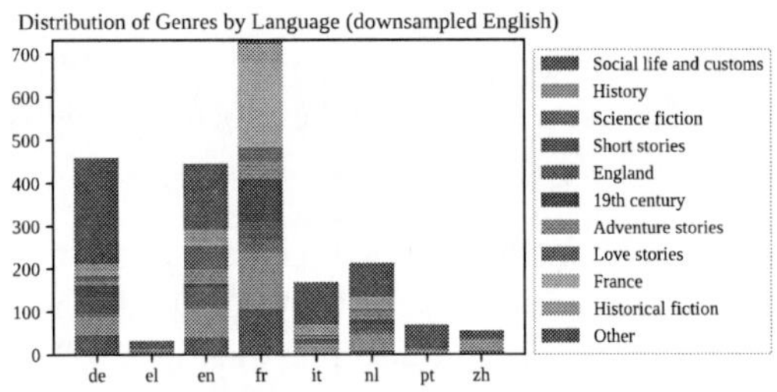

Figure 1: Number of fiction books compiled from Project Gutenberg, split by language and genres. Note that 13,565 English books were downsampled to form this set of 436 books shown here.

texts, keeping 436 books contained in the Project Gutenberg bookshelves "Best Books Ever Listings" or "Bestsellers, American, 1895-1923".

3.2 Word Dictionaries

We seek to quantify differences in narrative structure among stories of different languages. To this end, we study word category arcs using two sets of word lists: arc-of-narrative word lists (Boyd et al., 2020), and Linguistic Inquiry and Word Count (LIWC) dictionaries (Pennebaker et al., 2015). We describe each of these in turn.

Boyd et al. (2020) builds upon Gustav Freytag's pyramid of dramatic structure: exposition, rising action, climax, falling action, and resolution. They condensed Freytag's five-step model into three narrative phases: staging, plot progression, and cognitive tension. They find that the staging phase, associated with setting the scene of the story, is characterized by higher relative usage of function words such as prepositions and articles, which diminish as the story progresses. The plot progression phase is characterized by increased use of auxiliary verbs, pronouns, and connectives that help move the story forward. Finally, the cognitive tension phase is characterized by an increase in cognitive process words up until the climax of the narrative, at which point it then decreases. Boyd et al. (2020) constructed three lists of words correlated with these three patterns, which they call arcs of narrative.[2]

LIWC (Pennebaker et al., 2015) is a proprietary lexicon that associates word patterns with a range of psychological processes, including emotion, cognitive processes, perceptual processes, bodily processes, drives, personal concerns, and many others. LIWC is one of the most popular tools to analyze word usage in texts with respect to psychological processes.

We compute narrative arcs using word categories from both these dictionaries. By tracking the usage of a specific category of words (e.g. positive emotion words) longitudinally across the duration of the narrative, we can study the structure of narratives just as Vonnegut envisioned. Computationally, others have analyzed narratives in this way (Mohammad, 2011; Reagan et al., 2016; Boyd et al., 2020), but only on English text and with a limited number of word categories.

3.3 Translating Dictionaries

One goal of this work is to generalize the study of narrative arcs *across languages*. However, existing word lists are largely limited to English. In addition, some popular resources like LIWC are proprietary, and thus many researchers may not have access to LIWC and its translations. Thus, we develop a method to translate such dictionaries, including the arc of narratives list and LIWC, using Wiktionary,[3] a large, multilingual, crowdsourced dictionary freely available online.

Because these lists contain words as well as stem patterns (e.g. *happy* and *happi**), we first perform pattern expansion on each word, using the entries in Wiktionary as a comprehensive word list. Note that contrary to some traditional dictionaries, Wiktionary contains inflected forms as separate dictionary entries (e.g. *eat* and *eats*). Then, we use translations within Wiktionary (Wu and Yarowsky, 2020a,b) as a translation table to translate each word into seven target languages: German (de), Spanish (es), French (fr), Greek (el), Italian (it), Dutch (nl), and Chinese (zh). Each translation is then associated with the set of psychological categories of the original English word. This process is illustrated in Figure 2.

The process of pattern expansion on the three arc of narrative dictionaries expanded the original size of 916 words and patterns to 2,201 words. Pattern expansion on the English LIWC 2015 resulted in roughly 6.5K LIWC words and patterns expanded into 23K English words. The Wiktionary translation process generated a similar order of magnitude of translations into the target languages, as shown in Table 1. We use these translated dictionaries in the rest of this work.

Certain categories may be harder to translate: by

[2]Not to be confused with the broader term of *narrative arcs*.

[3]https://www.wiktionary.org

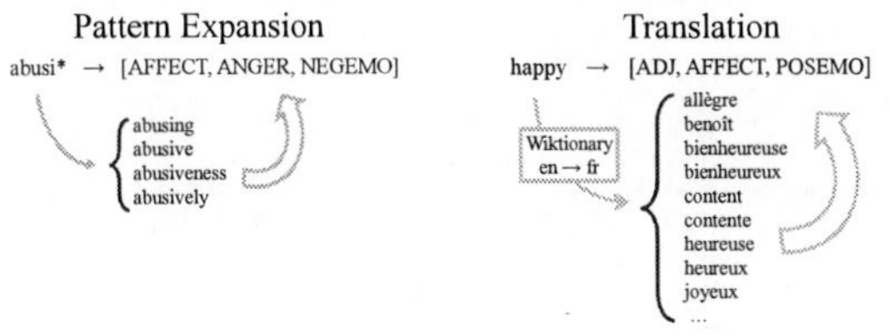

Figure 2: Illustration of the process of expanding LIWC asterisk patterns and performing automatic translation into French using Wiktionary. The resulting words inherit the original word's LIWC patterns.

Language	# Words
de	25k
el	11k
en	23k
es	23k
fr	20k
it	28k
nl	16k
zh	14k

Table 1: Translated LIWC dictionary sizes.

applying manually translated LIWC editions in English, Dutch, Romanian, and Brazilian Portuguese to analyze parallel texts in the four languages, Dudău and Sava (2021) found strong between-dictionary equivalences for function words that are not linguistically specific (e.g., negations, numbers, and I-statements), and several categories of content words (e.g., negative emotions, perceptual processes, biological processes, and personal concerns), while finding a weak correlation between many grammatical categories (e.g. third-person singular pronouns, auxiliary verbs, adverbs, conjugations, adjectives), the reward category, and the informal language category. Because of this, we ignore grammatical categories and limit our analysis of narrative arcs to psychological and cognitive categories, which are stable between languages (Dudău and Sava, 2021).

Case Study on Chinese. The Simplified Chinese version of LIWC (Huang et al., 2012) was created by manually translating the English LIWC 2007 and includes eleven new Chinese-specific categories that do not exist in the English version, as well as 106 words that occurred in the top 2000 most frequent words in the Sinica Corpus 3.0 (Chen et al., 1996). To validate our translation approach, we apply our method to automatically translate the English LIWC into Chinese and compare with the existing human-translated Chinese LIWC. The Chinese LIWC contains 6,828 words, while our translation of the English LIWC into Chinese contains 14,849 words. Because our translation contains both simplified and traditional characters, we convert all traditional Chinese characters to simplified characters using character conversion tables,[4] resulting in a total of 9,937 translations. In addition, because the English and Chinese word lists have slightly different LIWC categories, we remove the following categories that do not exist in both lists: all function words (FUNCT and subcategories); from the Chinese version, tense words (TENSEM and subcategories) and HUMANS; and from the English version: MALE, FEMALE, and certain informal words (INFORMAL, NETSPEAK, NONFLU, and FILLER).

Words in the Chinese LIWC have a mean number of categories of 2.46 (std. 1.04), while our translated list has a mean number of categories of 3.01 (std. 1.75), indicating that our automatic translation is slightly overproductive. The two lists' intersection contains 3,301 words, with a Jaccard distance of 0.54 indicating moderately high overlap. We compare a random selection of words in Table 2.

Though our translations are overproductive, the new word categories are often valid additions. For example, 哇 'wow!' is annotated as AFFECT and ASSENT in (Huang et al., 2012), but our translation adds the categories INFORMAL, NETSPEAK, and POSEMO. We believe these categories are actually omissions from the manual translation. Often the differences in categories lie at the superclass level because LIWC categories are hierarchical: a word labeled as WORK also falls under PERSONAL (the superclass of WORK). Similarly, all POWER words are DRIVES words by definition. For words that exist in our translation but do not exist in (Huang et al., 2012), a manual analysis indicates that many of them should be valid inclusions.

This case study on Chinese indicates that word-level translation of the English LIWC dictionaries is practical and feasible. Thus, we release our translations of the English LIWC into the seven non-English languages investigated in this paper, as well as the code to generate translations into over 4,000 languages supported by Wiktionary, in order to encourage further research in this area. We believe these automatically translated lexicons will serve as excellent starting points, saving hundreds of hours of manual translation. These can then be

[4] https://github.com/BYVoid/OpenCC

Word	Translation	LIWC Categories in Huang et al. (2012)	LIWC Categories in Our Translation
客人	guest	FRIEND, SOCIAL	FRIEND, SOCIAL
舐	to lick	PERCEPT	PERCEPT
消沉	depressed	AFFECT, NEGEMO, SAD	AFFECT, NEGEMO, SAD
哇	wow	AFFECT, ASSENT	AFFECT, INFORMAL, NETSPEAK, POSEMO
公安	public safety	PERSONAL, WORK	DRIVES, POWER, WORK
律师	lawyer	PERSONAL, WORK	DRIVES, POWER, WORK
节食	to diet	BIO, INGEST	BIO, HEALTH, INGEST
孙女	granddaughter	FAMILY, SOCIAL	FAMILY, FEMALE, SOCIAL
套房	hotel suite	HOME, PERSONAL	HOME
作孽	to sin	—	AFFECT, NEGEMO, RELIG
好站	warlike	—	ADJ, AFFECT, ANGER, NEGEMO
落败	to be defeated	—	ACHIEV, AFFECT, DRIVES, NEGEMO, POWER
滴	to drip	—	MOTION, RELATIV
乐观主义	optimism	—	AFFECT, DRIVES, POSEMO, REWARD
难吃	unpalatable	AFFECT, NEGEMO, PERCEPT	—
确立	to establish	CERTAIN, COGMECH	—
北面	northern side	RELATIV, SPACE	—
怒视	to glower	AFFECT, ANGER, NEGEMO, PERCEPT, SEE	—
远视	far-sighted	BIO, HEALTH	—

Table 2: Comparison of a random selection of words in the Chinese LIWC (Huang et al., 2012) and our automatic translation of the English LIWC into Chinese. Our translation tends to be overproductive but produces words that are associated with valid categories. Note that some categories are hierarchical. For example, PERSONAL encompasses WORK and HOME, while DRIVES encompasses POWER.

verified by human annotators to form larger, broad-coverage lexicons.

4 Quantifying Narrative Arcs

With our translated word dictionaries, we now investigate narrative arcs across languages.

4.1 Methods for Narrative Arcs

A narrative arc, also known as a word category arc, timeline, or trajectory, is a collection of word counts measured across segments of a narrative. Mathematically, a narrative arc is a word usage time series and can be conveniently visualized as a line plot, where the x-axis spans equally-spaced segments of the narrative, and the y-axis indicates the word usage computed within each segment. In previous work, the number of segments within a narrative varies from 5 (Boyd et al., 2020) to 20 (Mohammad, 2011), to a fixed window size of 10k words Reagan et al. (2016). For our experiments, we use 10 segments, a happy medium that balances granularity and computational cost. In addition, we follow Boyd et al. (2020) in z-score standardizing the word usage across each story in order to better analyze the difference in relative (rather than absolute) usage of words as a function of time.

4.2 Clustering and Interpreting Arcs

After computing arcs on all narratives in our dataset, we perform clustering of arcs within a word category to characterize stories that follow a particular arc. Reagan et al. (2016) discovered six arcs that correspond with Vonnegut's predictions (Vonnegut, 1999): 'Rags to riches' (rise), 'Tragedy' or 'Riches to rags' (fall), 'Man in a hole' (fall-rise), 'Icarus' (rise-fall), 'Cinderella' (rise-fall-rise), 'Oedipus' (fall-rise-fall). We ask: do these arcs also exist in non-English stories? To answer this question, we partition similar stories by their arcs using unsupervised clustering methods and then identify features of each group, a process reminiscent of topic models (Blei and Lafferty, 2009; Blei, 2012).

We perform k-means clustering on arcs of a specific LIWC category calculated on Fiction stories in Project Gutenberg across multiple languages, but using the downsampled English set (see Section 3.1), otherwise clustering will overemphasize English's contribution. We select the optimal number of clusters based on the elbow method with cluster inertia (the sum of squared distance between each point and the cluster centroid), a common metric for identifying the goodness of clusters. For many LIWC categories, we find that five to seven clusters are optimal.

Case Study on Positive Emotion Arcs. As a case study, we consider clusters of positive emotion (POSEMO) word usage trajectories. The elbow method indicates an optimal number of 5 clusters. The centroids of each cluster are shown in (Figure 3). To understand and interpret these clusters, a visual examination of each arc's peak pinpoints the

#	Shape	Size	Genres	Languages	Examples
0	rise-fall	236	History (18.2%), France (12.3%), Social life and customs 29 12.3%	en (29.7%), fr (28.8%), de (9.3%), nl (8.1%)	水滸傳 (Shi Nai'an), *L'île mystérieuse* (Jules Verne), *The Private Memoirs and Confessions of a Justified Sinner* (James Hogg), *Scaramouche: A Romance of the French Revolution* (Rafael Sabatini)
1	fall	222	History (17.6%), France (11.7%), Social life and customs (11.3%)	en (34.2%), fr (32.0%), es (8.6%), de (8.6%)	*The Awakening of Helena Richie* (Margaret Wade Campbell Deland), *Coniston — Volume 04* (Winston Churchill), *Trois contes* (Gustave Flaubert), *Elpénor* (Jean Giraudoux)
2	fall-rise-fall	218	History (21.1%), France (13.3%), Social life and customs (11.0%)	fr (34.9%), en (26.6%), de (12.4%), nl (8.3%)	*Die Klerisei* (N. S. Leskov), *The Reign of Law; a tale of the Kentucky hemp fields* (James Lane Allen), *The Right to Read* (Richard Stallman), *The Monk: A Romance* (M. G. Lewis)
3	fall-rise-fall-rise	211	History (18.5%), Historical fiction (10.4%), Love stories (10.4%)	en (50.7%), fr (18.5%), de (10.4%), it (7.1	狂人日記 (Lu Xun), *Jane Cable* (George Barr McCutcheon), *Robinson Crusoe (II/II)* (Daniel Defoe), *Le nabab, tome II* (Alphonse Daudet)
4	rise-fall-rise	224	History (18.3%), France (12.1%), Social life and customs (11.6%)	en (32.1%), de (32.1%), fr (22.3%), it (6.7	*The Expedition of Humphry Clinker* (Tobias Smollett), *La Marquise* (George Sand), *Les petites alliées* (Claude Farrère), *Du côté de chez Swann* (Marcel Proust)

Table 3: Interpretation of clustering on Positive Emotion arcs of stories across languages.

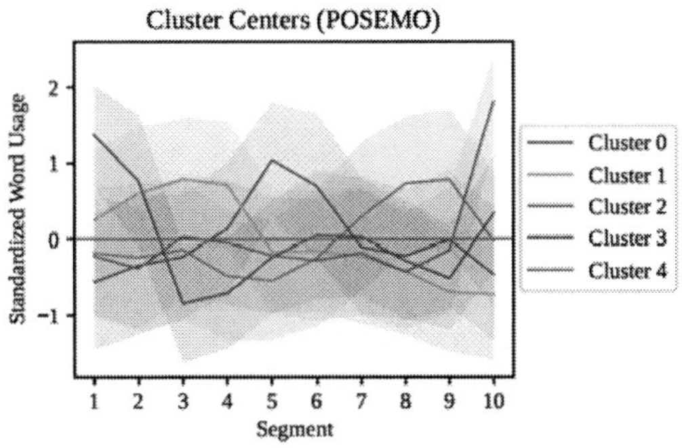

Figure 3: Cluster centroids of positive emotion (POSEMO) arcs computed on Fiction stories in Project Gutenberg (rebalanced English). Error bars indicate standard deviation.

location in the story where the most frequent use of positive emotion words occurs. We now dive deeper within each cluster, characterizing specific aspects including the languages and genres of the stories within in Table 3.

We find that the five clusters closely correspond to the following Vonnegut shapes: cluster 0 (blue) corresponds to 'Icarus' (rise-fall), cluster 1 (orange) corresponds to 'riches to rags' (fall), cluster 2 (green) corresponds to 'Oedipus' (fall-rise-fall), cluster 3 (red) corresponds to 'double man in a hole' (fall-rise-fall-rise), and cluster 4 (purple) corresponds to 'Cinderella' (rise-fall-rise). We do not see a 'man-in-the-hole' (fall-rise) -shaped arc, although at a high level, cluster 3 can be interpreted as fall-rise. If we specify six clusters, we find a sixth arc with a rise-fall-rise-fall shape that again may be a more specific form of the more general rise-fall shape.

In terms of cluster size, k-means tends to generate similarly sized clusters. We performed additional experiments clustering with HDBSCAN (McInnes et al., 2017), a hierarchical density-based clustering algorithm. HDBSCAN automatically identified 11 optimal clusters when computing POSEMO clusters. However, the majority of narratives were considered noise by this algorithm, and were thus not assigned a cluster, so we do not further analyze the HDBSCAN results here.

When analyzing genres, we find that History, France, and Social life are the top three genres in the entire dataset. Within a cluster, the only cluster that stands out is cluster 3, which is characterized by a larger portion of Historical fiction and Love stories, indicating that these genres tend to prefer this story structure. This cluster is also made up of over 50% English novels.

For non-English stories, the highest percentage of French novels appeared in cluster 2, while the highest percentage of German novels appeared in cluster 4. This may indicate a preference for these arc shapes by speakers of these languages. Such a preference could be cultural: from France and Germany originated Charles Perrault and the Grimm Brothers, respectively, whose fairy tale compilations have been read by children of numerous generations. Thus, the clustering of arcs allows us to examine similarities and differences between groups of narratives. While we consider positive emotion arcs here, due to their similarity with Vonnegut's story structure, future work will investigate other categories and their relevance to narrative structure.

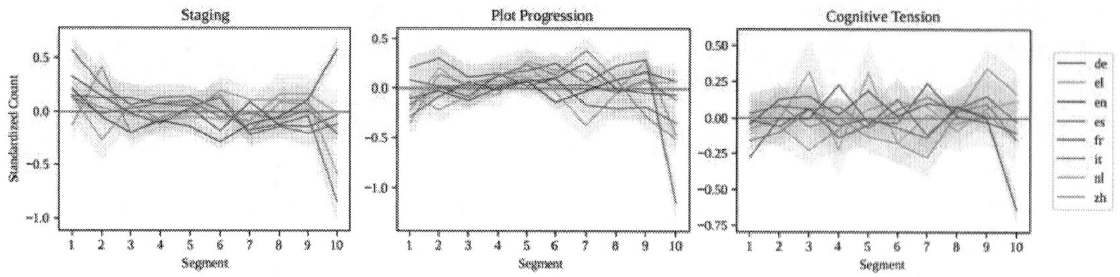

Figure 4: Boyd et al. (2020)'s word categories translated and computed on fiction narratives in other languages.

	Staging		Plot Prog		Cog Ten	
Lang	r	p	r	p	r	p
de	-0.075	0.836	0.241	0.502	0.604	0.064
es	0.723	0.018*	0.727	0.017*	-0.543	0.105*
fr	0.779	0.008**	0.801	0.005**	0.435	0.209
it	0.634	0.049*	0.789	0.007**	0.009	0.981
nl	0.721	0.019*	0.756	0.011*	0.086	0.813
zh	0.693	0.026*	0.858	0.002**	-0.198	0.583

Table 4: Correlation between narrative arcs to the English arcs in fiction stories. r is the Pearson correlation coefficient, and p is the p-value. A single asterisk indicates p-values ≤ 0.05, while double asterisks indicate p-values ≤ 0.01.

Category 1	Category 2	Corr.	Overlap
DISCREP	PLOTPROG	0.987	0.05
SOCIAL	YOU	0.986	0.01
FEMALE	I	0.973	0
AFFECT	REWARD	-0.972	0.04
AFFILIATION	WE	0.970	0.01
FEEL	WE	0.967	0
FILLER	NONFLU	0.962	0
FILLER	RELIG	-0.957	0
DEATH	NONFLU	-0.955	0

Table 5: Most strongly correlated narrative arcs (including negatively correlated). All correlations are significant ($p < 0.001$). PLOTPROG is from Boyd et al. (2020) and is not a LIWC category. Corr is the Pearson correlation coefficient, and Overlap is the Jaccard similarity between the words in each category.

5 Narrative Arcs Across Languages and Genres

5.1 Story Structure Processes

We now investigate narrative arcs' implications on narrative structure across languages by comparing them with an established study of narrative structure in English. Boyd et al. (2020) constructed three word categories corresponding to primary story structure processes: staging, plot progression, and cognitive tension. They then computed narrative arcs using these word categories, experimenting on various domains of text. We examine whether these three categories also apply to stories in languages other than English. We translate Boyd et al. (2020)'s word lists and apply them to a set of Fiction stories, standardizing the word counts within each story in order to allow fair comparison of relative word usage across stories. We compute the mean narrative arcs for fiction stories (shown in Figure 4), where error bars indicate standard error, and we calculate the Pearson correlation between each non-English narrative arc in Table 4.

Overall, we find strong support for Boyd et al. (2020)'s notion of staging and plot progression across languages, with most languages except for German showing a strong, statistically-significant correlation with the English narrative arc. For cognitive tension, we find that German, Spanish, and French arcs are weakly correlated, with Spanish surprisingly negatively correlated.

5.2 Arcs by Category

In addition to identifying similar stories, word usage arcs can also inform us about similarities between *word categories*, especially those with seemingly little or no overlap. Such analysis is similar to the idea of burstiness (Schafer and Yarowsky, 2002), where similar words occur at similar frequencies across time, an idea that was one of the precursors to the modern notion of embeddings computed based on some aspect of word usage.

We compute narrative arcs on all books within the Fiction genre in Project Gutenberg for each LIWC category and compute the Pearson correlation between the means of the arcs within each category. We show the most correlated categories in Table 5; the correlations between all categories are shown in Figure 7 in the Appendix.

Most of these correlations have a natural explanation. PLOT PROGRESSION words (from Boyd et al.

(2020)) are strongly correlated with LIWC DISCREPANCY words (*should, would, could*), which help to drive the plot forward. SOCIAL words (including social actions as well as relationships) already encompass a large percentage of You words (*you, y'all*), so high correlation is expected. However, some pairs of categories have zero overlap. FEMALE words (*girl, her, mom*) and I words (*I, me*) have high correlation; these words tend to occur in similar contexts (a paradigmatic relationship), as do FILLER words (*anyway, y'know*) and NONFLUENCIES (*er, um*). FEELING words (related to the perceptual process of touch, such as *feel, touch, cool, warm*) and WE words (*we, us, our*) in contrast have a syntagmatic relationship: they occur together but cannot be substituted for one another. The negatively correlated category pairs are also interesting. AFFECT words (related to emotion) and REWARD words (*take, prize, benefit*) have slight overlap and a strong negative correlation, the explanation of which needs further investigation. FILLER words and RELIGION words, as well as DEATH words and NONFLUENCIES, can be considered complete opposites: death and religion are heavy topics not often discussed with inconsequential or informal language such as filler words, and thus show a negative correlation.

5.3 Arcs By Genre

While certain plot structures may be universal, different genres may prefer different narrative structures. In this section, we discover structural differences between genres through the lens of word category arcs.

Consider Figure 5, containing all arcs computed on the LIWC category PERCEPT, which includes perception processes (e.g. seeing, hearing, and feeling). Through a visual inspection, we find that a large number of narratives in the History genre (total 1.2k books) exhibit a downward usage in perception words between segments 9 and 10, while in Science fiction (total 1.6k books), a visible portion of books have already dropped their usage of Perception words starting around segment 7.

To concretely quantify the difference between genres, we compute narrative arcs for all word categories over the eight most frequent genres within Fiction in Project Gutenberg: Social life and customs, History, Science fiction, Short stories, England, 19th century, Adventure stories, and Love stories. We identify word categories that maximally separate these genres by minimizing the mean absolute correlation between each pair of genres $\text{MAC}_d = \frac{1}{n}\sum_{g_1,g_2} |\text{r}(\overline{\text{arc}}_d(g_1), \overline{\text{arc}}_d(g_2))|$ for word category d, n pairs of genres g_1 and g_2 in the set of top 8 genres, $\overline{\text{arc}}_d(g)$ indicating the mean narrative arc computed on word usage of dimension d on stories in genre g, and r is the Pearson correlation coefficient.

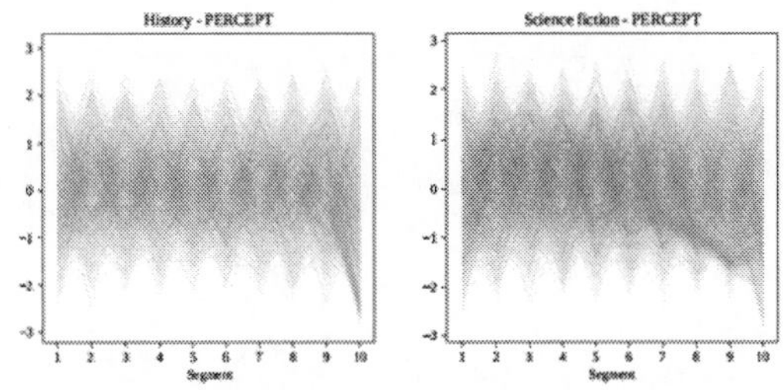

Figure 5: All Perception narrative arcs plotted for the genres History and Science fiction. Notice the clear difference in where usage of Perception words drops off.

The LIWC categories that maximally separate the top eight genres are SEXUAL (MAC = 0.29), ADVERBS (MAC = 0.37), and FILLER (MAC = 0.42), shown in Figure 6. We see, for example, that science fiction and short stories on average have a higher usage of SEXUAL words (*love, lust*) at the beginning of the narrative, which subsequently declines. The inclusion of love scenes at the beginning of a novel is a technique frequently used by authors to hook the reader. On the other hand, love stories on average are more likely to use Sexual words both at the beginning and the end of the story, perhaps indicating a happy ending. The next most distinguishable categories, Adverbs and Filler words, are harder to interpret due to their non-content nature. The categories that have the least distinguishing power are WE words (MAC = 0.91), CAUSE words (MAC = 0.92), and AFFILIATION words (MAC = 0.94); these arcs are very similar regardless of the genre.

5.4 Arcs by Language

Finally, we investigate how arcs differ with respect to language. We perform this analysis by correlating arcs computed for different word categories on stories in different languages, grouping stories by language. Correlation between languages for the same category is presented in Table 6.

When evaluating arcs across languages, we find that the most highly correlated categories are mem-

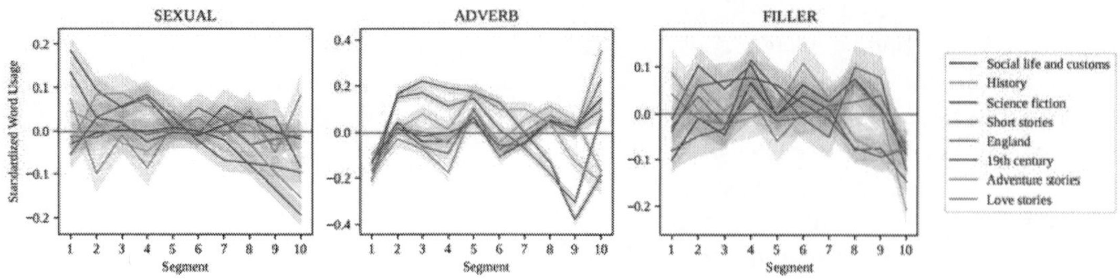

Figure 6: Top three word categories that maximally separate genres. Error bars indicate standard error.

Lang1	Lang2	Category	r
en	fr	DEATH	0.956
es	zh	NONFLU	0.956
es	nl	INFORMAL	0.956
es	fr	INFORMAL	0.94
fr	nl	INFORMAL	0.931
fr	nl	FOCUSPAST	0.931
es	fr	NUMBER	0.921
es	fr	NETSPEAK	0.909
es	nl	NETSPEAK	0.898
es	fr	ASSENT	0.896
de	es	ASSENT	0.884
es	fr	STAGE	0.881
en	fr	MOTION	0.88
en	fr	INFORMAL	0.878
de	fr	NEGATE	0.876
en	zh	NONFLU	0.876

Table 6: Most correlated categories across languages. All categories are from LIWC except STAGE, which is from Boyd et al. (2020). All correlations are statistically significant ($p < 0.001$).

bers of the INFORMAL category (including ASSENT, NONFLUENCIES, and NETSPEAK). For the other prominent categories, we already showed in Section 5.2 that DEATH words are highly correlated. For FOCUSPAST, a category that includes words that indicate focusing on past action (e.g. *was, has, been*), the high correlation between French and Dutch may be due to the fact that French and Dutch have some similarities in their past tenses.[5] For NEGATE, in both French and German, the negation word often comes after the verb (e.g. French *nous ne mangeons pas* vs. German *wir essen nicht*. Thus, narrative arcs also enable the study of language typology through careful selection of word categories.

[5]The French *passé simple* and *imparfait*, along with the Dutch *onvoltooid verleden tijd* (OVT), are morphologically simplex, while the French *passé composé* and Dutch *voltooid tegenwoordige tijd* (VTT) are morphologically complex.

6 Conclusion

Narrative arcs, operationalized as word category arcs, model word usage across the timeline of a narrative. They are powerful tools that allow us to not only gain a high-level overview of a narrative's structure but also enable us to identify similarities across languages and genres. In order to quantify narrative arcs across languages, we present a method for automatically translating wordlists such as LIWC, which we validate with an existing Chinese translation of LIWC. We then apply our translated dictionaries in eight languages to analyze narrative arcs in Project Gutenberg fiction books.

We first investigate clustering to interpret narrative structure according to Kurt Vonnegut's claims. Next, we investigate story structure, showing that Boyd et al. (2020)'s created word categories findings largely hold across languages. We then perform correlation studies, interpreting narrative arcs with respect to word categories, genres, and languages. Analyzing categories, we discover and explain positive correlations between several categories, even when they have no words in common. Analyzing genres, science fiction and short stories have a higher usage of SEXUAL words at the beginning of the story in order to hook the reader. Analyzing languages, we find that a high correlation between certain categories like DEATH and INFORMAL words can indicate a typological relation.

This work investigates how narrative arcs differ across various dimensions; we leave the question of *why* to future work.

Limitations

Corpus. In this paper, we use fiction novels from multiple languages in Project Gutenberg. One assumption of this work is that the text is representative of the culture surrounding the language. While this may or may not be true (e.g. Handler and Segal, 1999), our investigation's focus is on the structure, or narrative arc, of stories and how arcs may differ across languages. Naturally, our findings may differ for other genres, such as history or self-help. We focus on fiction because the vast majority of research on narratives has focused on fiction, though we believe non-fiction and other genres would be interesting for future work. Future work can also consider the addition of other corpora to enhance Project Gutenberg, such as MegaLite Moreno-Jiménez et al. (2021), a corpus of about 5,000 Spanish, French, and Portuguese narrative texts, poetry, or plays. However, multilingual corpora of this kind are few and far between, even for high-resource languages like Spanish and French.

Dictionaries. This work heavily relies on LIWC, which is proprietary software. Many researchers (including ourselves) may not have access to all LIWC dictionaries. In addition, as a dictionary of psychometric properties, LIWC is constantly evolving and improving with new research in psychology and linguistics.

Acknowledgements

This work is supported in part by the Air Force Office of Scientific Research (#FA9550-22-1-0099) and by the Templeton Foundation (#62256). Any opinions, findings, and conclusions or recommendations expressed in this material are those of the authors and do not necessarily reflect the views of AFOSR or of the Templeton Foundation. We would also like to thank the members of the LIT and LAUNCH labs at the University of Michigan, and especially Aylin Gunal, for helpful feedback on an early draft of this work.

References

David M Blei. 2012. Probabilistic topic models. *Communications of the ACM*, 55(4):77–84.

David M Blei and John D Lafferty. 2009. Topic models. In *Text mining*, pages 101–124. Chapman and Hall/CRC.

Christopher Booker. 2004. *The seven basic plots: Why we tell stories*. A&C Black.

Peter Boot, Hanna Zijlstra, and Rinie Geenen. 2017. The dutch translation of the linguistic inquiry and word count (liwc) 2007 dictionary. *Dutch Journal of Applied Linguistics*, 6(1):65–76.

Ryan L Boyd, Kate G Blackburn, and James W Pennebaker. 2020. The narrative arc: Revealing core narrative structures through text analysis. *Science advances*, 6(32):eaba2196.

Keh-Jiann Chen, Chu-Ren Huang, Li-Ping Chang, and Hui-Li Hsu. 1996. Sinica Corpus : Design methodology for balanced corpora. In *Proceedings of the 11th Pacific Asia Conference on Language, Information and Computation*, pages 167–176, Seoul, Korea. Kyung Hee University.

Diana Paula Dudău and Florin Alin Sava. 2020. The development and validation of the romanian version of linguistic inquiry and word count 2015 (ro-liwc2015). *Current Psychology*, pages 1–18.

Diana Paula Dudău and Florin Alin Sava. 2021. Performing multilingual analysis with linguistic inquiry and word count 2015 (liwc2015). an equivalence study of four languages. *Frontiers in Psychology*, 12:2860.

William Foster-Harris. 1959. *The basic patterns of plot*. University of Oklahoma Press.

Gustav Freytag. 1894. *Die technik des dramas*. S. Hirzel.

Richard Handler and Daniel Segal. 1999. *Jane Austen and the fiction of culture: An essay on the narration of social realities*. Rowman & Littlefield.

Chin-Lan Huang, Cindy K Chung, Natalie Hui, Yi-Cheng Lin, Yi-Tai Seih, Ben CP Lam, Wei-Chuan Chen, Michael H Bond, and James W Pennebaker. 2012. The development of the chinese linguistic inquiry and word count dictionary. *Chinese Journal of Psychology*.

Evgeny Kim, Sebastian Padó, and Roman Klinger. 2017. Investigating the relationship between literary genres and emotional plot development. In *Proceedings of the Joint SIGHUM Workshop on Computational Linguistics for Cultural Heritage, Social Sciences, Humanities and Literature*, pages 17–26, Vancouver, Canada. Association for Computational Linguistics.

Guillem Massó, Patrik Lambert, Carlos Rodríguez Penagos, and Roser Saurí. 2013. Generating new liwc dictionaries by triangulation. In *Asia Information Retrieval Symposium*, pages 263–271. Springer.

Allyssa McCabe. 1997. Cultural background and storytelling: A review and implications for schooling. *The Elementary School Journal*, 97(5):453–473.

Leland McInnes, John Healy, and Steve Astels. 2017. hdbscan: Hierarchical density based clustering. *J. Open Source Softw.*, 2(11):205.

Tabea Meier, Ryan L Boyd, James W Pennebaker, Matthias R Mehl, Mike Martin, Markus Wolf, and Andrea B Horn. 2019. "liwc auf deutsch": The development, psychometrics, and introduction of de-liwc2015. *PsyArXiv*, (a).

Saif Mohammad. 2011. From once upon a time to happily ever after: Tracking emotions in novels and fairy tales. In *Proceedings of the 5th ACL-HLT Workshop on Language Technology for Cultural Heritage, Social Sciences, and Humanities*, pages 105–114, Portland, OR, USA. Association for Computational Linguistics.

Saif M Mohammad and Peter D Turney. 2013. NRC emotion lexicon. *National Research Council, Canada*, 2.

Luis-Gil Moreno-Jiménez, Juan-Manuel Torres-Moreno, et al. 2021. Megalite: a new spanish literature corpus for nlp tasks. In *Computing Conference*.

Jessica Ouyang and Kathleen McKeown. 2015. Modeling reportable events as turning points in narrative. In *Proceedings of the 2015 Conference on Empirical Methods in Natural Language Processing*, pages 2149–2158, Lisbon, Portugal. Association for Computational Linguistics.

Monisha Pasupathi, Risha M Henry, and Laura L Carstensen. 2002. Age and ethnicity differences in storytelling to young children: Emotionality, relationality and socialization. *Psychology and Aging*, 17(4):610.

James W Pennebaker, Ryan L Boyd, Kayla Jordan, and Kate Blackburn. 2015. The development and psychometric properties of liwc2015. Technical report.

Andrew Piper, Richard Jean So, and David Bamman. 2021. Narrative theory for computational narrative understanding. In *Proceedings of the 2021 Conference on Empirical Methods in Natural Language Processing*, pages 298–311, Online and Punta Cana, Dominican Republic. Association for Computational Linguistics.

Georges Polti. 1917. *The thirty-six dramatic situations*. Editor Company.

Andrew J Reagan, Lewis Mitchell, Dilan Kiley, Christopher M Danforth, and Peter Sheridan Dodds. 2016. The emotional arcs of stories are dominated by six basic shapes. *EPJ Data Science*, 5(1):1–12.

Charles Schafer and David Yarowsky. 2002. Inducing translation lexicons via diverse similarity measures and bridge languages. In *COLING-02: The 6th Conference on Natural Language Learning 2002 (CoNLL-2002)*.

Swapna Somasundaran, Xianyang Chen, and Michael Flor. 2020. Emotion arcs of student narratives. In *Proceedings of the First Joint Workshop on Narrative Understanding, Storylines, and Events*, pages 97–107, Online. Association for Computational Linguistics.

Ronald B Tobias. 2012. *20 master plots: And how to build them*. Penguin.

Leon Van Wissen and Peter Boot. 2017. An electronic translation of the liwc dictionary into dutch. In *Electronic lexicography in the 21st century: Proceedings of eLex 2017 conference*, pages 703–715. Lexical Computing.

Kurt Vonnegut. 1999. *Palm Sunday: an autobiographical collage*. Dial Press.

Winston Wu and David Yarowsky. 2020a. Computational etymology and word emergence. In *Proceedings of the 12th Language Resources and Evaluation Conference*, pages 3252–3259, Marseille, France. European Language Resources Association.

Winston Wu and David Yarowsky. 2020b. Wiktionary normalization of translations and morphological information. In *Proceedings of the 28th International Conference on Computational Linguistics*, pages 4683–4692, Barcelona, Spain (Online). International Committee on Computational Linguistics.

A Appendix

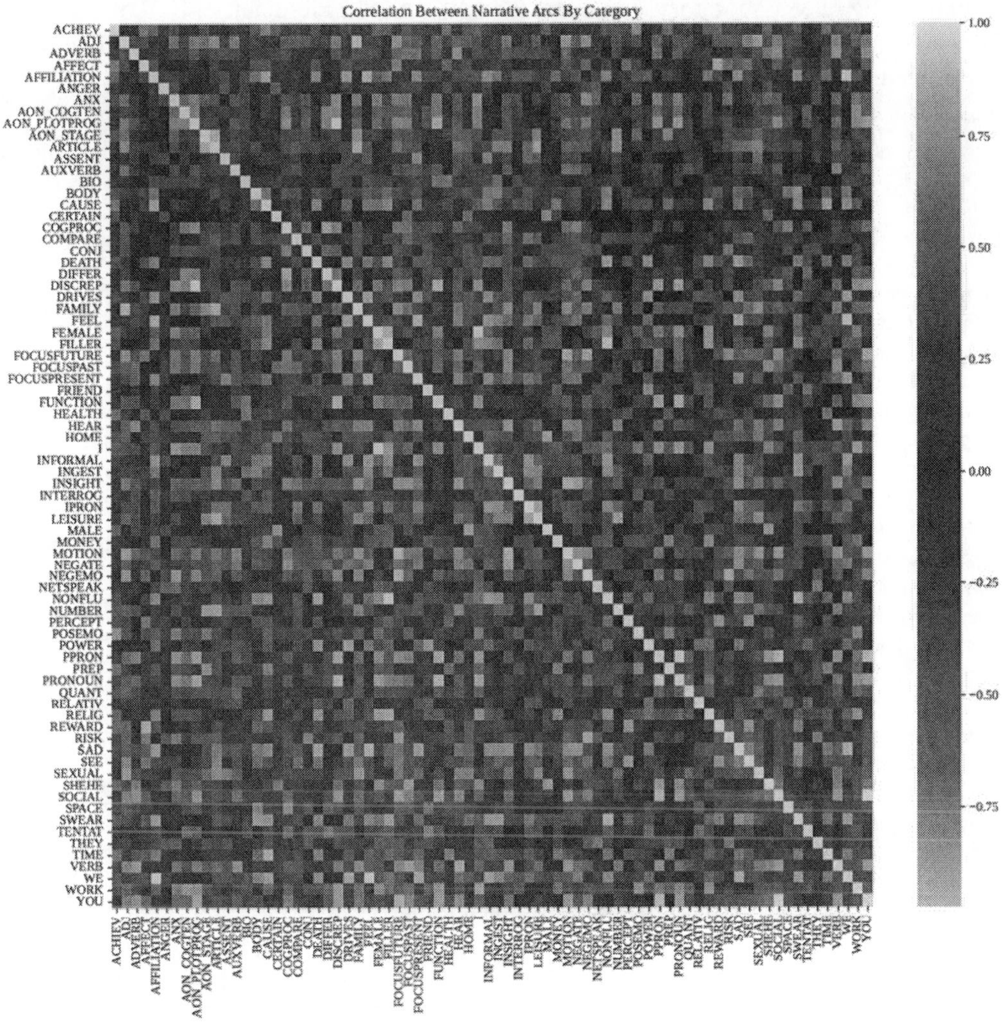

Figure 7: Correlation between narrative arcs for each LIWC category, with the addition of the three categories starting with AON_ from Boyd et al. (2020). The most highly correlated categories (including negative correlation) are in light blue and light red and are analyzed in Section 5.2.

The Candide Model: How Narratives Emerge Where Observations Meet Beliefs

Paul Van Eecke[1] and **Lara Verheyen**[1] and **Tom Willaert**[2,3] and **Katrien Beuls**[4]
[1]Artificial Intelligence Laboratory, Vrije Universiteit Brussel, Pleinlaan 2, B-1050 Brussels
[2]Brussels School of Governance, Vrije Universiteit Brussel, Pleinlaan 2, B-1050 Brussels
[3]imec-SMIT, Vrije Universiteit Brussel, Pleinlaan 2, B-1050 Brussels
[4]Faculté d'informatique, Université de Namur, rue Grandgagnage 21, B-5000 Namur
paul@ai.vub.ac.be, lara.verheyen@ai.vub.ac.be,
tom.willaert@vub.be, katrien.beuls@unamur.be

Abstract

This paper presents the Candide model as a computational architecture for modelling human-like, narrative-based language understanding. The model starts from the idea that narratives emerge through the process of interpreting novel linguistic observations, such as utterances, paragraphs and texts, with respect to previously acquired knowledge and beliefs. Narratives are personal, as they are rooted in past experiences, and constitute perspectives on the world that might motivate different interpretations of the same observations. Concretely, the Candide model operationalises this idea by dynamically modelling the belief systems and background knowledge of individual agents, updating these as new linguistic observations come in, and exposing them to a logic reasoning engine that reveals the possible sources of divergent interpretations. Apart from introducing the foundational ideas, we also present a proof-of-concept implementation that demonstrates the approach through a number of illustrative examples.

1 Introduction

Today's natural language processing (NLP) systems excel at exploiting the statistical properties of huge amounts of textual data to tackle a wide variety of NLP subtasks. They meticulously capture the co-occurrence of characters, words and sentences, sometimes in relation to an annotation layer, and make use of numerical operations over these co-occurrences to perform mappings between linguistic input on the one hand and task-specific linguistic or non-linguistic output on the other. As a result of recent advances in neural machine learning techniques and infrastructure (see e.g. Sutskever et al., 2014; Vaswani et al., 2017; Devlin et al., 2018), combined with the availability of huge text corpora, impressive results are now being achieved on many tasks, including machine translation, speech recognition, text summarisation, semantic role labelling and sentiment analysis (for an overview, see Lauriola et al., 2022).

Yet, current NLP systems are everything but capable of modelling human-like, narrative-based language understanding. One reason is that this capacity is hard to cast in the predominant machine learning paradigm. Indeed, human-like narrative understanding is hard to define in the form of an annotation scheme. Narratives are not captured in texts as such, but are construed through an interpretation process. This process is personal, and different individuals may construe different narratives given the same linguistic observations (Steels, 2022). This diversity in perspectives reflects the richness of human language and cognition, and modelling divergent interpretations constitutes a crucial challenge to the broader computational linguistics community today.

The primary objective of this paper is to introduce a novel approach to narrative-based language understanding that starts from the idea that narratives emerge through the process of interpreting novel observations with respect to previously acquired knowledge and beliefs. Concretely, we present a computational model of this interpretation process. The model integrates three main components: (i) a personal dynamic memory that holds a frame-based representation of the knowledge and beliefs of an individual agent, (ii) a construction grammar that maps between linguistic observations and a frame-based representation of their meaning, and (iii) a reasoning engine that performs logic inference over the information stored in the personal dynamic memory.

Crucially, the representations that result from the language comprehension step take the same form as those stored in the personal dynamic memory. Not only does this mean that these representations can dynamically be merged into the personal dynamic memory to update the knowledge and beliefs of an agent, it also facilitates the use of information

Proceedings of the The 5th Workshop on Narrative Understanding, pages 48–57
July 14, 2023 ©2023 Association for Computational Linguistics

stored in the personal dynamic memory to inform the language comprehension process. The information stored in the personal dynamic memory can be queried through a logic reasoning engine, with each answer being supported by a human-interpretable chain of reasoning operations. This chain of reasoning operations explains how the background knowledge and beliefs of an agent guide its conclusions, thereby revealing the narrative construed through the agent's interpretation process.

Personal, dynamic and interpretable models of narrative-based language understanding are of great interest to the fields of computational linguistics and artificial intelligence alike. To the field of computational linguistics, they contribute a perspective that emphasises the individual and contextualised nature of linguistic communication, which contrasts with the static and perspective-agnostic models that dominate the field of NLP today. In the field of artificial intelligence, they respond to the growing interest in the development of artificial agents that combine human-like language understanding with interpretable, value-aware and ethics-guided reasoning (see e.g. Steels, 2020; Montes and Sierra, 2022; Abbo and Belpaeme, 2023).

The remainder of this paper is structured as follows. Section 2 lays out the background and overall architecture of our model. Section 3 presents its technical operationalisation and provides a number of illustrative examples. Finally, Section 4 reflects on the contribution of our paper and discusses avenues for further research.

2 The Candide Model

The model for narrative-based language understanding that we introduce in this paper is named after Voltaire's "*Candide ou l'optimisme*" (Voltaire, 1759). It is inspired by one of the main themes of the novel, namely that a character's belief system and history of past experiences shape the way in which they interpret the world in which they live. As such, different characters in the novel represent different philosophical positions and thereby construe different narratives to explain the same situations and events. The main protagonist, Candide, starts out as a young, naive 'blank slate'. Through conversations with the Leibnizian optimist Pangloss and the fatalistic pessimist Martin, and as a result of long travels that make him experience the hardships of the world, Candide gradually develops his own belief system in light of which he ever more wisely interprets the situations and events he witnesses.

Following the main theme of the novel, our aim is not to model a single 'true' interpretation of an observation, but to show that different beliefs can lead to different interpretations. Moreover, we consider the belief system of an agent to be dynamic, with the interpretations and conclusions of an agent shifting as more experience and knowledge are gathered. In order to formalise these high-level ideas, we introduce the following operational definitions:

Personal dynamic memory (PDM) The personal dynamic memory of an agent is a data structure that stores the knowledge and beliefs of the agent in a logic representation that supports automated reasoning. The PDM is conceived of as a dynamic entity to which new knowledge and beliefs can be added at any point in time. Reasoning over the PDM is non-monotonic, as updated beliefs can alter conclusions.

Belief system The belief system of an agent at a given point in time equals all information that is stored in the agent's PDM at that moment in time. Each entry in the PDM carries a confidence score, which reflects the degree of certainty of the agent with respect to that entry. However, there exists no formal or conceptual distinction between entries based on their epistemological status, avoiding the need to distinguish between 'knowledge', 'facts', 'opinions' and 'beliefs' for example.

Conclusion A conclusion is a piece of information that logically follows from a reasoning operation over the belief system of an agent. A typical example would be the answer to a question.

Narrative A narrative is defined as a chain of reasoning operations that justifies a conclusion based on the belief system of an agent as it is stored in its PDM. Logically, it corresponds to a proof for the conclusion. It is possible that multiple narratives that support the same or different conclusions can be construed by an individual agent. An agent can use the certainty scores carried by the beliefs that constitute its PDM to rank its conclusions and the narratives that support them.

Language comprehension Language comprehension is the process of mapping a linguistic observation, such as an utterance, paragraph or text,

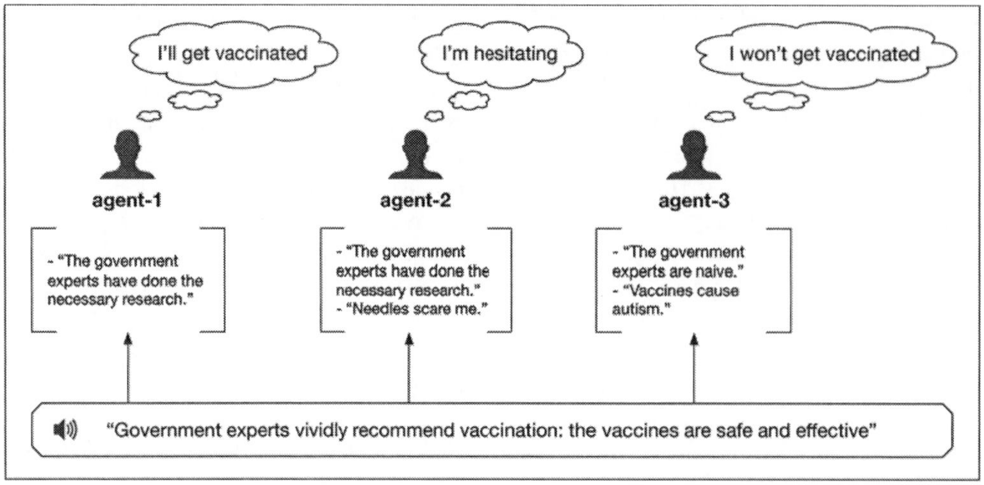

Figure 1: Informal sketch of the Candide model. The model conceives of narrative-based language understanding as the interpretation of a linguistic observation with respect to an agent's individual belief system. Narratives are defined as argumentation structures on the basis of which conclusions are drawn.

to a logic representation of its meaning. While language comprehension is primarily concerned with retrieving the information captured in the linguistic input, rather than its integration with respect to the personal dynamic memory, it is heavily intertwined with other aspects of the interpretation process as well. Indeed, the linguistic knowledge needed to support language comprehension is personal and dynamic, and thereby unavoidably constitutes a first layer of individual interpretation.

Interpretation The interpretation process comprises all aspects involved in narrative-based language understanding, from the linguistic input to the construction of a narrative that justifies a conclusion. This involves both the language comprehension process, which maps from linguistic input to a logic representation of its meaning, and the reasoning processes that corroborate this meaning representation with the information stored in the PDM, thereby construing narratives that support conclusions.

An informal example of the main ideas underlying the Candide model is shown in Figure 1. Here, three agents observe the same broadcasted message "*Government experts vividly recommend vaccination: the vaccines are safe and effective*" and are asked whether they plan to get vaccinated. In order to answer the question, the three agents individually interpret this message with respect to the beliefs stored in their PDM and construe a narrative that justifies a conclusion in the form of an answer to the question. The first agent comes to the conclusion that they will get vaccinated, justifying their choice through the narrative that the government experts are competent. The second agent is hesitant to get vaccinated, construing the narrative that vaccines are beneficial but that they are scared of needles. The third agent will not get vaccinated, as they construe the narrative that vaccines are dangerous and that the government experts are being misled.

The example illustrates three properties of narratives that, in our view, constitute crucial challenges in operationalising narrative-based language understanding. First of all, a model of analysis can only be adequate if it captures the personal nature of narratives. Whether or not a conclusion is justified does not depend on its truth or falsehood from an external perspective, but only on whether it is supported by the beliefs held by an agent. Second, narratives are not captured as such in linguistic artefacts. While authors convey messages that are grounded in their belief systems, these messages do not encode the belief systems themselves. Indeed, the intended meaning underlying a message needs to be reconstructed inferentially based on the belief system of the receiver (Grice, 1967; Sperber and Wilson, 1986). Finally, it is essential that the interpretation process that is modelled is transparent and human-interpretable. The goal is not merely to draw conclusions given linguistic input, but to reveal the background knowledge, beliefs and reasoning processes that underlie the conclusions that are drawn.

3 Technical Operationalisation

This section presents the technical operationalisation of an initial proof-of-concept of the Candide model. We discuss the proof-of-concept's language comprehension component, its personal dynamic memory, and its processes of reasoning and narrative construction.

3.1 Language Comprehension

The language comprehension component is responsible for mapping between linguistic input, in particular utterances, paragraphs and texts, and a formal representation of their underlying meaning. The language comprehension component is operationalised using the Fluid Construction Grammar framework (FCG – `https://fcg-net.org`; Steels, 2004; van Trijp et al., 2022; Beuls and Van Eecke, 2023). The FCG framework provides a computational operationalisation of the basic tenets of construction grammar (Fillmore, 1988; Goldberg, 1995; Croft, 2001; Fried and Östman, 2004; Beuls and Van Eecke, 2024). It includes a formalism for representing construction grammars, a processing engine that supports construction-based language comprehension and production, and a library of operators for learning construction grammars in a usage-based fashion.

The choice for FCG as the backbone of the language comprehension component of our proof-of-concept is motivated by four main reasons. First of all, in line with its theoretical grounding in usage-based construction grammar, FCG offers a uniform way to represent and process linguistic phenomona, whether or not they can be analysed compositionally (Beuls and Van Eecke, 2023). Second, FCG is compatible with a wide variety of meaning representations (van Trijp et al., 2022), including the frame-semantic representation that will be used to represent the knowledge and beliefs captured in the personal dynamic memory of the agents. Third, FCG's symbolic learning operators are especially designed to facilitate the one-shot learning of constructions given new linguistic observations, thereby maximally reflecting the personal and dynamic nature of an agent's linguistic capacities (Van Eecke, 2018; Nevens et al., 2022; Doumen et al., 2023). Finally, the symbolic data structures and unification-based processing algorithms employed by FCG ensure that the representation of an agent's linguistic knowledge, as well as its language comprehension, production and learning processes, are transparent and human-interpretable (Van Eecke and Beuls, 2017).

We opt for a semantic representation that captures the meaning underlying linguistic expressions in the form of semantic frames (Fillmore, 1976; Fillmore and Baker, 2001). Semantic frames represent situations, which are evoked by linguistic expressions, along with their participants. As such, the meaning of the utterance "*Sam sent Robin a postcard*" could be represented through a SENDING frame, with "*Sam*", "*Robin*" and "*a postcard*" respectively taking up the roles of SENDER, RECIPIENT and THEME. In terms of data structures, we represent instances of semantic frames through two types of predicates: entities and roles. Entity predicates are used to represent referents, i.e. objects, people, events and situations that can be referred to. In our example, *Sam*, *Robin*, *the postcard*, *the sending event* and *the transfer situation* serve as entities. Role predicates are used to represent relations between entities. Each role predicate expresses a relation between a frame role (e.g. SENDER), the frame to which that role is associated (SENDING), the entity that is taking up the role (*Sam*), the entity that represents the frame instance (*the sending event*) and the entity that represents the situation about which the frame is expressed (*the transfer situation*). There exists a subtle yet important distinction between frame instances and situations. A situation is defined in terms of an agent's world model, while a frame instance assumes a linguistically expressed perspective on a situation. In our example, the transfer situation is linguistically expressed as a sending event, while the same situation could also have been expressed as a receiving event (e.g. "*Robin received a postcard from Sam*"). Note that both the frame instance and the situation are reified as entities and can thus be referred to. The entity and role predicates follow the FrameNet conventions (`https://framenet.icsi.berkeley.edu`) and are represented in standard Prolog syntax (ISO/IEC 13211), as exemplified in Listing 1.

The exact way in which the FCG engine maps between utterances and their frame-semantic representation, as well how FCG grammars can be designed or learnt, fall outside the scope of this paper. Instead, we refer the interested reader to van Trijp et al. (2022), Nevens et al. (2022), Doumen et al. (2023) and Van Eecke et al. (2022).

```
% Entity predicates

entity(sam).
entity(robin).
entity(postcard).
entity(sending_event).
entity(transfer_situation).

% Role predicates

role(sender,sending,sam,sending_event,transfer_situation).
role(recipient,sending,robin,sending_event,transfer_situation).
role(theme,sending,postcard,sending_event,transfer_situation).
```

Listing 1: Frame-semantic representation underlying the utterance "*Sam sent Robin a postcard*" as a combination of entity and role predicates expressed in standard Prolog syntax.

3.2 Personal Dynamic Memory

The personal dynamic memory of an agent holds a frame-based representation of the agent's belief system. Technically, it consists of a collection of Prolog facts and rules. Instances of semantic frames are expressed by means of entity and role predicates, just like those resulting from the language comprehension process. For the purposes of this section, we will assume that our agents observe the utterance "*Sam sent Robin a postcard*", comprehend it into the frame-based semantic representation shown in Listing 1, and add this representation to their personal dynamic memory. We will also assume that our agents already hold a number of previously acquired beliefs, in particular about the relation between the semantic frames of SENDING and RECEIVING. As such, they believe that the DONOR role in an instance of the RECEIVING frame, cast over a particular situation, is taken up by the same entity that takes up the SENDER role in an instance of the SENDING frame cast over the same situation. However, this alignment only holds under the condition that the postal services are operational. In other terms, each sending event corresponds to a receiving event if the postal services are operational, and the sender of the sending event corresponds to the donor of the receiving event. At the same time, the agents believe that a similar alignment can be made for the other roles of the SENDING and RECEIVING frames. Moreover, they believe that the postal services are operational if no general strike is taking place. A formal encoding of these beliefs is shown in Listing 2.

While our agents hold the same beliefs about the relation between the SENDING and RECEIVING frames, as well as the conditions under which the postal services are operational, they hold differ-

```
% Belief about the operationality of the mail

mail_operational :- not(general_strike).

% Beliefs about the relation between the sending
% frame and the receiving frame

role(donor,receiving,Entity,_,Situation) :-
    role(sender,sending,Entity,_,Situation),
    !, mail_operational.

role(recipient,receiving,Entity ,_,Situation) :-
    role(recipient,sending,Entity,_,Situation),
    !, mail_operational.

role(theme,receiving,Entity,_,Situation) :-
    role(theme,sending,Entity,_,Situation),
    !, mail_operational.

role(sender,sending,Entity,_,Situation) :-
    role(donor,receiving,Entity,_,Situation),
    !, mail_operational.

role(recipient,sending,Entity,_,Situation) :-
    role(recipient,receiving,Entity,_,Situation),
    !, mail_operational.

role(theme,sending,Entity,_,Situation) :-
    role(theme,receiving,Entity,_,Situation),
    !, mail_operational.
```

Listing 2: The beliefs of our example agents concerning the operationality of the mail and the conditional alignment between the SENDING and RECEIVING frames.

```
% Belief about the state of social unrest

general_strike :- false.
```

Listing 3: Agent 1's belief that there is no general strike.

```
% Belief about the state of social unrest

general_strike :- true.
```

Listing 4: Agent 2's belief that there is a general strike.

```
% Query

?- role(theme,receiving,What,Event,Situation),
   role(recipient,receiving,robin,Event,Situation),
   role(donor,receiving,sam,Event,Situation).

% Answer by Agent 1:

What = postcard,
Situation = transfer_situation.

% Answer by Agent 2:

false.
```

Listing 5: Frame-semantic representation underlying the question "*What did Robin receive from Sam?*" with two different answers as computed by the Prolog engine based on the PDMs of Agent 1 and Agent 2.

ent beliefs about the current state of social unrest. As such, Agent 1 believes that there is no general strike, while Agent 2 believes that a general strike is going on at the moment. These beliefs are formally encoded in Listing 3 and 4 respectively.

We define the PDM of Agent 1 to be the combination of the facts and rules specified in Listings 1, 2 and 3, and the PDM of Agent 2 to consist of the facts and rules specified in Listings 1, 2 and 4. Our proof-of-concept implementation does not address the issue of modelling the confidence of an agent with respect to its individual beliefs. The most straightforward way to operationalise this in the current proof of concept would be to use probabilistic logic programming, e.g. through ProbLog (De Raedt et al., 2007).

Our model does not make any assumptions about the origin of the beliefs captured in the personal dynamic memory of an agent. Beliefs can result from the language comprehension process, from abductive reasoning processes, or could even by designed by a knowledge engineer.

3.3 Reasoning and narrative construction

As the beliefs stored in the personal dynamic memory of an agent and the meaning of natural language utterances as comprehended by an agent are both represented as a collection of Prolog facts and rules, logical reasoning can naturally be operationalised through SLD-resolution-based inference. This means that agents can be asked to prove logic formulae that correspond to natural language questions. The conclusion of the proof then constitutes the answer to the question, while the proof itself corresponds to the narrative that explains the reasoning behind it (see Section 2).

Suppose that we ask our two example agents to answer the question "*What did Robin receive from Sam?*". The agents first use their grammar to comprehend this question into its frame-semantic representation, as shown at the top of Listing 5. The interrogative nature of the question is reflected by the presence of variables in the semantic representation, denoted by symbols starting with a capital letter. In this case, we are primarily interested in the entity taking up the role of THEME in the receiving event, represented by the variable `What`. The agents are then asked to find a proof for the meaning representation of the question, given the beliefs stored in their respective personal dynamic memories.

Agent 1 reasons that the `transfer_situation` that was previously described (see Listing 1) can be viewed as an instance of the RECEIVING frame, given the facts (i) that there is no general strike, (ii) that the mail service is therefore operational, and (iii) that the `transfer_sitation` is already believed to be an instance of the SENDING frame in which `robin` takes up the role of RECIPIENT and `sam` the role of SENDER. The agent comes to the conclusion that this reasoning process is (only) valid under the condition that the variables `What` and `Situation` are bound to the values `postcard` and `transfer_situation` respectively. In other terms, Agent 1 comes to the conclusion that Robin received the postcard that was sent to them by Sam.

Agent 2 on the other hand reasons that it knows of no situation that could be viewed as a receiving event in which `sam` and `robin` take up the roles of DONOR and RECIPIENT respectively. Although this agent holds the same beliefs as Agent 1 when it comes to the link between the `sending`

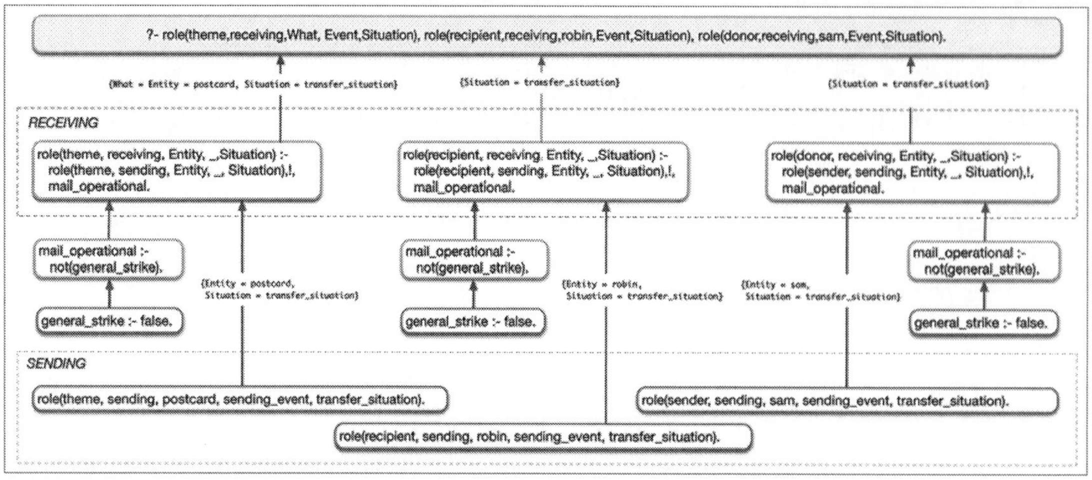

Figure 2: Narrative constructed by Agent 1 for responding to the question "*What did Robin receive from Sam?*" based on the frame-semantic information captured in its PDM (cf. Listings 1, 2 and 3).

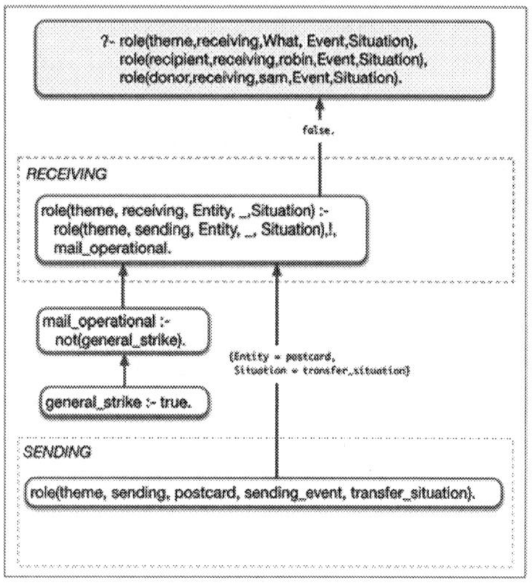

Figure 3: Narrative constructed by Agent 2 for responding to the question "*What did Robin receive from Sam?*" based on the frame-semantic information captured in its PDM (cf. Listings 1, 2 and 4).

and `receiving` frames, Agent 2's belief that a general strike is going on leads to the belief that the postal services are disfunctional, which in turn leads to the belief that the sending event cast over `transfer_situation` does not correspond to any receiving event. In other terms, Agent 2 beliefs that, while a postcard was sent by Sam to Robin, it was never received at Robin's end because of a general strike that paralysed the postal services.

Figures 2 and 3 show a schematic overview of the different steps involved in the respective reasoning processes of Agent 1 and Agent 2 when asked to answer the question "*What did Robin receive from Sam?*". The meaning representation of the question is shown in the yellow boxes at the top of the figures and corresponds to a Prolog query. The facts and rules that can be used to prove the query are those stored in the personal dynamic memories of the agents and correspond to those presented in Listings 1, 2 and 3 (Agent 1) and Listings 1, 2 and 4 (Agent 2).

The conjunction of three clauses that constitutes the query can indeed be proven by Agent 1 through a chain of subproofs that establish the link between there not being a general strike, the operationality of the postal services and the alignment of the SENDING and RECEIVING frames. The solid arrows denote the subproofs that were used to prove the top-level query. The labels on the arrows denote the variable bindings that resulted from the subproofs. While the set of bindings that result from proving the top-level query can be considered the conclusion of the reasoning process, it is the chain of subproofs that constitutes the narrative of the agent with respect to this conclusion. The same query cannot be proven by Agent 2, where the proof already fails at the first conjunct. Indeed, Agent 2 fails to prove the alignment between instances of the RECEIVING and SENDING frames, as its belief that a general strike is going on leads to a failure to prove that the postal services are operational, which is a precondition for the link between the two frames to be established. Note that when a conclusion cannot be proven, the narrative needs to be constructed abductively. Indeed, it consists here in finding a minimal explanation for why a conclusion does not follow from a collection of facts and rules.

4 Discussion and Conclusion

In this paper, we have introduced the Candide model as a computational architecture for modelling human-like, narrative-based language understanding. As such, we have presented an approach that radically breaks with today's mainstream natural language processing paradigm. Rather than modelling the co-occurrence of characters and words in huge amounts of textual data, our approach focusses on the logic reasoning processes that may justify different interpretations of the same linguistic observations. While this forces us to take an enormous leap back, it bears the promise of contributing a perspective that emphasises the individual and contextualised nature of linguistic communication to the fields of computational linguistics and artificial intelligence.

We have defined narratives to be chains of reasoning operations that underlie the conclusions drawn by an individual based on their belief system. This belief system is personal and dynamic in nature, as it is continuously being shaped by new linguistic and non-linguistic experiences. Narratives are thus not captured in texts as such, but need to be construed through a personal interpretation process. A narrative thereby reflects the perspective of an individual on the world, as the process of narrative construction necessarily takes one's entire belief system into account.

The construction of a narrative is a means rather than an end. While the end is to reach a conclusion, for example to answer a question, to resolve a coreference, or to make sense of a novel observation or experience, the means to reach that end is to construe a narrative that is consistent with one's belief system. In this view, the construction of a narrative is not a task in itself, but serves the purpose of solving an external task through human-interpretable reasoning processes. As narratives highly depend on external tasks and individual belief systems, they are hard to annotate in linguistic resources. Indeed, whether a narrative is justified or not only depends on whether it is consistent with the input that is observed in combination with the beliefs held by an individual. Narrative-based language understanding therefore largely coincides with the use of explainable methods for solving a variety of NLP tasks, including question answering, text summarisation and sentiment analysis, with the difference that the focus in evaluation shifts from the task accuracy to the soundness of the reasoning processes involved.

The Candide model operationalises this vision through a combination of frame-based constructional language processing and logic reasoning. As such, the belief system of an agent is represented as a collection of facts and rules that support automated reasoning through logic inference. The Fluid Construction Grammar-based language comprehension component is used to map between natural language utterances and a frame-based representation of their meaning. This semantic representation makes use of the same format as the one used to represent the agent's belief system, facilitating the straightforward integration of new beliefs into the agent's personal dynamic memory. The Prolog-based reasoning component can be leveraged to solve external tasks by proving logic formulae based on the facts and rules stored in the agent's personal dynamic memory. It is during this process of logic inference that narratives emerge as logical explanations that justify the conclusions drawn by an agent. We have illustrated our proof-of-concept implementation of the Candide model by means of a didactic example that shows how two agents who hold slightly different beliefs interpret the same linguistic observation differently, as they construe different narratives that lead to substantially different conclusions.

While this paper has laid the conceptual foundations of a novel approach to narrative-based language understanding, it has left the issue of operationalising the approach on a larger scale unaddressed. We envision an agent to start out as a blank slate, with an empty belief system and grammar. Through experience, an agent would then gradually build up linguistic and non-linguistic beliefs in a constructivist manner through the processes of intention reading and pattern finding. These processes have abundantly been attested in children (see e.g. Pine and Lieven, 1997; Tomasello, 2003) and have more recently been operationalised at scale in artificial agents through abductive reasoning processes (see e.g. Nevens et al., 2022; Doumen et al., 2023; Beuls and Van Eecke, 2023). We consider these preliminary results to be modest yet promising steps towards the moonshot of building personal, dynamic and human-interpretable models of narrative-based language understanding.

Limitations

This paper presents the conceptual foundations of a novel architecture for narrative-based language understanding, along with an illustrative proof-of-concept implementation. As such, it has been operationalised on a small scale only. Scaling up the approach to real-world applications is a highly non-trivial task that would not only require large investments but also significant innovative research efforts. Moreover, important aspects of the theoretical model have not been included in the proof-of-concept implementation, in particular when it comes to modelling the confidence of an agent with respect to its beliefs and narratives.

Acknowledgements

We are especially grateful to Remi van Trijp for his important contributions to the insightful discussions that led up to the development of the Candide model, as well as for his constructive feedback on a first version of this manuscript.

The research reported on in this paper received funding from the European Union's Horizon 2020 research and innovation programme under grant agreements no. 951846 (MUHAI - Meaning and Understanding in Human-centric AI) and no. 101094752 (SoMe4Dem - Social Media for Democracy – understanding the causal mechanisms of digital citizenship), from the Research Foundation Flanders (FWO) through a postdoctoral grant awarded to Paul Van Eecke (grant no. 75929) and from the Flemish Government under the 'Flanders AI Research Program'.

References

Giulio Antonio Abbo and Tony Belpaeme. 2023. Users' perspectives on value awareness in social robots. In *HRI2023, the 18th ACM/IEEE International Conference on Human-Robot Interaction*, pages 1–5, New York, NY, USA. Association for Computing Machinery.

Katrien Beuls and Paul Van Eecke. 2023. Fluid Construction Grammar: State of the art and future outlook. In *Proceedings of the First International Workshop on Construction Grammars and NLP (CxGs+NLP, GURT/SyntaxFest 2023)*, pages 41–50, Washington, D.C., USA. Association for Computational Linguistics.

Katrien Beuls and Paul Van Eecke. 2024. Construction grammar and artificial intelligence. In Mirjam Fried and Kiki Nikiforidou, editors, *The Cambridge Handbook of Construction Grammar*. Cambridge University Press, Cambridge, UK.

William Croft. 2001. *Radical construction grammar: Syntactic theory in typological perspective*. Oxford University Press, Oxford, United Kingdom.

Luc De Raedt, Angelika Kimmig, and Hannu Toivonen. 2007. Problog: A probabilistic prolog and its application in link discovery. In *Proceedings of the Twentieth International Joint Conference on Artificial Intelligence*, pages 2468–2473, San Francisco, CA, USA. Morgan Kaufmann Publishers Inc.

Jacob Devlin, Ming-Wei Chang, Kenton Lee, and Kristina Toutanova. 2018. Bert: Pre-training of deep bidirectional transformers for language understanding. In *Proceedings of NAACL*, pages 4171–4186.

Jonas Doumen, Katrien Beuls, and Paul Van Eecke. 2023. Modelling language acquisition through syntactico-semantic pattern finding. In *Findings of the Association for Computational Linguistics: EACL 2023*, pages 1317—-1327, Dubrovnik, Croatia. Association for Computational Linguistics.

Charles J. Fillmore. 1976. Frame semantics and the nature of language. In *Annals of the New York Academy of Sciences: Conference on the origin and development of language and speech*, volume 280, pages 20–32. New York, NY, USA.

Charles J. Fillmore. 1988. The mechanisms of "construction grammar". In *Annual Meeting of the Berkeley Linguistics Society*, volume 14, pages 35–55.

Charles J. Fillmore and Collin F. Baker. 2001. Frame semantics for text understanding. In *Proceedings of WordNet and Other Lexical Resources Workshop, NAACL*, volume 6.

Mirjam Fried and Jan-Ola Östman. 2004. Construction grammar: A thumbnail sketch. In Jan-Ola Östman and Mirjam Fried, editors, *Construction grammar in a cross-language perspective*, pages 1–86. John Benjamins, Amsterdam, Netherlands.

Adele E. Goldberg. 1995. *Constructions: A construction grammar approach to argument structure*. University of Chicago Press, Chicago, IL, USA.

Paul Grice. 1967. Logic and conversation. In Paul Grice, editor, *Studies in the Way of Words*, pages 41–58. Harvard University Press, Cambridge, MA, USA.

Ivano Lauriola, Alberto Lavelli, and Fabio Aiolli. 2022. An introduction to deep learning in natural language processing: Models, techniques, and tools. *Neurocomputing*, 470(C):443–456.

Nieves Montes and Carles Sierra. 2022. Synthesis and properties of optimally value-aligned normative systems. *Journal of Artificial Intelligence Research*, 74:1739–1774.

Jens Nevens, Jonas Doumen, Paul Van Eecke, and Katrien Beuls. 2022. Language acquisition through intention reading and pattern finding. In *Proceedings of the 29th International Conference on Computational Linguistics*, pages 15–25, Gyeongju, Republic of Korea. International Committee on Computational Linguistics.

Julian M. Pine and Elena V. M. Lieven. 1997. Slot and frame patterns and the development of the determiner category. *Applied Psycholinguistics*, 18(2):123–138.

Dan Sperber and Deirdre Wilson. 1986. *Relevance: Communication and cognition*. Harvard University Press, Cambridge, MA, USA.

Luc Steels. 2004. Constructivist development of grounded construction grammar. In *Proceedings of the 42nd Annual Meeting of the Association for Computational Linguistics (ACL-04)*, pages 9–16.

Luc Steels. 2020. Personal dynamic memories are necessary to deal with meaning and understanding in human-centric AI. In *Proceedings of the First International Workshop on New Foundations for Human-Centered Artificial Intelligence (NeHuAI@ECAI)*, pages 11–16.

Luc Steels. 2022. Towards meaningful human-centric AI. In Luc Steels, editor, *Foundations for meaning and understanding in human-centric AI*, pages 5–28. Venice International University, Venice, Italy.

Ilya Sutskever, Oriol Vinyals, and Quoc V. Le. 2014. Sequence to sequence learning with neural networks. In *Advances in Neural Information Processing Systems*, volume 27, pages 3104–3112, Red Hook, NY, USA. Curran Associates, Inc.

Michael Tomasello. 2003. *Constructing a Language: A Usage-Based Theory of Language Acquisition*. Harvard University Press, Harvard, MA, USA.

Paul Van Eecke. 2018. *Generalisation and specialisation operators for computational construction grammar and their application in evolutionary linguistics Research*. Ph.D. thesis, Vrije Universiteit Brussel, Brussels: VUB Press.

Paul Van Eecke and Katrien Beuls. 2017. Meta-layer problem solving for computational construction grammar. In *The 2017 AAAI Spring Symposium Series*, pages 258–265, Palo Alto, CA, USA. AAAI Press.

Paul Van Eecke, Jens Nevens, and Katrien Beuls. 2022. Neural heuristics for scaling constructional language processing. *Journal of Language Modelling*, 10(2):287–314.

Remi van Trijp, Katrien Beuls, and Paul Van Eecke. 2022. The FCG editor: An innovative environment for engineering computational construction grammars. *PLOS ONE*, 17(6):e0269708.

Ashish Vaswani, Noam Shazeer, Niki Parmar, Jakob Uszkoreit, Llion Jones, Aidan N. Gomez, Lukasz Kaiser, and Illia Polosukhin. 2017. Attention is all you need. In *Advances in Neural Information Processing Systems*, volume 30, pages 6000–6010, Red Hook, NY, USA. Curran Associates, Inc.

Voltaire. 1759. *Candide ou l'Optimisme*. Gabriel Cramer, Genève.

What is Wrong with Language Models that Can Not Tell a Story?

Ivan P. Yamshchikov
CAIRO, THWS
Würzburg, Germany
CEMAPRE,
University of Lisbon, Portugal
ivan@yamshchikov.info

Alexey Tikhonov
Inworld.AI
Berlin, Germany
altsoph@gmail.com

Abstract

In this position paper, we contend that advancing our understanding of narrative and the effective generation of longer, subjectively engaging texts is crucial for progress in modern Natural Language Processing (NLP) and potentially the broader field of Artificial Intelligence. We highlight the current lack of appropriate datasets, evaluation methods, and operational concepts necessary for initiating work on narrative processing.

1 Introduction

Since the linguistic turn in the early 20th century (Wittgenstein, 1921), human language has been considered fundamental to shaping human cognition. This notion positions language as a core aspect of intelligence, often equating intelligence with the ability to generate natural language. In (Turing, 1950), Turing famously suggests that the capacity for meaningful natural language interaction is critical for artificial intelligence. While most contemporary researchers narrow the Turing test's scope to day-to-day conversations, the original essay emphasizes that artificial intelligent agents should convincingly imitate humans in creative tasks expressed in natural language. Framing the problem in Turing's original terms reveals the current limitations of artificial systems, which can only partially imitate human dialogue in specific contexts and struggle to generate engaging stories (van Stegeren and Theune, 2019) or jokes (Niculescu, 2021).

Modern Natural Language Generation (NLG) leverages increased computational power and vast training data (Brown et al., 2020; Raffel et al., 2020; Chowdhery et al., 2022; Bajaj et al., 2022; Zoph et al., 2022), focusing on computation-heavy solutions rather than on statistical methods and mathematical models to qualitatively advance our understanding of language. A century after Andrey Markov developed his eponymous chains to analyze poetry, NLG concepts remain similar, and their limitations could hardly be overcome solely through quantitative means. This is particularly evident in narrative processing, where automatic generation of textual narratives often requires significant human intervention or relies on predefined narrative structures (van Stegeren and Theune, 2019).

Efforts to generate longer text blocks[1] exist, such as (Kedziorski, 2019) and (Agafonova et al., 2020), see Figure 1, but they succeed only under certain stylistic and topical constraints that preclude genuine narrative generation. While recent advancements have been made in suspense generation (Doust and Piwek, 2017), narrative personalization (Wang et al., 2017), and short context-based narratives (Womack and Freeman, 2019), generating extended stories remains a challenge (van Stegeren and Theune, 2019).

Philosophers and linguists have attempted to conceptualize plot, narrative arc, action, and actor notions for nearly a century (Shklovsky, 1925; Propp, 1968; Van Dijk, 1976), but few of these concepts have proven useful for modern NLP. In (Ostermann et al., 2019), a machine comprehension corpus is presented for end-to-end script knowledge evaluation, revealing that existing machine comprehension models struggle with tasks humans find relatively easy. Despite these setbacks, some progress in narrative generation has been made within the NLP community (Fan et al., 2019; Ammanabrolu et al., 2020). However, narrative generation is still largely considered a fringe research topic.

We argue that the concept of *narrative* is crucial for further NLP progress and should become a focal point within the NLP community. This paper raises vital questions for narrative processing to establish itself as a well-defined sub-field in NLP research. We begin by presenting several arguments for why breakthroughs in narrative pro-

[1]https://github.com/NaNoGenMo

Proceedings of the The 5th Workshop on Narrative Understanding, pages 58–64
July 14, 2023

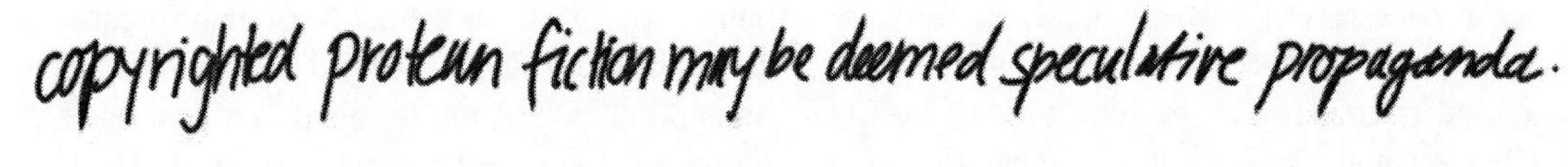

Figure 1: "Copyrighted protein fiction may be deemed speculative propaganda" — a line from a generative art project "Paranoid Transformer — a diary of an artificial neural network", (Agafonova et al., 2020). The diary was generated end-to-end without any human post-processing and published as a hardcover book. This is one of the examples of long-form generated artistic text, however the text is devoid of narrative.

cessing could be pivotal for artificial intelligence research in general. We then explore the bottlenecks hindering progress in narrative processing and decompose the question "why don't we have an algorithm to generate good stories?" into three systemic components: data, evaluation methods, and concepts. We contend that these three areas present significant challenges, with only data being partially addressed.

2 On the Importance of Narrative

Before addressing the three fundamental bottlenecks that separate us from achieving qualitatively advanced narrative generation models, let's briefly present a case for why narrative processing is crucial for further NLP development. Recent years have witnessed the success of language models driven by the distributional hypothesis (Harris, 1954). Although these models primarily focus on local input and training, they have been transformative even beyond the scope of classical NLP. For instance, (Lu et al., 2021) show that pretraining on natural language can enhance performance and compute efficiency in non-language downstream tasks. (Zeng et al., 2022) propose a new approach to AI systems, wherein multimodal tasks are formulated as guided language-based exchanges between different pre-existing foundation models. (Tam et al., 2022) discuss how language provides useful abstractions for exploration in a reinforcement learning 3D environment. Given these advancements, is narrative processing still necessary? Can all verbal cognition, like politics, be local?

We argue that narrative processing as a research field would significantly impact two other core aspects of natural language processing, which are essential for expanding the adoption of NLP products and technologies. The first aspect is causality and natural language inference. Causal inference from natural language is crucial for further NLP progress, and current language models still underperform in this area. Although narrative could be considered a sub-category within a broader family of causal texts, we contend that narrative generation is an ideal task for validating and testing hypotheses around natural language inference, paving the way for more explainable AI. The second area where narrative processing is indispensable is the continued development of human-machine interaction. People are known to remember stories more than facts (Wiig, 2012), but NLP-based natural language interfaces exhibit the opposite tendency, processing and "remembering" facts more easily than stories. These factors make narrative essential for further NLP progress.

Another field in which narrative processing could prove pivotal is explainable AI. One could argue that a feasible path to explainable artificial intelligence involves a set of dedicated models trained to communicate with humans in natural language, clarifying specific aspects of a given decision. These models would necessarily need to be capable of causal inference in natural language. Although this technically leads to the same bottleneck discussed earlier, we believe this field is so critical for the continued development and adoption of artificial intelligence in the industry that it warrants explicit mention here.

3 Where Do We Fail?

This position paper aims to highlight critical gaps in our conceptual understanding, benchmarking, and evaluation within the field of narrative processing. We contend that these three significant layers require the immediate focus of the research community. In this section, we examine each of these layers in depth and propose potential avenues for progress.

3.1 Data

Many existing datasets labeled as narrative datasets in academic literature deviate significantly from a common-sense understanding of a "story." Some authors even refer to their datasets as *scenarios* rather than stories or narratives. Additionally, these datasets are often too small for meaningful use with modern transformer-based language models. In (Regneri et al., 2010), authors collect 493 event sequence descriptions for 22 behavior scenarios. In (Modi et al., 2016), authors present the InScript dataset, consisting of 1,000 stories centered around 10 different scenarios. (Wanzare et al., 2019) provide 200 scenarios and attempt to identify all references to them in a collection of narrative texts. (Mostafazadeh et al., 2016) present a corpus of 50k five-sentence commonsense stories.

As we progress towards longer stories, the landscape of available data splits into two major fields: collections of narrative written in various natural languages and labelled data that facilitates narrative understanding. The examples of the latter direction include (Bamman et al., 2020) who annotate longer stories to aid narrative understanding, (Zhao et al., 2022) who pair plot descriptions with corresponding abstractive summaries, and (Pang et al., 2022; Wang et al., 2022) with QA/summarization datasets for longer stories from Project Gutenberg. The former filed of longer narrative datasets is still relatively sparse. (Fan et al., 2018) collect a large dataset of 300K human-written stories paired with writing prompts from an online forum. The MPST dataset contains 14K movie plot synopses, (Kar et al., 2018), and WikiPlots[2] comprises 112,936 story plots extracted from the English Wikipedia. (Malysheva et al., 2021) provided a dataset of TV series along with an instrument for narrative arc analysis. The rise of large language models in the last year significantly stimulated the interest of the community to the datasets that collect longer stories. For example, (Bamman et al., 2020) annotate longer stories to aid narrative understanding, (Zhao et al., 2022) pair plot descriptions with corresponding abstractive summaries, and (Pang et al., 2022; Wang et al., 2022) are QA/summarization datasets on longer stories from Project Gutenberg. We are sure that this interest will grow in the nearest future, since high-quality annotated longer narrative datasets are still rare.

Another aspect of narrative data that is still rarely addressed is multilingual narrative data. A vast majority of the narrative datasets are only available in English. In (Tikhonov et al., 2021) authors present StoryDB — a broad multilanguage dataset of narratives. With stories in 42 different languages, the authors try to amend the deficit of multilingual narrative datasets. This is one of the early attempts to amend the lack of mulilitngual narrative datasets that we know of yet we expect more in the next years.

While data is the only area of narrative processing exhibiting positive progress, it is essential to acknowledge the current state: limited datasets with longer narrative texts are available, primarily in English, and rarely include human labeling regarding narrative structure and quality. Furthermore, there is minimal discussion about the necessary narrative datasets for advancing narrative generation within the community.

3.2 Evaluation

Before delving into the narrative itself, let's first discuss the evaluation techniques available for natural language generation in general. In (Hämäläinen and Alnajjar, 2021), the authors review numerous recent generative papers, covering both automated and manual methods, where native speakers are instructed to evaluate specific properties of the generated text. This review encompasses over twenty papers on text generation that evaluate various aspects of generated texts using human labels. We believe that the scope of this paper represents the field as a whole.

Examining the evaluation aspects addressed in these 20+ papers on text generation, we find a range of methods, approaches, and concepts. For details, we refer the reader to (Hämäläinen and Alnajjar, 2021); however, in the context of this discussion, we can broadly categorize the majority of the proposed methods into five major groups:

Fluency; these methods estimate whether a generated text contains grammatical and syntactic mistakes. These metrics are relatively well-defined and can be automated to some extent. At least 13 out of the 23 NLG papers in the study utilize one or more fluency metrics for evaluation.

Topic/style/genre matching; these metrics can also be automated, typically relying on a pretrained classifier, as seen in (Ficler and Goldberg, 2017). 12 papers in the study use one or more evaluation criteria of this type.

Coherence; this group of metrics is more arbitrary, with at least three major types of coherence evaluation approaches. First, some estimate coherence on a linguistic pragmatics level, focusing on coherent causal statements that include words

[2]https://github.com/markriedl/WikiPlots

like "hence/so/thus/etc." The second approach evaluates whether the generated text aligns with the reader's general world knowledge. These questions are more subjective, especially since fictional texts often describe alternative realities[3]. Lastly, the most abstract methods assess if the text is coherent within the internal logic of the "world" it describes. This high level of abstraction leads to greater misalignment between human annotators and lower potential for automated evaluation.

Even this brief overview demonstrates that there is no consensus on the coherence evaluation, yet 10 out of the 23 papers in (Hämäläinen and Alnajjar, 2021) used coherence evaluation understanding the term 'coherence' differently. However, there is a trend that might solidify the understanding of coherence in the field and move it towards the third line of reasoning that we described above, namely, coherence within the internal logic of the "world" that the text describes. The arrival of large language models that can process longer sequences of text brings to light a recursive approach to narrative generation, see (Yang et al., 2022). The idea to generate the outline of the story first and then extend separate blocks of the story while keeping some necessary information in the prompt to control coherence seems promising. Similarly, (Goldfarb-Tarrant et al., 2020) suggest an approach that combines overall story planning, generative language model and an ensemble of scoring models that each implement an aspect of good story-writing.

Overall emotional effect; these metrics are more challenging to automate, as they rely on human emotional response. However, with enough human labels, it is possible to train a classifier for this task. 11 out of the 23 papers in the study utilize some form of emotional effect evaluation.

Novelty/originality/interestingness; these metrics are even more difficult to formalize and automate. Most papers that ask human labelers to assess interestingness imply a certain level of novelty. Nevertheless, human labelers may interpret interestingness as a topic-related category. 7 out of 23 papers in the review use human evaluation of novelty.

The first two evaluation types dominate automated evaluation methods, while coherence and novelty are seldom assessed rigorously. Numerous NLG papers employing automatic evaluation fall within these five categories, emphasizing our limited tools for evaluating generated narratives.

Coherence is something humans can intuitively estimate, but it is notoriously difficult to automate. Meanwhile, we still struggle to understand even the most basic tools, such as semantic similarity metrics for short texts, as seen in (Yamshchikov et al., 2021; Solomon et al., 2021).

Novelty depends on a deeper understanding of semantics, and it may entail an additional layer of complexity. After all, human experience typically suggests that comprehending something presented to us is less challenging than creating something new from scratch.

In summary, we must conclude that among the five groups of metrics used in human evaluation, first two could be automated yet hardly advance our understanding of narrative, while three others could hardly be fully automated and applied to narrative evaluation. They are either automated but operate on a lower level with shorter texts or address high-level conceptual questions that are not quantified in a manner that permits automatic evaluation. This surprising realization leads us to the following logical conclusion: we cannot explain to humans how to evaluate a narrative. Despite the existence of literary criticism, narratology that represents a separate scientific field and a variety of approaches proposed in NLP, i.e. (Castricato et al., 2021), we still lack a universal formalized understanding of what a narrative is and how to assess it. Let us discuss this in the further subsection.

3.3 Concepts

In a review paper, (Gervás et al., 2019) authors present a compelling argument that the concept of storytelling encompasses a diverse set of operations. These operations are sometimes executed independently to create simple stories or specific story components, while other times they are combined to produce more complex narratives. The authors propose "deconstructing" storytelling into the following approaches: stories as narrative structures; stories as simulations; stories as evolving networks of character affinity; stories as narrations of observed facts; and stories as suspense-driven entertainment.

Upon closer examination, the proposed taxonomy reveals similar issues to those encountered in the evaluation process. There are no universally agreed-upon mechanisms for narrative representa-

[3]Still, we intuitively understand that some science fiction or fantasy novels are coherent, even if not realistic.

tion with high coherence among human labelers. Most methods are either deeply subjective (such as the well-known anthology of four plots first presented in (Borges, 1972)) or extremely low-level, working for causal inference on a short time scale but unable to extend to the level of a short story, let alone a novel.

It is essential to emphasize that each conceptual approach can yield practical results. However, there is no clear understanding of how these approaches structure the broader field of narrative processing, which we argue should be the primary focus of the NLP and AI communities in the near future. Is one approach sufficient to develop new models capable of generating entertaining stories? Do we need a combination of these pipelines? Should there be qualitative and quantitative interactions between these pipelines, and if so, how should they be organized? Finally, there is a set of even more general question. For example, could be have a narrative representation that would ne non-textual? What are independent properties of such representation if it exists? How one could quantify them? We hope this position paper could help intensifying the discussion of these questions.

4 Conclusion

This position paper puts forth two primary assertions:

- The generation of novel, entertaining narratives is a crucial task that could propel the progress of artificial intelligence across various fields and industries.
- Despite the critical importance of this task, the current NLP and AI communities are far from reaching a shared understanding of suitable datasets for narrative generation, appropriate evaluation methods, and the need for rigorous definition of concepts to address these problems effectively.

We hope this paper stimulates further discussion on these topics and attracts the attention of the NLP and AI community towards the challenges surrounding narrative generation.

Limitations

This is a position paper thus we do not see what the potential limitations could be. The only potential limitation might be the incompleteness of the list of relevant publications.

Ethics Statement

This paper complies with the ACL Ethics Policy. We have used generative AI for editing of the final text of the paper, since some of the authors might not be native speakers of English.

References

Yana Agafonova, Alexey Tikhonov, and Ivan P Yamshchikov. 2020. Paranoid transformer: Reading narrative of madness as computational approach to creativity. *Future Internet*, 12(11):182.

Prithviraj Ammanabrolu, Ethan Tien, Wesley Cheung, Zhaochen Luo, William Ma, Lara J Martin, and Mark O Riedl. 2020. Story realization: Expanding plot events into sentences. In *Proceedings of the AAAI Conference on Artificial Intelligence*, volume 34, pages 7375–7382.

Payal Bajaj, Chenyan Xiong, Guolin Ke, Xiaodong Liu, Di He, Saurabh Tiwary, Tie-Yan Liu, Paul Bennett, Xia Song, and Jianfeng Gao. 2022. Metro: Efficient denoising pretraining of large scale autoencoding language models with model generated signals. *arXiv preprint arXiv:2204.06644*.

David Bamman, Olivia Lewke, and Anya Mansoor. 2020. An annotated dataset of coreference in english literature. In *Proceedings of the Twelfth Language Resources and Evaluation Conference*, pages 44–54.

Jorge Luis Borges. 1972. El oro de los tigres. In *Emece, Buenos Aires*.

Tom Brown, Benjamin Mann, Nick Ryder, Melanie Subbiah, and others (OpenAI). 2020. Language models are few-shot learners. In *Advances in Neural Information Processing Systems*, volume 33, pages 1877–1901.

Louis Castricato, Stella Biderman, Rogelio E Cardona-Rivera, and David Thue. 2021. Towards a formal model of narratives. *arXiv preprint arXiv:2103.12872*.

Aakanksha Chowdhery, Sharan Narang, Jacob Devlin, Maarten Bosma, Gaurav Mishra, Adam Roberts, Paul Barham, Hyung Won Chung, Charles Sutton, Sebastian Gehrmann, et al. 2022. Palm: Scaling language modeling with pathways. *arXiv preprint arXiv:2204.02311*.

Richard Doust and Paul Piwek. 2017. A model of suspense for narrative generation. In *Proceedings of the 10th International Conference on Natural Language Generation*, pages 178–187.

Angela Fan, Mike Lewis, and Yann Dauphin. 2018. Hierarchical neural story generation. In *Proceedings of the 56th Annual Meeting of the Association for Computational Linguistics (Volume 1: Long Papers)*, pages 889–898.

Angela Fan, Mike Lewis, and Yann Dauphin. 2019. Strategies for structuring story generation. In *Proceedings of the 57th Annual Meeting of the Association for Computational Linguistics*, pages 2650–2660.

Jessica Ficler and Yoav Goldberg. 2017. Controlling linguistic style aspects in neural language generation. In *Proceedings of the Workshop on Stylistic Variation*, pages 94–104.

Pablo Gervás, Eugenio Concepción, Carlos León, Gonzalo Méndez, and Pablo Delatorre. 2019. The long path to narrative generation. *IBM Journal of Research and Development*, 63(1):8–1.

Seraphina Goldfarb-Tarrant, Tuhin Chakrabarty, Ralph Weischedel, and Nanyun Peng. 2020. Content planning for neural story generation with aristotelian rescoring. In *Proceedings of the 2020 Conference on Empirical Methods in Natural Language Processing (EMNLP)*, pages 4319–4338.

Mika Hämäläinen and Khalid Alnajjar. 2021. Human evaluation of creative nlg systems: An interdisciplinary survey on recent papers. In *Proceedings of the 1st Workshop on Natural Language Generation, Evaluation, and Metrics (GEM 2021)*, pages 84–95.

Z Harris. 1954. Distributional hypothesis. *Word*, 10(23):146–162.

Sudipta Kar, Suraj Maharjan, A Pastor López-Monroy, and Thamar Solorio. 2018. Mpst: A corpus of movie plot synopses with tags. In *Proceedings of the Eleventh International Conference on Language Resources and Evaluation (LREC 2018)*.

Richard Koncel Kedziorski. 2019. *Understanding and Generating Multi-Sentence Texts*. Ph.D. thesis.

Kevin Lu, Aditya Grover, Pieter Abbeel, and Igor Mordatch. 2021. Pretrained transformers as universal computation engines. *arXiv preprint arXiv:2103.05247*.

Anastasia Malysheva, Alexey Tikhonov, and Ivan P Yamshchikov. 2021. Dyplodoc: Dynamic plots for document classification. In *Modern Management based on Big Data II and Machine Learning and Intelligent Systems III*, pages 511–519. IOS Press.

Ashutosh Modi, Tatjana Anikina, Simon Ostermann, and Manfred Pinkal. 2016. Inscript: Narrative texts annotated with script information. In *Proceedings of the Tenth International Conference on Language Resources and Evaluation (LREC'16)*, pages 3485–3493.

Nasrin Mostafazadeh, Nathanael Chambers, Xiaodong He, Devi Parikh, Dhruv Batra, Lucy Vanderwende, Pushmeet Kohli, and James Allen. 2016. A corpus and cloze evaluation for deeper understanding of commonsense stories. In *Proceedings of the 2016 Conference of the North American Chapter of the Association for Computational Linguistics: Human Language Technologies*, pages 839–849.

Andreea I Niculescu. 2021. Brief considerations on the phenomenon of humor in hci. In *Asian CHI Symposium 2021*, pages 152–156.

Simon Ostermann, Michael Roth, and Manfred Pinkal. 2019. Mcscript2. 0: A machine comprehension corpus focused on script events and participants. In *Proceedings of the Eighth Joint Conference on Lexical and Computational Semantics (* SEM 2019)*, pages 103–117.

Richard Yuanzhe Pang, Alicia Parrish, Nitish Joshi, Nikita Nangia, Jason Phang, Angelica Chen, Vishakh Padmakumar, Johnny Ma, Jana Thompson, He He, et al. 2022. Quality: Question answering with long input texts, yes! In *Proceedings of the 2022 Conference of the North American Chapter of the Association for Computational Linguistics: Human Language Technologies*, pages 5336–5358.

Vladimir Propp. 1968. Morphology of the folktale, trans. *Louis Wagner, 2d. ed.*

Colin Raffel, Noam Shazeer, Adam Roberts, Katherine Lee, Sharan Narang, Michael Matena, Yanqi Zhou, Wei Li, and Peter J Liu. 2020. Exploring the limits of transfer learning with a unified text-to-text transformer. *Journal of Machine Learning Research*, 21:1–67.

Michaela Regneri, Alexander Koller, and Manfred Pinkal. 2010. Learning script knowledge with web experiments. In *Proceedings of the 48th Annual Meeting of the Association for Computational Linguistics*, pages 979–988.

Viktor Shklovsky. 1925. Theory of prose (b. sher, trans.). *Champaign, IL: Dalkey Archive Press. Original work published.*

Shaul Solomon, Adam Cohn, Hernan Rosenblum, Chezi Hershkovitz, and Ivan P Yamshchikov. 2021. Rethinking crowd sourcing for semantic similarity. *arXiv preprint arXiv:2109.11969*.

Allison C Tam, Neil C Rabinowitz, Andrew K Lampinen, Nicholas A Roy, Stephanie CY Chan, DJ Strouse, Jane X Wang, Andrea Banino, and Felix Hill. 2022. Semantic exploration from language abstractions and pretrained representations. *arXiv preprint arXiv:2204.05080*.

Alexey Tikhonov, Igor Samenko, and Ivan Yamshchikov. 2021. Storydb: Broad multi-language narrative dataset. In *Proceedings of the 2nd Workshop on Evaluation and Comparison of NLP Systems*, pages 32–39.

A. Turing. 1950. Computing machinery and intelligence. *Mind*, 59(236):433.

Teun A Van Dijk. 1976. Philosophy of action and theory of narrative. *Poetics*, 5(4):287–338.

Judith van Stegeren and Mariët Theune. 2019. Narrative generation in the wild: Methods from nanogenmo. In *Proceedings of the Second Workshop on Storytelling*, pages 65–74.

Alex Wang, Richard Yuanzhe Pang, Angelica Chen, Jason Phang, and Samuel R Bowman. 2022. Squality: Building a long-document summarization dataset the hard way. *arXiv preprint arXiv:2205.11465*.

Pengcheng Wang, Jonathan P Rowe, Wookhee Min, Bradford W Mott, and James C Lester. 2017. Interactive narrative personalization with deep reinforcement learning. In *IJCAI*, pages 3852–3858.

Lilian Diana Awuor Wanzare, Michael Roth, and Manfred Pinkal. 2019. Detecting everyday scenarios in narrative texts. In *Proceedings of the Second Workshop on Storytelling*, pages 90–106.

Karl Wiig. 2012. *People-focused knowledge management*. Routledge.

Ludwig Wittgenstein. 1921. Logisch-Philosophische Abhandlung. *Annalen der Naturphilosophie*.

Jon Womack and William Freeman. 2019. Interactive narrative generation using location and genre specific context. In *International Conference on Interactive Digital Storytelling*, pages 343–347. Springer.

Ivan P Yamshchikov, Viacheslav Shibaev, Nikolay Khlebnikov, and Alexey Tikhonov. 2021. Style-transfer and paraphrase: Looking for a sensible semantic similarity metric. In *Proceedings of the AAAI Conference on Artificial Intelligence*, volume 35, pages 14213–14220.

Kevin Yang, Nanyun Peng, Yuandong Tian, and Dan Klein. 2022. Re3: Generating longer stories with recursive reprompting and revision. *arXiv preprint arXiv:2210.06774*.

Andy Zeng, Adrian Wong, Stefan Welker, Krzysztof Choromanski, Federico Tombari, Aveek Purohit, Michael Ryoo, Vikas Sindhwani, Johnny Lee, Vincent Vanhoucke, et al. 2022. Socratic models: Composing zero-shot multimodal reasoning with language. *arXiv preprint arXiv:2204.00598*.

Chao Zhao, Faeze Brahman, Kaiqiang Song, Wenlin Yao, Dian Yu, and Snigdha Chaturvedi. 2022. Narrasum: A large-scale dataset for abstractive narrative summarization. *arXiv preprint arXiv:2212.01476*.

Barret Zoph, Irwan Bello, Sameer Kumar, Nan Du, Yanping Huang, Jeff Dean, Noam Shazeer, and William Fedus. 2022. Designing effective sparse expert models. *arXiv preprint arXiv:2202.08906*.

Story Settings: A Dataset

Kaley Rittichier
University of Connecticut
kaley.rittichier@uconn.edu

Abstract

Understanding the settings of a given story has long been viewed as an essential component of understanding the story at large. This significance is not only underscored in academic literary analysis but also in kindergarten education. However, despite this significance, it has received relatively little attention regarding computational analyses of stories. This paper presents a dataset of 2,302 time period setting labeled works and 6,991 location setting labeled works. This dataset aims to help with Cultural Analytics of literary works but may also aid in time-period-related questions within literary Q&A systems.

1 Introduction

The setting of a story is the time and place in which the events in the story are purported to occur. Understanding the setting of a story is important to understanding the story's composite pieces, such as characters, events, and plot. This significance is even unscored in children's early education with the United States Common Core standards having setting detection as a key area of English education for kindergartners (Pearson, 2013). Part of the reason for the significance is that settings can enable us to make inferences as varied as customs/practices, technology, and character limitations. The inferences we can make have various levels of granularity depending on our knowledge of the time period or location.

Apart from such inferences, story settings are advantageous when conducting Cultural Analytics using literature. One of the reasons is what is called in philosophy the epistemic role of fiction (Green, 2022; García-Carpintero, 2016). Stories have a remarkable impact on people's understanding of the world. Empirical studies have shown this is the case even when people know the story is fictional (Murphy, 1998; Strange and Leung, 1999; Strange, 1993, 2002). This carries particular weight with historical fiction. These studies seem to suggest that it is hard to read or watch "War and Peace" without it shaping our view of the actual transpiring of the War of 1812.

Such epistemic uses of fiction seem to have had large social effects. For instance, the carefully researched 1852 novel "Uncle Tom's Cabin" was said to have a profound effect on the public's negative perception and consequential response to slavery (Reynolds, 2011). However, some works have been said to misrepresent racial relations, such as "Gone With The Wind"'s portrayal of the Civil War (Coates, 2018).

Having a dataset that distinguishes the time period the work was written in and the time period of its setting enables analysis of how truthful the work is in comparison to historical records. It also enables additional literary analysis. For instance, when doing cultural analysis of fictional character presentations, we may analyze not only how Victorian authors presented women in their "modern-day" novels but also how they presented women of the past.

However, despite the value of identifying a story's time period and location, there are currently no large or diverse datasets for this purpose. This paper presents such a dataset. The dataset is available for download under a Creative Commons Attribution 4.0 license at `https://github.com/krittichier/StorySettings`.

This paper is organized as follows: Section 2, describes related work that focused on determining time period and location from texts. In Section 3, the time period dataset is outlined, including the retrieval process as well as the cleaning, labeling, and baseline classification from the data. Section 4, outlines the location dataset construction and classification using simple metrics. Section 5, concludes the paper.

Proceedings of the The 5th Workshop on Narrative Understanding, pages 65–72
July 14, 2023 ©2023 Association for Computational Linguistics

2 Related Work

There has been some work focused on the time period setting or other temporal aspects of stories. The first Narrative Q & A dataset (Kočiský et al., 2018) was offered in 2018 to evaluate reading comprehension. Of the over 1,500 textual works, only 6% had a time period setting Q & A combo and 7.5% had a location setting Q & A combo. Although there were some that dealt with the setting for a particular event, these also had low representation.

There was a publication on the passage of time within fictional works (Kim et al., 2020), where segments of text are labeled by the time of day they take place (i.e., morning, daytime, evening, and night.) Similarly, an annotation guideline for temporal aspects was published as part of the SANTA (Systematic Analysis of Narrative levels Through Annotation) project. This dataset addresses the issue of how to deal with jumps in the story timeline, such as Analepsis (a flashback) or Prolepsis (a flashforward).

A few projects have focused on time period classification for non-story texts. Most of the literature focuses on news data (Ng et al., 2020). The problem with this, as with many other cases of news data's use in natural language processing, is that news data is often written more explicitly than other text of text (Bamman et al., 2020); in this case particularly, temporal aspects are very clear, sometimes down to the hour (Ng et al., 2020). Additionally, news text is often much shorter, and therefore its time spans are smaller. Another example of non-story detection is EVALITY's 2020 task (Basile et al., 2020; Brivio, 2020). In this task, works were collected about the former prime minister of Italy, Alcide De Gasperi (Menini et al., 2020; Massidda, 2020). In this task, there were 2,759 works that were then split into five different categories for coarse-grained analysis and 11 different ranges for fine-grained analysis.

There have also been two attempts at identifying the time period of a text using time series(Mughaz et al., 2017; HaCohen-Kerner and Mughaz, 2010). These two papers are written by some of the same authors using different approaches. Their work differs from this one in that it deals more with the publication time period than the setting time period. The term frequency-based approach they use is not able to draw this distinction and therefore is less suited for the tasks of Digital Humanities and Cultural Analytics.

3 Time Period Dataset

`Project Gutenberg`[1] is the source of the literary works. Project Gutenberg is a resource that contains textual works in the public domain. At the time of this, The United States has the copyright set to expire 70 years after the author dies. As of 2019, all works written prior to 1924 are in the public domain. Although there are some public domain works that have been recently published, the majority of the works were published before that date. Around 80 percent of the works in Project Gutenberg are in English. Of these English texts, 40 percent are fictional texts. To determine the work's fictional status, a combination of LoC classification (namely sub-classifications of "P: Language and Literature", which were reviewed to be literature labels rather than language or literary criticism) and header terms (such as "fiction", "story", and "tale") were used.

Three primary resources were used for identifying the time period setting of the work. These resources are Library of Congress Subject Classification[2], `Wikipedia API`[3], and `SparkNotes`[4]. Library of Congress classifications of works are expert-labeled topics that include setting information. Wikipedia has categories of text related to the time period, such as "Set in the 1920s" or "Set during the Civil War." SparkNotes consist of expert reviews of works for study purposes. `BeautifulSoup`[5] was used to scrape the HTML SparkNotes webpages and retrieve the information about the works. Like many issues within machine learning, the difficulty lies in the scarcity of the data, as there were 2,302 works labeled with time periods settings after cleaning.

3.1 Resource 1: Library of Congress Data

Each work on Project Gutenberg has at least one Library of Congress subject. Most works contain multiple subjects. Each subject itself can be composed of what the Library of Congress (henceforth LoC) refers to as headers, which are separated in the subject by "– ". LoC, they are the same across

[1] https://www.gutenberg.org/

[2] https://www.loc.gov/aba/publications/FreeLCSH/freelcsh.html

[3] https://www.mediawiki.org/wiki/API:Main_page

[4] https://www.sparknotes.com/lit/

[5] https://beautiful-soup-4.readthedocs.io/en/latest/

both copies of the work. For instance, "The Scarlet Letter" has 11 subjects: "Adultery – Fiction", "Historical fiction", "Revenge – Fiction", "Psychological fiction", "Married women – Fiction", "Clergy – Fiction", "Triangles (Interpersonal relations) – Fiction", " Illegitimate children – Fiction", "Women immigrants – Fiction", "Puritans – Fiction", "Boston (Mass.) – History – Colonial period, ca. 1600-1775 – Fiction".

In order to make these headings useful, review was required. One problem was that many of the names were missing a beginning/end or listed multiple beginning dates. In these cases, the information for the person was found and filled in by hand using Wikipedia or a historical website as a resource. Sometimes different birth/death years are given than the LoC classification; in such a case, either the default or the one that offers a longer range is used.

Sometimes the reason a date is missing is more historically significant, such as in the case of the historical figure Pocahontas, where the birth is unknown. Additionally, sometimes fictional characters are the people listed with a range. This sometimes includes "(fictional character)" and other times does not but was only determined by searching. These do not have dates of death because the death of the character never took place in the book. The date for all these is approximated by using an approximate average lifespan of real people in the dataset.

Some of the ranges express uncertainty or have typos. For instance, some people have approximated deaths (and birth) times given on Wikipedia, such as Edmund Brokesbourne, whose Wikipedia page lists him as dying in either 1396 or 1397. Some cases lead to distinctly bigger ranges, but in all cases, the year that offers the longest range is selected. In order to deal with shortened versions of the names, we make sure that each piece of the names that were found has a historical name connected to it.

Lastly, there is a category of works that are "To X"; there are 47 works with only this label for the time period setting. In investigating the full subjects, the heading "To X" is embedded; there is no clear option for what to label these as. Therefore, the range used is simply (X, X) for all instances of this label. When splitting for classification, most of the works with this give a larger range than this, making it not affect the classification. However, this is made clear in the dataset and is able to be altered.

After the initial cleaning was completed, we conducted inspections to remove time period labels that indicate the time period the work was written in rather than the actual setting of the work. A notable case for this is the century label. When it is a setting, it is indicated with the heading "History" immediately preceding it. Of all the time period labels, 1,229 had only centuries as their label. Of these, 148 had "History" before it. Additionally, 47 others had those combined with other time period indicators. These history century labels were only used for the ones that did not have other time period labels, given the that they were too large of a range and the distribution: 68% of the centuries after the "History" subcategory is "19th century," while 89% span "17th century" to "19th century". Additionally, another time period indicating header that is indicative of the time written and not the setting is when author labels are included, such as "Shakespeare, William, 1564-1616". These were removed from the headings.

The total number of LoC headings for time period is 759. All of these headings were reviewed by hand to identify whether they represent a person, event, or simply a time period. Of these labels, 404 of these labels are names of people accompanied by their lifespan. 261 of the headers are events, which are broadly construed to include conspiracies and locations at particular times, such as "New Plymouth, 1620-1691". Of the remaining 93, 67 indicate year ranges, 18 of these indicate "ToX", and the remaining 8 indicate the centuries spanning from the 13th to the 20th century.

Of the 1923 works with time period labels that are not simply a century, 1,641 have only one subject (header), and 280 of them have multiple time periods indicating labels (people, events, etc.). 182 of these have at least one range that encompasses all of the other ranges. When this is not the case, a span of all of them is taken. The range of the setting years for all the works is 1000 to 2099 as "Two thousand, A.D." was used to describe two books set in the 2000s, which were written in the 1800s.

3.2 Resource 2: Wikipedia

Categories are a way that Wikipedia pages are organized and can be retrieved through the Wikipedia

API[6]. To gather the works from Wikipedia, the categories listed in the table where X stands for a number and '|' indicate different options. "BC" sometimes followed the century category:

- Novels|Fiction|Plays set in the Xth|Xst|Xnd century
- Novels|Fiction|Plays set in the Xs
- Novels|Fiction|Plays set in the X
- Novels|Fiction|Plays set in the Middle Ages

From these categories, there were 1,497 titles retrieved, and 311 (21%) were found to be unique works on Project Gutenberg. In order to avoid fiction of the same title getting mistaken for a work on Gutenberg, the Wikipedia pages were reviewed to find the author's name presented in the article. A few of the works contained the exact names of the authors. However, a by hand inspection of the remaining was needed as the authors' names come in many different variations, such as with/without accent marks, shortened/lengthened versions (e.g., Sam vs. Samuel), initials in place of names, missing middle name(s), and misspellings. The resulting number of books was 236. Part of the reason for the significant drop is that Wikipedia labels tend to focus on more recently published books, in other words, not those that are typically available on Project Gutenberg.

3.3 Resource 3: SparkNotes

In this section, we discuss the SparkNotes data. As of August 2021, the SparkNotes website has 710 works [7] of which it offers study guides that consist of descriptions and explanations. 464 of these works have a factsheet[8] associated with them containing information on specific details of the novel, such as Setting (Time Period), Setting (Location), tense, date of publication, etc. 156 of the works on the website are supplied by The Project Gutenberg, but only 101 of these works contain "factsheets" detailing aspects of the novel such as setting. By hand review of all of the 464 was done to verify the same title as SparkNotes sometimes does not use official names but rather what the work is commonly called, such as "Alice's Adventures in Wonderland" title being "Alice in Wonderland."

Of these 101 works, 10 of these are not literature/fiction. 5 of these are not the same book but simply the same title. The reference of the title to the correct work, and not another by the same title, is verified by the author's being reviewed by hand. Another 5 are removed because the time period could not be determined. The reason for this is that some have the setting marked as "unknown", and others are too vague such as in the case of "The Alchemist", where no time indications are given except for the advancements of technology. This would leave us with 81 works, yet one of the entries on SparkNotes is for both parts 1 and 2, which are separate books that cover the same time span, so these were split up. We are, therefore, left with 82 time period works from SparkNotes. In the dataset, the key is the URL for the work, and the id and filename are for Project Gutenberg retrieval.

Given that literary works do not always offer specific dates for the time period setting, this ambiguity is reflected in SparkNotes labeling. For instance, the time period of "The American" by Henry James is labeled by SparkNotes as "May 1868 and the several years thereafter". Of the 82 works, only 24 contain specific ranges. To deal with the variance, each 58 with the remaining, certain rules were used. Regular expressions and named-entity recognition was used to aid the labeling of the works, but each of the works was inspected by hand. A table for numerical interpretations of terms such as "mid", "late", and "early" (and their synonyms)is given in Appendix A as well as an explanation of the rules followed for other vague terms.

3.4 Resource Overlap

Some of the resources had overlap in works attributed values LoC and Wikipedia had 51 works that overlapped: 35 of these works the range fell within one another, 12 of these works had overlap (with an overlap average of 40 years), and 4 were disjoint from one another which was, on average, only a difference of 4 years. LoC and SparkNotes had 7 works in-common and 6 of the SparkNotes within the AoC label ranges. The only one that did not was the LoC label' Revolution, 1789-1799' for "The Tale of Two Cities," which takes place "1775–1793". Between Wikipedia and SparkNotes, Wikipedia was often too large of a range. There were 3 works that were in all 3 of the datasets. Be-

[6] `https://en.wikipedia.org/wiki/Wikipedia:Contents/Categories`

[7] `https://www.sparknotes.com/lit/`

[8] For an example of a factsheet, namely A Tale of Two Cities: `https://www.sparknotes.com/lit/a-tale-of-two-cities/facts/`

cause SparkNotes is the most precise and expert reviewed, its value takes precedence over all other labelings. Second is Wikipedia, i.e., Wikipedia's labels are used when Wikipedia and LoC both label the same work.

3.5 Dataset Construction

For time period setting, the dataset contains a zipped folder of all 2,302 works. For labels, it contains a JSON file that can be read in as a table. In the table, the time period is in the form of a tuple indicating its range. It also includes Project Gutenberg data/metadata: file name, id, title, author and years alive (e.g., "Hawthorne, Nathaniel, 1804-1864"), the list of LoC subjects, and the list of LoC classifications (such as "PR: English literature").

For interpreting the LoC headings, a JSON dictionary is supplied. Within this, each heading has a type label (year, event, or person), a start date, and an end date. So, "William I, Prince of Orange, 1533-1584" is labeled as a person and has a start date of 1533 and an end date of 1584. Given restrictions on distributing SparkNotes data, there are no such dictionaries offered. However, A offers a breakdown of the general rules applied. Also, due to the simplicity of the Wikipedia labels, no such dictionary for it is supplied.

3.6 Results

For the classification task, we use the TF-IDF score. This score is commonly used for document classification. It works by calculating the term frequency of a document and dividing it by the inverse document frequency. By doing this, the formula captures the significance of the words to the document rather than simply prominence in the document. This can be seen in the formula 1. In this formula, $tf_{i,j}$ is the frequency of the term i in file j, df_i is the number of files that contain i, and N is the total number of files.

$$w_{i,j} = tf_{i,j} \times \log(\frac{N}{df_i}) \quad (1)$$

Before running the TF-IDF algorithm on the works, they were cleaned to remove stopwords and lemmatized.

Given the various ranges the labels offer, they must be split into categories. The difficulty of this lies in the lack of clear thresholds. For instance, some novels may cover the first few years of the Revolution, while others cover the duration and the aftermath. Given that the dataset is already fairly small, we don't want to lose many of the works. For this reason, we give some wiggle room to thresholds in comparing the works to the threshold. The formula for softening the thresholds is allowing them to be up to 10 years off as long as the difference is less than 10% of the range. This metric was used because it appeared to best represent our concept of "close", and that the majority of the work would be in that range. In future work, other metrics may be tested.

The data was tested on three different numbers of categories:

- 3-way split where the soft thresholds are 1746 and 1877
- 4-way split where the soft thresholds are 1698, 1803, and 1898
- 5-way split where the soft thresholds are 1605, 1792, 1859, and 1912

The 3-way split reduced the total works down to 1850 split 545:681:624. The 4-way split reduced the total number of works down to 1686 split 471:211:454:550. The 5-way split reduced the total works down to 1595 split 286:303:207:326:473. Given that the 3-way split offers the evenest distribution and a similar breakdown to the EVALITY task mentioned in Section 2, split-3 was used for the baseline results. Table 1 shows the results using the top 100 TF-IDF features alone. Both Random Forest and Support Vector were able to give an F1 score of 0.81.

4 Location Dataset and Baseline Classification

In order to detect location data, LoC headings are used, as well as some SparkNotes headings. Additionally, datasets from `Simple Maps` are used for some of the world cities[9], The USA[10] and Great Britain[11]. Additionally, given the variance in state names, in LoC classification, much of the data consists of states which are abbreviated with either standard abbreviations (e.g., "AZ") or postal abbreviations (e.g., "ARIZ"). A table containing alternative state names (full and abbreviated) and postal was used. The reason for using these resources is that it enables a more robust part-whole classification than WordNet currently offers. Having the

[9] https://simplemaps.com/data/world-cities
[10] https://simplemaps.com/data/us-cities
[11] https://simplemaps.com/data/gb-cities

	Random Forest	SVM	KNN	Naïve Bayes	Decision Tree
Accuracy	0.8090	0.8090	0.7351	0.6955	0.6649
Precision	0.8260	0.8198	0.7569	0.6962	0.6717
Recall	0.8092	0.8104	0.7362	0.7049	0.6721
F1	0.8141	0.8125	0.7399	0.6985	0.6719

Table 1: Time period classification results using the TF-IDF score

part-whole relation offered a way to detect which country/state it was falling in and whether the city location was legitimate.

The results for both LoC headings and SparkNote location labels were reviewed by hand due to non-locations with the same term. For instance, though Battle is a place in England, but many battles took place in England, which is what is most often referred to with the term Battle and England in the heading labels.

The dataset included 6,962 gathered with LoC subjects. 689 of these works are labeled as having more than one location classification. There are 556 headings with identified locations. There are also 75 SparkNotes works with location(s), with around 22 having multiple location labels. 46 works are in both the LoC headers and SparkNotes, resulting in 6,991 works.

Baseline classification results using location setting were achieved using simple term occurrence metrics. 34.5% had the setting location as the most often mentioned location. 60.5% had the setting location (or the larger location it falls within, such as the country) as mentioned. The remaining 5% did not have any terms to indicate the location, and it remains an open question what content in the stories the annotators relied on in assigning the label.

This dataset covers a more simple version of location setting, namely geolocation. Other important features for location are whether it takes place in a house or, better yet, a certain character's house. However, this more nuanced version is only reflected in a few of the SparkNotes labels we see, with most having simple geolocation (e.g., country, city, state), which indicates a need for even simple location setting labels.

The dataset for the location settings is similar to the the one for time period described in section 3.5. It has a zipped folder of the works and a table that includes all of the same Project Gutenberg information. However, instead of each work having a location label column, there is a list of location-specific headings. These headings can be used as keys in the accompanying dictionary. Each key has an associated country and may also have a city and/or state based on the granularity of the label.

5 Conclusion

This paper presents a dataset of 2,302 time period setting labeled works and 6,991 location setting labeled works. The aim is for these to help with the detection of settings within stories and interesting Cultural Analytic findings by enabling analysis of cross-time-period writing and the role settings serve for story understanding. It can also help offer refinement/investigation into literary Q&A systems.

Additionally, this project serves as a way to investigate how beneficial metadata on Project Gutenberg or from LoC can be. The aim is that this will enable the use of the LoC classifications, which, to our knowledge, have not been capitalized on in natural language processing, at least at this scale or for this aim. There is also room for tracking more carefully where different portions of the work take place as can be seen to be important in the SparkNotes' labeling.

Limitations

Some of the limitations of this dataset include that of much of the time periods and locations given are simply approximations of the time period that the work is actually set in; this is most notable in the case of Library of Congress and Wikipedia labels which make up the majority of the work. These datasets offer more coarse-grained settings of a work, such as years and geolocation, which have limitations for some purposes. An additional limitation is that the works are in English and also are more commonly set/written in the West, which should be taken into account when used for analytics.

References

David Bamman, Olivia Lewke, and Anya Mansoor. 2020. An annotated dataset of coreference in English literature. In *Proceedings of the Twelfth Language Resources and Evaluation Conference*, pages 44–54, Marseille, France. European Language Resources Association.

Valerio Basile, Maria Di Maro, Croce Danilo, and Lucia C Passaro. 2020. Evalita 2020: Overview of the 7th evaluation campaign of natural language processing and speech tools for italian. In *Seventh Evaluation Campaign of Natural Language Processing and Speech Tools for Italian*, pages 1–7. CEUR-ws.

Matteo Brivio. 2020. matteo-brv@ dadoeval: An svm-based approach for automatic document dating. In *Proceedings of Seventh Evaluation Campaign of Natural Language Processing and Speech Tools for Italian. Final Workshop (EVALITA 2020), Online. CEUR. org*.

Ta-Nehisi Coates. 2018. Why do so few blacks study the civil war?

Manuel García-Carpintero. 2016. Introduction: Recent debates on learning from fiction. *Teorema: Revista Internacional de Filosofía*, 35(3):5–20.

Mitchell Green. 2022. Fiction and epistemic value: State of the art. *British Journal of Aesthetics*, 62(2):273–289.

Yaakov HaCohen-Kerner and Dror Mughaz. 2010. Estimating the birth and death years of authors of undated documents using undated citations. In *International Conference on Natural Language Processing*, pages 138–149. Springer.

Allen Kim, Charuta Pethe, and Steve Skiena. 2020. What time is it? temporal analysis of novels. In *Proceedings of the 2020 Conference on Empirical Methods in Natural Language Processing (EMNLP)*, pages 9076–9086, Online. Association for Computational Linguistics.

Tomáš Kočiský, Jonathan Schwarz, Phil Blunsom, Chris Dyer, Karl Moritz Hermann, Gábor Melis, and Edward Grefenstette. 2018. The NarrativeQA reading comprehension challenge. *Transactions of the Association for Computational Linguistics*, 6:317–328.

Riccardo Massidda. 2020. rmassidda@ dadoeval: Document dating using sentence embeddings at evalita 2020. In *EVALITA*.

Stefano Menini, Giovanni Moretti, Rachele Sprugnoli, and Sara Tonelli. 2020. Dadoeval@ evalita 2020: Same-genre and cross-genre dating of historical documents. In *7th Evaluation Campaign of Natural Language Processing and Speech Tools for Italian. EVALITA 2020*, pages 391–397. Accademia University Press.

Dror Mughaz, Yaakov HaCohen-Kerner, and Dov Gabbay. 2017. Mining and using key-words and key-phrases to identify the era of an anonymous text. In *Transactions on Computational Collective Intelligence XXVI*, pages 119–143. Springer.

Sheila T Murphy. 1998. The impact of factual versus fictional media portrayals on cultural stereotypes. *The Annals of the American academy of political and social science*, 560(1):165–178.

Victoria Ng, Erin E Rees, Jingcheng Niu, Abdelhamid Zaghool, Homeira Ghiasbeglou, and Adrian Verster. 2020. Application of natural language processing algorithms for extracting information from news articles in event-based surveillance. *Canada Communicable Disease Report*, 46(6):186–191.

P David Pearson. 2013. Research foundations of the common core state standards in english language arts. *Quality reading instruction in the age of Common Core State Standards*, pages 237–262.

David S Reynolds. 2011. *Mightier than the Sword: Uncle Tom's cabin and the Battle for America*. WW Norton & Company.

Jeffrey J Strange. 2002. How fictional tales wag real-world beliefs. *Narrative impact: Social and cognitive foundations*, pages 263–286.

Jeffrey J Strange and Cynthia C Leung. 1999. How anecdotal accounts in news and in fiction can influence judgments of a social problem's urgency, causes, and cures. *Personality and Social Psychology Bulletin*, 25(4):436–449.

Jeffrey John Strange. 1993. *The facts of fiction: The accommodation of real-world beliefs to fabricated accounts*. Ph.D. thesis, Columbia University.

A Appendix

Type	Term	Start	End
Century	turn-century	XX00	XX10
	early-century	XX00	XX40
	mid-century	XX35	XX75
	late-century	XX60	XX99
Decade	early-decade	0	4
	mid-decade	3	7
	late-decade	6	9

Table 2: Conversions for SparkNotes' ambiguity

Phrases like "shortly after the turn of the 20th century" is assumed to be 10 years longer than the dates given. In other smaller cases, "several years after" is assumed to mean 5 years after that time. Likewise, terms like "around" are 5 years added to both sides. Additionally, there are some eras used, such as Renaissance, Medieval, and Victorian eras. For these, historical references were used. In the case of multiple years given for different sections of the works (chapters, acts, etc.), the highest range is used. Also, with the presence of terms like "specifically" or "especially," the more specific range is what is used.

There are also times when multiple years, centuries, decades, or eras are given. Sometimes the variance refers to different sections of the work, such as the first chapter being set in X year and the second being set in Y. In these cases, the full range is used.

An Analysis of Reader Engagement in Literary Fiction through Eye Tracking and Linguistic Features

Rose Neis
University of Minnesota
neis@umn.edu

Karin de Langis
University of Minnesota
dento019@umn.edu

Zae Myung Kim
University of Minnesota
kim01756@umn.edu

Dongyeop Kang
University of Minnesota
dongyeop@umn.edu

Abstract

Capturing readers' engagement in fiction is a challenging but important aspect of narrative understanding. In this study, we collected 23 readers' reactions to 2 short stories through eye tracking, sentence-level annotations, and an overall engagement scale survey. We analyzed the significance of various qualities of the text in predicting how engaging a reader is likely to find it. As enjoyment of fiction is highly contextual, we also investigated individual differences in our data. Furthering our understanding of what captivates readers in fiction will help better inform models used in creative narrative generation and collaborative writing tools. The interactive demo is available here[1].

1 Introduction

The question of reader engagement in fiction has been studied in the psychology field for decades, with some of the foundational theoretical work from Gerrig (1993) on Transportation Theory paving the way for more recent theoretical frameworks and experimental setups, notably the work by Melanie C. Green (2004) and Busselle and Bilandzic (2009).

However, as Jacobs (2015) emphasized in his article on the neurocognitive science of literary reading, the samples normally collected are small and not enough to compensate for individual differences in reading patterns due to reader context and other situational factors. In order to help close the experimental gap, one contribution of this study is to provide a data set of reader reactions to natural stories, which Jacobs refers to as "hot" experimental research. This data, along with the extraction of linguistic features, allows us to test theories around reader engagement and discover which textual qualities have the most impact.

In our study, we have the following research questions:

- **RQ1: Does absorption in a story lead to longer dwell times?** To answer this question, we looked at how well the different annotations correlated with dwell time to see if there is a relationship between dwell time and different modes of reading – one being immersed and the other more reflective. We also looked at whether linguistic features of the text related to a more affective reading mode led to higher dwell times as Jacobs predicts.
- **RQ2: How much is engagement dependent on reader context vs. linguistic features?** In order to address this question, we evaluated how well the features we extracted could predict whether a sentence was highlighted by readers.
- **RQ3: Are dwell time patterns consistent across readers?** We scaled dwell times per participant and evaluated the pattern over the story to see if dwell times increased and decreased in the same areas of the story for different readers.

With respect to RQ1, our findings indicated that negatively-valenced, concrete sentences had higher dwell times. No relationship was found between the highlights and dwell times. This may be due to the fact that the highlighting data is sparse. For RQ2, we found that features such as valence, sentiment, and emotion were significant across readers, although the reader context accounted for much of the variance in highlighting annotations. Regarding RQ3, there was a high amount of variance between readers for dwell time. However, once dwell times were individually scaled, we could see some consistency in their patterns, particularly when looking only at highly engaged readers.

For future studies, a modified highlighting exercise in which participants must select a category for each sentence — including none — could result in less sparse annotation data. A more complete an-

[1] https://bookdown.org/bishop_pilot/acldemo2/ACLDemo.html

Proceedings of the The 5th Workshop on Narrative Understanding, pages 73–81
July 14, 2023 ©2023 Association for Computational Linguistics

	Ours	Kunze et al. (2015)	Magyari et al. (2020)	Hsu et al. (2015)	Maslej et al. (2019)
Data gathered					
Eye tracking	x	x	x		
Saccade angle		x	x		
fMRI				x	
Engagement survey	x	x	x		x
Engagement annotation	x			x	
Textual features extracted					
Emotional arc	x				
Lexical categories	x			x	x
Description category			x		

Table 1: Comparison between our study and other similar experiments.

notation of the story text would allow us to explore the connection between dwell time and different modes of engagement. As new methods are created for representing complex features of stories, such as character relationships and story tension, data sets like ours can be used to find more meaningful relationships between the story text and how engaging it is.

2 Related Work

In his model for the neurocognitive poetics of literary reading, Jacobs (2015) proposed two modes of reading: one fast track — "immersion" and one slow — "aesthetic trajectory". The former is proposed to be brought on by things like familiarity, suspense, sympathy, and vicarious hope; whereas the latter is a more reflective and connected mode brought on by aesthetic appreciation, more complex emotion, and unfamiliar situations. We used this framework to inform what variables we expected to have an impact on dwell time.

Busselle and Bilandzic (2009) conducted a series of studies to narrow down the salient aspects of reader engagement and created a general media engagement scale. The aspects they defined are narrative understanding, attentional focus, emotional engagement, and narrative presence, and the scale they created include questions related to those aspects. We adapted this scale for written narrative to gauge overall interest in the stories used in our study. In addition, in order to obtain more granular information, we used these aspects to design an annotation task that would provide sentence-level feedback. Using visualizations and linear mixed effect models, we explored textual features that had an impact on engagement and dwell time across readers. There have been several other eye tracking as well as fMRI studies in the area of reader engagement (a few are shown in Table 1). One 13-participant study showed that words in enactive passages had on average longer fixation durations and dwell times (Magyari et al., 2020). Based on survey responses, the authors hypothesized that in the enactive texts, the ease of imagery contributes to greater involvement in imagination and results in an overall slower reading speed. Hsu et al. (2015) conducted an fMRI study and found valence and arousal scores as good predictors of overall emotional experience of the reader.

3 Methods

Participant study design The study asked 31 English speakers (17 female, 11 male, 3 other, average age: 26) to read two short stories by Anton Chekhov[2] while their eyes were tracked, and then answer an engagement scale survey:

- I was curious about what would happen next. (+)
- The story affected me emotionally. (+)
- While reading my body was in the room, but my mind was inside the world created by the story. (+)
- At times while reading, I wanted to know what the writer's intentions were. (+)
- While reading, when a main character succeeded, I felt happy, and when they suffered in some way, I felt sad. (+)
- The characters were alive in my imagination. (+)

[2]"Expensive Lessons" and "Schoolmistress"

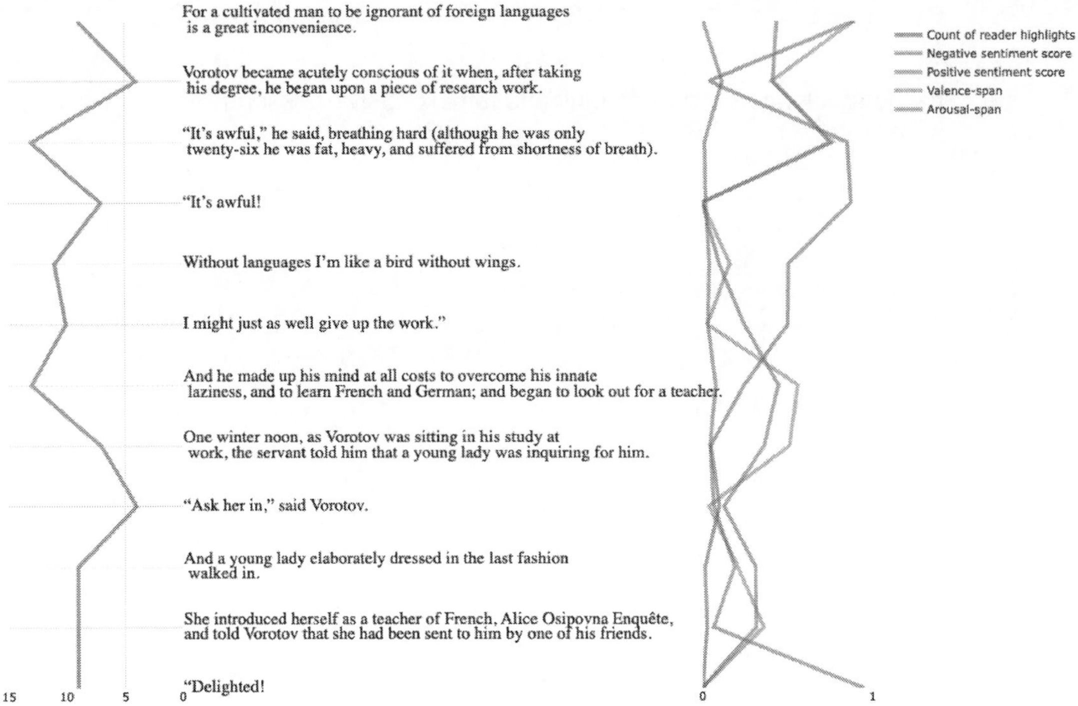

Figure 1: Engagement highlight counts (left) and linguistic feature scores (right) for Expensive Lessons. More examples and interactive demos are available in `https://bookdown.org/bishop_pilot/acldemo2/ACLDemo.html`

- I found my mind wandering while reading the story. (-)
- I could vividly imagine the scenes in the story. (+)
- At points, I had a hard time making sense of what was going on in the story (-)

After reading through both stories, they completed a highlighting exercise where they highlighted areas according to the following categories:

- *Present*: Able to vividly picture the scene in the story
- *Confused*
- *Curious*: Curious about what will happen next
- *Connected*: Connected to the character; able to identify with them or feel their emotions
- *Other*: Enjoyed it for a different reason

Eye-tracking data Due to calibration issues, 8 samples were discarded, leaving 23 (13 female, 8 male, 2 other, average age: 28, std.: 10). See Table 4 for more details on the participants. The eye tracking results were drift corrected and interest area reports were exported using words as interest areas. Outliers for dwell time were removed using the inner quartile range method (1.7% of the data). The data was aggregated to the sentence level and dwell time values were normalized by sentence character count. To handle missing data, null values for the eye tracking features were filled with the average of the 5 nearest sentences (5.7% of all sentences read across participants). Dwell times were then scaled individually per participant using min-max scaling. This allowed each participant's dwell time patterns to be preserved when scaling.

Linguistic and discourse features We extracted the following features from the stories to create sentence-level predictors: negative and positive sentiment scores using the RoBERTa sentiment base model, emotion categories using the DistilRoBERTa emotion base model[3], concreteness scores from the Brysbaert et al. (2014) corpus, valence and arousal from the NRC-VAD corpus (Warriner et al., 2013), word frequency from the subtlex corpus (Brysbaert, 2015), and average word length. Emotions extracted were based on the basic emotions described by Ekman and Cordaro (2011) plus a neutral category: anger, disgust, fear, joy, neutral, sadness, surprise. Sentence level scores for concreteness, valence, arousal, and word frequency were obtained by using the scores of each lemma

[3]RoBERTa sentiment model and DistilRoBERTa emotion model

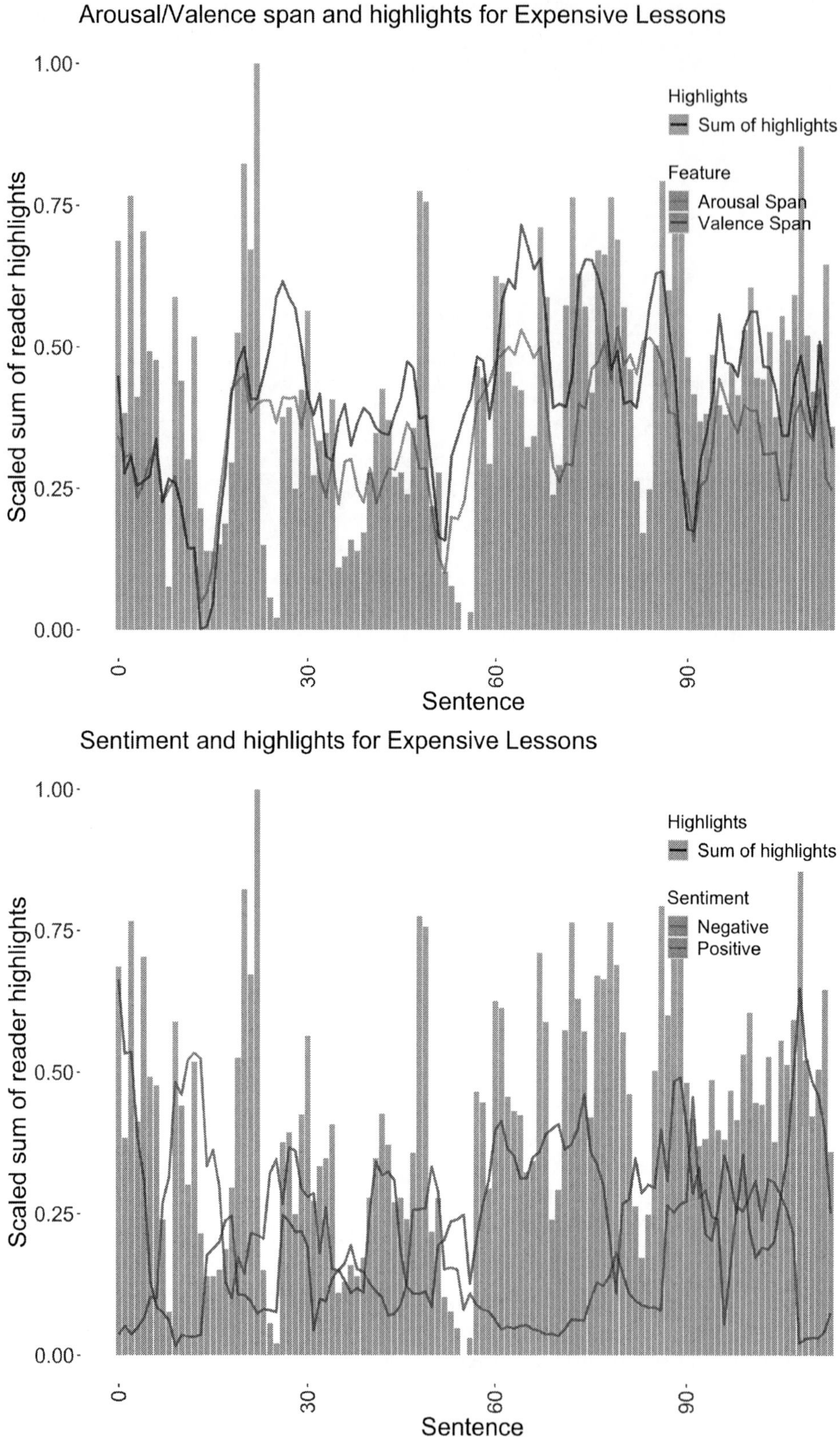

Figure 2: Highlights and features.

and then computing the mean and difference between minimum and maximum scores. To obtain lemmas, we used the BookNLP [4] code package. All feature scores used in our models are scaled to $[0, 1]$.

As these sentence-level features can have high variability on their own, we performed low-pass filtering by Fourier transformation on sliding windows of ten sentences. As a result, we were able to filter out extreme features and smoothly track the patterns of features that persist over a longer context.

Limitations There are a few issues with the data that should be mentioned. Since the participants were asked to read two stories in a row, it is best to make sure there is a balance in which story is read first. However, due to poor tracking of reading order, our data ended up with a skew towards one story (Expensive Lessons: 16, Schoolmistress: 7), which may affect level of attention for the second story.

In addition, the stories did not receive high scores on average in the engagement survey. On a scale from 0-4, Expensive Lessons got an average of 2.09 and Schoolmistress averaged 1.92. Ideally, stories used for such studies should be more widely popular in order to make engagement more likely. Perhaps in part due to the low average score, the highlighting data is sparse, making it difficult to find relationships between dwell time and engagement categories.

Finally, although efforts were made to recruit participants from the larger community, a majority of the participants were University students and staff, with a minority from outside the University community. As seen in Table 4, this resulted in a skew towards younger, college-educated participants. Observations from this study may not generalize well to other groups.

4 Results

Other studies have shown that valence and arousal play an important role in predicting interest in a story (Maslej et al., 2019; Hsu et al., 2015) and Jacobs (2015) emphasized the importance of affective processes in his framework. In order to determine the importance of these values for our data, we used linear mixed model analysis. Using lme4 (Bates et al., 2015) and lmerTest (Kuznetsova et al., 2017), we fit predictions of the proportion of the sentence highlighted and dwell time, with random effects of participant (n=23) and story (n=2). Variables were tested for collinearity using the variance inflation factor (VIF) method outlined by Zuur et al. (2010), and no variables exceeded the recommended threshold of 3. Observations and fixed effects are on a $[0, 1]$ scale. See Appendix B for exact model definitions.

4.1 Predicting engagement highlights

	Slope	$Pr(>\|t\|)$	Sig.	VIF
(Intercept)	-0.05	0.49		
char. ct.	0.16	< 0.001	$***$	2.19
word freq.	0.07	0.08	.	1.23
positive	0.03	0.09	.	1.58
negative	0.09	< 0.001	$***$	1.73
concrete	0.02	0.15		1.24
valence	0.11	0.011	$*$	1.39
arousal	-0.02	0.68		1.11
val.-span	0.11	< 0.001	$***$	2.75
ar.-span	0.11	< 0.001	$***$	2.61
surprise	0.08	0.001	$**$	1.11
disgust	0.03	0.059	.	1.15

Table 2: Fixed Effects: predicting highlights

We fit a model for predicting the proportion of a sentence highlighted by a reader in order to see how significant the textual features were across readers to address RQ2. Table 2 shows major results in predicting annotated highlights with different linguistic and discourse features.

Our results support a significance of valence mean (p=0.01), similar to Hsu et al. (2015). Unlike in other studies, we found that arousal mean had no significance (p=0.686). However, similar to Hsu et al. (2015), valence-span — the difference between valence max and valence min (p<0.001) and arousal-span — the difference between arousal max and arousal min (p<0.001) were significant. The positive slope for both (0.1) suggests that the reader was more engaged in sentences with a higher range of valence and arousal.

Of the emotion categories (i.e. anger, disgust, fear, joy, neutral, sadness, surprise), surprise was found to be a significant effect (p=0.001) with a positive slope (0.08). Other features that had an impact were negative sentiment score (p<0.001) and character count (p<0.001). The positive slope for negative sentiment (0.09) partially align with

[4]BookNLP

the Maslej et al. (2019) study, where negative emotion predicted higher story ratings, although unlike their findings, there was no relationship between concreteness and engagement.

When including random effects that model individual participants, the model explains 23% of the variance; without these effects the explained variance drops to 3.7%. So, with respect to RQ2, the reader context is important in elucidating the relationships of the fixed effects with engagement.

Since the proportion is bounded between 0 and 1, the model residuals are not normally distributed. We therefore also fit a generalized mixed model with a binomial distribution, with the observed outcome a binary variable representing whether or not the sentence had any highlighting. Table 5 shows largely the same results, except that word frequency and positive sentiment are not significant when predicting the binary outcome.

4.2 Predicting eye movement dwell time

	Slope	$Pr(>\|t\|)$	Sig.	VIF
(Intercept)	0.10	< 0.001	$***$	
word freq.	0.18	< 0.001	$***$	1.19
positive	0.01	0.045	$*$	1.57
negative	0.01	0.1		1.68
concrete	0.01	0.0002	$***$	1.21
valence	-0.06	< 0.001	$***$	1.37
arousal	-0.01	0.34		1.09
val.-span	-0.02	0.0029	$**$	2.40
ar.-span	-0.06	< 0.001	$***$	2.24
surprise	-0.03	< 0.001	$***$	1.07

Table 3: Fixed Effects: predicting dwell time

To address RQ1, we fit a model that predicted dwell time (Table 3). In our findings, valence mean was significant (p<0.001) with a negative slope (-0.06) and arousal mean was not (p=0.349). Valence-span (p=0.0029) and arousal-span (p<0.001) were found to be significant. The negative relationship between valence mean and dwell time supports part of Jacobs' proposed framework, which states that passages that engage our emotions, particularly negative valence, would likely result in higher dwell times. There was no relationship between highlights and dwell time, however, so we were not able to confirm whether the different categories of engagement correlated with different modes of reading.

There was also a positive relationship between concreteness and dwell time (p<0.001, slope=0.01). According to the prevailing theory in neuroscience, "words referring to easily perceptible entities coactivate the brain regions involved in the perception of those entities" (Brysbaert et al., 2014). This observation may indicate that this leads to longer processing times. So indirectly our observation has some overlap with the findings of Maslej et al. (2019), where enactive passages had higher dwell times, although the linguistic features of their study differed.

To evaluate how consistent dwell time patterns were across readers (RQ3), we examined the dwell time graphs of participants to see if there was a similar pattern. We noticed an especially striking similarity in patterns amongst readers who were highly engaged (see Figure 3).

Although removing word-level outliers for dwell time improved the skewness of the data, it is still heavily skewed to the left. This resulted in residuals with a fat tail and therefore not perfectly normal. A log transformation improved the normality of the data, but it resulted in less normal residuals. This may impact the reliability of the above results.

5 Conclusion

By collecting reader feedback and eye tracking data on literary fiction, we were able to support findings of other studies that emphasized the importance of affective language for reader immersion. Although we found no direct relationship between dwell times and highlighted text, the dwell time model and the highlight model shared some predictors, such as valence and arousal. One possibility to explore for future studies would be to look at whether this overlap is related to two different modes of engagement — one that leads to higher dwell times and one that leads to lower dwell times.

However, as mentioned, this exploration would require a more complete annotation. This could be achieved by selecting more engaging stories and modifying the highlighting exercise to require readers to annotate each sentence with a category or select none. Further analysis on our data set could be done by extracting more complex features. This would expand the analysis beyond the lexical level would allow us to find more interesting relationships.

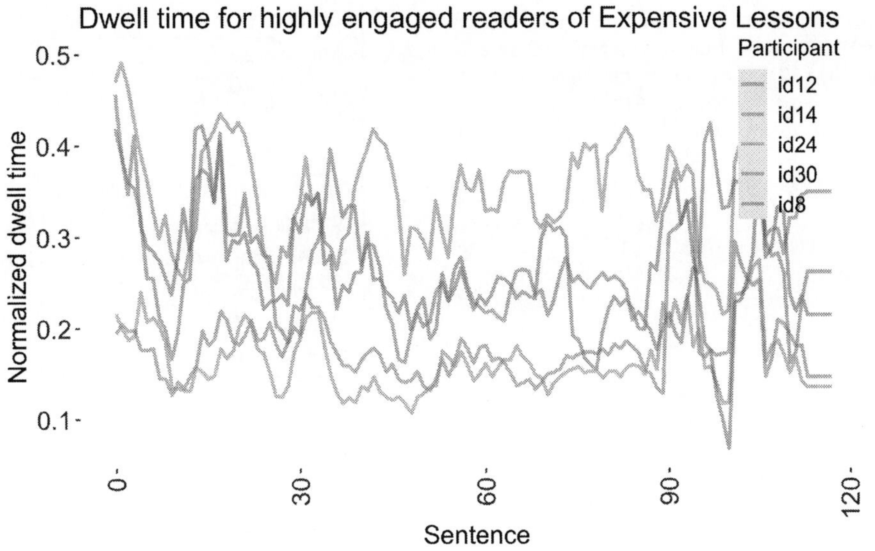

Figure 3: Dwell time for engaged readers

References

Booknlp. https://github.com/booknlp/booknlp.

Dealing with multicollinearity using vifs. Link. Accessed: 2023-05-30.

Exploring the shapes of stories using python and sentiment apis. https://indicodata.ai/blog/plotlines/. Accessed: 2022-12-21.

Francesco Barbieri, Jose Camacho-Collados, Luis Espinosa Anke, and Leonardo Neves. 2020. TweetEval: Unified benchmark and comparative evaluation for tweet classification. In *Findings of the Association for Computational Linguistics: EMNLP 2020*, pages 1644–1650, Online. Association for Computational Linguistics.

Douglas Bates, Martin Mächler, Ben Bolker, and Steve Walker. 2015. Fitting linear mixed-effects models using lme4. *Journal of Statistical Software*, 67(1):1–48.

Ryan Boyd, Ashwini Ashokkumar, Sarah Seraj, and James Pennebaker. 2022. The development and psychometric properties of liwc-22.

Marc Brysbaert. 2015. Subtlex us word frequency database.

Marc Brysbaert, Amy Beth Warriner, and Victor Kuperman. 2014. Concreteness ratings for 40 thousand generally known english word lemmas. *Behavior Research Methods*, 46(3):904–911.

Rick Busselle and Helena Bilandzic. 2009. Measuring narrative engagement. *Media Psychology*, 12(4):321–347.

Gianluca Consoli. 2018. Preliminary steps towards a cognitive theory of fiction and its effects. *Journal of Cultural Cognitive Science*, 2:85–100.

Pablo Delatorre, Alberto Salguero, Carlos León, and Alan Tapscott. 2019. The impact of context on affective norms: A case of study with suspense. *Frontiers in Psychology*, 10.

Paul Ekman and Daniel Cordaro. 2011. What is meant by calling emotions basic. *Emotion review*, 3(4):364–370.

Richard J. Gerrig. 1993. *Experiencing Narrative Worlds: On the Psychological Activities of Reading*. Yale University Press.

Melanie C. Green, Timothy C. Brock, and Geoff F. Kaufman. 2006. Understanding media enjoyment: The role of transportation into narrative worlds. *Communication Theory*, 14(4):311–327.

Jochen Hartmann. 2022. Emotion english distilroberta-base. Link.

Chun-Ting Hsu, Arthur M. Jacobs, Francesca M.M. Citron, and Markus Conrad. 2015. The emotion potential of words and passages in reading harry potter – an fmri study. *Brain and Language*, 142:96–114.

Arthur M. Jacobs. 2015. *Towards a neurocognitive poetics model of literary reading*, page 135–159. Cambridge University Press.

Arthur M. Jacobs. 2017. Quantifying the beauty of words: A neurocognitive poetics perspective. *Frontiers in Human Neuroscience*, 11.

Arthur M. Jacobs and Roel M. Willems. 2018. The fictive brain: Neurocognitive correlates of engagement in literature. *Review of General Psychology*, 22(2):147–160.

Kai Kunze, Susana Sanchez, Tilman Dingler, Olivier Augereau, Koichi Kise, Masahiko Inami, and Terada Tsutomu. 2015. The augmented narrative: Toward estimating reader engagement. In *Proceedings of the 6th Augmented Human International Conference*, AH '15, page 163–164, New York, NY, USA. Association for Computing Machinery.

Alexandra Kuznetsova, Per B. Brockhoff, and Rune H. B. Christensen. 2017. lmerTest package: Tests in linear mixed effects models. *Journal of Statistical Software*, 82(13):1–26.

Lilla Magyari, Anne Mangen, Anežka Kuzmičová, Arthur M. Jacobs, and Jana Lüdtke. 2020. Eye movements and mental imagery during reading of literary texts with different narrative styles. *Journal of Eye Movement Research*, 13(3):10.16910/jemr.13.3.3.

Marloes Mak and Roel M. Willems. 2019. Mental simulation during literary reading: Individual differences revealed with eye-tracking. *Language, Cognition and Neuroscience*, 34(4):511–535.

Marta M Maslej, Raymond A. Mar, and Victor Kuperman. 2019. The textual features of fiction that appeal to readers: Emotion and abstractness. *Psychology of Aesthetics, Creativity, and the Arts*.

Geoff F. Kaufman Melanie C. Green, Timothy C. Brock. 2004. Understanding media enjoyment: The role of transportation into narrative worlds. *Communication Theory*, 14(4):311–327.

P. Stockwell. 2002. *Cognitive Poetics: An Introduction*. Routledge.

Amy Beth Warriner, Victor Kuperman, and Marc Brysbaert. 2013. Norms of valence, arousal, and dominance for 13,915 english lemmas. *Behavior Research Methods*, 45(4):1191–1207.

Alain F. Zuur, Elena N. Ieno, and Chris S. Elphick. 2010. A protocol for data exploration to avoid common statistical problems. *Methods in Ecology and Evolution*, 1(1):3–14.

6 Acknowledgements

We would like to thank the University of Minnesota Text Group for initial feedback on experiment setup and the Blue Lantern Writing Group for additional feedback.

A Participants

Category	Count
Age: 18-24	10
Age: 25-40	10
Age: 40+	3
Native English speaker	17
Speaks English with friends	23
Speaks English with family	22
Speaks English at work	23
Gender: Female	13
Gender: Male	8
Gender: Other	2

Table 4: Participant info (n=23)

B Model Definition

Predicting engagement highlights:

```
lmer(proportion_highlighted ~ 1 +
↪ norm_dwell_time +
↪ character_count_norm +
↪ word_freq_avg + positive +
↪ negative + concreteness +
↪ valence_avg + arousal_avg +
↪ valence_span + arousal_span +
↪ surprise + disgust + (1 |
↪ participant_id) + (1 |
↪ story), data=all_data)
```

Predicting dwell time:

```
lmer(norm_dwell_time ~ 1 +
↪ word_freq_avg + positive +
↪ negative + concreteness +
↪ valence_avg + arousal_avg
↪ +valence_span + arousal_span
↪ + surprise +
↪ proportion_highlighted + (1 |
↪ participant_id) + (1 |
↪ story), data=all_data)
```

Predicting engagement highlights — binary:

```
glmer(highlight ~ 1 +
↪ norm_dwell_time +
↪ character_count_norm +
↪ word_freq_avg + positive +
↪ negative + concreteness +
↪ valence_avg + arousal_avg +
↪ valence_span + arousal_span +
↪ surprise + disgust + (1 |
↪ RECORDING_SESSION_LABEL) + (1
↪ | story), data=all_data,
↪ family=binomial)
```

Variable	Estimate	Pr(> $|z|$)	Sig
(Intercept)	-2.51	<0.001	***
norm_dt	0.28	0.279	
char. count	2.05	< 0.001	***
word freq.	0.17	0.569	
positive	0.08	0.548	
negative	0.44	0.001	***
concreteness	0.01	0.876	
valence	0.88	0.006	**
arousal	-0.32	0.392	
val.-span	0.90	<0.001	***
ar.-span	0.78	<0.001	***
surprise	0.51	0.002	**
disgust	0.19	0.049	*

Table 5: Results from binomial engagement highlights model

C Further Experiments

We asked ChatGPT to highlight the most engaging parts of the beginning of "Expensive Lessons", and here was the response:

Highlighted engaging portions:

- The opening sentence immediately grabs the reader's attention by presenting an idea that they may not have considered before.
- Vorotov's struggle with his lack of language skills is relatable and adds a sense of realism to the story.
- The description of Vorotov's physical appearance and breathing difficulties creates a vivid image of the character and adds depth to his struggle.
- The use of dialogue between Vorotov and the servant adds a sense of immediacy to the story and keeps the reader engaged.
- The introduction of Alice Osipovna Enquête as a young lady dressed in the latest fashion creates intrigue and mystery around her character.
- The revelation that Alice was sent by one of Vorotov's friends adds a layer of unexpectedness to the story and piques the reader's curiosity.

This shows good potential for automatically detecting the most engaging passages to provide an engaging summary of stories.

Identifying Visual Depictions of Animate Entities in Narrative Comics: An Annotation Study

Lauren Edlin and **Joshua Reiss**
School of Electronic Engineering and Computer Science
Queen Mary University of London
L.Edlin@qmul.ac.uk, Joshua.Reiss@qmul.ac.uk

Abstract

Animate entities in narrative comics stories are expressed through a number of visual representations across panels. Identifying these entities is necessary for recognizing characters and analysing narrative affordances unique to comics, and integrating these with linguistic reference annotation, however an annotation process for animate entity identification has not received adequate attention. This research explores methods for identifying animate entities visually in comics using annotation experiments. Two rounds of inter-annotator agreement experiments are run: the first asks annotators to outline areas on comic pages using a Polygon segmentation tool, and the second prompts annotators to assign each outlined entity's animacy type to derive a quantitative measure of agreement. The first experiment results show that Polygon-based outlines successfully produce a qualitative measure of agreement; the second experiment supports that animacy status is best conceptualised as a graded, rather than binary, concept.

1 Introduction

Comics are a rich multi-modal medium for automatic discourse processing, yet empirical work investigating their narrative structures is still a nascent research area. Current approaches include computational descriptions of narrative structures that are used to automatically generate comics from chat scripts (Kurlander et al., 1996), video game logs (Shamir et al., 2006; Thawonmas and Shuda, 2008), or video (Yang et al., 2021). Approaches applying linguistic methods includes Visual Narrative Grammar, which categorizes panels based on their narrative function and describes grammar-like constraints distinguishing valid from invalid panel sequences (Cohn, 2013, 2020), and deriving relationships between high-level narrative structures and patterns of low-level text and image parts (Bateman et al., 2018).

This research is part of a larger project that seeks to identify narrative affordances in comics by examining compositions of units such as panels, text, symbols, characters, backgrounds, etc. Taking inspiration from annotation schemes for text narrative, we explore a method of annotation and assess the reliability with inter-annotator agreement experiments. This paper focuses on identifying animate entities in images. Our previous work examined coreference agreement of characters, and we hope to link image and discourse referents in the text in future work. We hope this work contributes to a full-fledged annotation scheme that can be applied to future corpora which would contain both annotations in the non-text areas of comics, as we look at here, and annotation of the textual areas of comic pages, for a truly multi-modal approach to discourse referents.

1.1 Identifying animate entities in comics

Identifying animate entities in comics is important for narrative analyses, as animate entities give rise to unique narrative affordances. A distinct feature of comics is that unlike other media such as film and literature, readers are prompted to infer an entity's movements, actions or intentions from static images and text. Information given in one panel primes the readers expectations for the next panel. A comic creator will therefore compose panels in a way that distinguishes entities that are not expected to move and think from animate entities, the latter of which structures events that progress the plot.

One narrative element of which animacy is foundational component is the concept of *character*. Successful annotation schemes used for corpus analyses of narrative in text have defined characters as "an animate being that is important

Proceedings of the The 5th Workshop on Narrative Understanding, pages 82–91
July 14, 2023 ©2023 Association for Computational Linguistics

Figure 1: An example of the character Ms. Marvel changing her appearance, and arguably her animacy status, over several panels (Wilson et al., 2015, p. 1)

to the plot" (Jahan and Finlayson, 2019, p. 13). Binary (Moore et al., 2013) and hierarchical (Zaenen et al., 2004) animacy annotation schemes have been developed to describe animate entities types that constitute characters. While work on character tracking for cohesion analysis is being applied to comics (Tseng et al., 2018; Tseng and Bateman, 2018), adding animacy as a criteria of character could aid in character identification (Jahan et al., 2018), as well as recording non-character animate entities and potential characters.

Determining whether a drawing depicts an animate entity, however, is not straightforward. Cases where animacy is ambiguous or uncertain regularly appear in comics as they often tell narratives about fantastical scenarios; many science fiction and fairy tale stories include things like talking animals, zombies, aliens and robots, which may or may not meet a threshold for animacy. Furthermore, an entity's animacy status may change or be hidden from the reader. An example of this is depicted in Figure 1 where Ms. Marvel (Kamala Kahn) is a superhero with shape-shifting powers. In these panels, Ms. Marvel is disguised as a sofa before transforming back to her typical appearance. Ideally, an annotated corpus or computational model would track these two depictions as the same referent while also accounting for this change of animacy status.

Consequently, a satisfactory annotation scheme should include relevant animate entities beyond the notion of character. This research proposes and tests an initial annotation scheme for identifying areas on images visually representing animate entities on comic pages through two annotation experiments. Experiment 1 asks annotators to identify animate entities by outlining them on a digital comic page, and experiment 2 prompts annotators to select the type of animacy for each annotated entity from experiment 1. The levels of inter-annotator agreement are measured for each, with conclusions drawn about the causes of disagreement for each task to inform future work.

2 Experiment 1: Identifying animate entities using outlines on comic pages

This first experiment tests a method for delineating animate entities according to reader judgments. Annotators are prompted to outline areas directly onto comics pages where they believe shows a depiction of an animate being. Having annotators draw on the page circumvents the researcher's assumptions about what should be considered animate, since the researcher is not pre-selecting potential candidates for annotators to judge. The areas outlined by each annotator are compared against one another to produce a qualitative measure of agreement.

2.1 Methods

2.1.1 Annotation scheme and implementation

Annotators are given an annotation scheme and a digital comic within a responsive browser-based tool to outline areas directly onto a given comic page. The Comics Annotation Tool (CAT) is an online interface that facilitates remote annotation. The main CAT interface is shown in Figure 2 - comic pages are given one at a time on the left, and annotation prompts are given on the right. Annotators use their keyboard and mouse to create closed polygons on the digital canvas. Panels, shown in red, are pre-segmented to guide annotators when making their outlines. The panels are pre-segmented because panel identification has very high inter-annotator agreement according to previous work (Edlin and Reiss, 2021). Animate entities are outlined in purple, and each closed

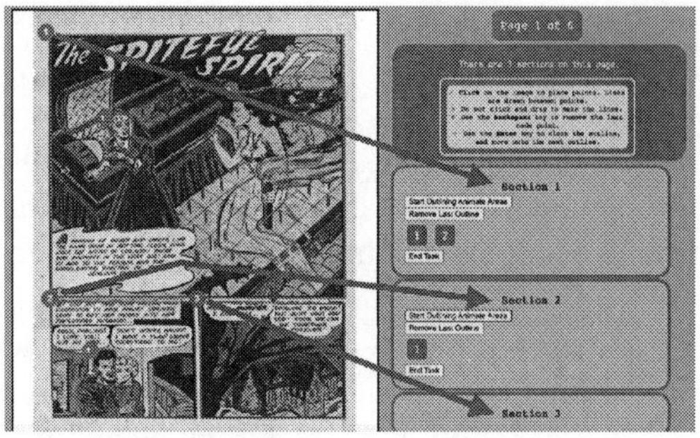

Figure 2: The main interface of the CAT. The red arrows point the panel ID number to the corresponding section.

outline generates a corresponding purple number in the panel/section where it was drawn.

The intent of this annotation project is to capture the build-up of information in the reader's mental model, rather than the comic authors perspective. Annotators are therefore instructed to try their best to segment areas within each panel in the order they would normally read, and make outlines based on the information they have up to the current point that they've read; they are not to go back and revise their outlines based on information unavailable at that point in the narrative, as this would not accurately capture how their mental model developed. Annotators are given whole pages to facilitate a natural reading experience, and to allow the use of all information, including visual cues and text, to make their annotations in both experiments.

The full annotation scheme and instructions can be downloaded directly from the CAT. The definition of an animate being or thing given to annotators is: *a depiction of an entity that displays human or higher animal-like behaviours, and/or can communicate autonomously and move intentionally.*[1] Some examples of animate versus inanimate representations from the annotation scheme are given in Table 1.

Four comics were selected from the *Alarming Tales*, which is a comics magazine that ran for six issues between 1957 and 1958. These comics were chosen as they are out of copyright, and exhibit a common artistic style of illustration that

Animate	Inanimate
Talking tree	Tree blowing in the wind
Wolf	A dead wolf
Sentient A.I	Supercomputer
Sleeping teacup	Self-playing piano

Table 1: Examples of animate and inanimate entities from the annotation scheme.

Story no.	**Age** (mean/range)	**Gender**
1	31.4 (21-37)	1F/4M
2	36.4 (22-50)	1NB/2F/4M
3	35.2 (21-51)	4F/1M
4	29.2 (22-38)	4F/1M

F=female, M=male, NB=non-binary

Table 2: Participant demographics for experiment 1.

persisted throughout the silver age of comics, and are all of the same sci-fi fantasy genre. Except for one four-page comic, all other stories are five pages which gives a total of 19 pages for annotation. Three of these comics were used in previous annotation experiments, allowing for comparison between studies. Finally, all stories appear to exhibit entities with unclear animacy according to the lead author's judgment. The comics were downloaded from Comic Book Plus,[2] which is an internet archive of open source and copy right free comics.

2.1.2 Participants

Five participants produced annotations per story for a total of 20 annotators. All participants were required to be fluent in English and have UK or US nationality. No participants annotated more than one story to prevent some annotators becoming familiar with using the CAT than others. An overview of participant demographics are given in Table 2.

All participants were recruited on the online crowd-sourcing platform Prolific. Crowd-sourcing has been shown to be an efficient method for comics annotation (Tufis and Ganascia, 2018), and annotation experiments in our previous work found that word-of-mouth and crowd-sourcing recruitment produced similar results on similar tasks (forthcoming). Participants were compensated £11/hour through the Prolific platform.

[1] All supplementary material is available at `https://github.com/le300/CAT_Annotation_Experiment_3`, including the full annotation schemes for both experiments with examples and more detailed explanations, the comics used for annotation, and all code implemented in the evaluations.

	Animacy mean IOU scores			Character mean IOU scores		
Story no.	Mapped-only	Unmapped-included	Diff.	Mapped-only	Unmapped-included	Diff.
1	0.725	0.649	0.076	0.725	0.694	0.031
2	0.704	0.695	0.009	0.802	0.795	0.007
3	0.693	0.629	0.064	0.603	0.538	0.065
4	0.716	0.641	0.075	-	-	-

Table 3: Results for animacy outline agreement compared with results from previous work on character outline agreement.

2.1.3 Inter-annotator agreement metrics

A rough estimate of annotator agreement is counting the number of overlapping outlined areas through the researcher's judgment - the more annotators that outlined the same areas, the higher the agreement. However, the precision of outlines between annotators will differ, as some annotators may leave a larger gap between the boundaries of the illustration part they intend to indicate. A qualitative judgment is therefore insufficient to count outline overlaps, especially if a panel is crowded with lots of outlines.

To confirm whether two outlines sufficiently overlap, we use the quantitative metric of *Intersection over Union* (IOU, or Jaccard Index). IOU is a similarity metric of two sets - more precisely, the size of the intersection divided by the size of the union of given sets A and B: $IOU(A, B) = |A \cap B| / |A \cup B|$. In this case, set elements are the pixels within an outline. IOU scores are calculated using the Python Shapely library, which defines the annotator's outlines as closed polygon objects. We use in-built intersection and union functions to determine the IOU score between two polygons.

An IOU score is between $[0, 1]$. The threshold for sufficient overlap between two outlines is not established as there is no ground truth for comparison. A similar experiment in our previous work, with tested agreement for identifying characters, found an overlap threshold of 0.6 was adequate for rectangular bounding boxes, although the agreement threshold between stories ranged from 0.6 to 0.8. We use the same technique here to determine an overlap threshold for polygon outlines.

Overall IOU agreement between a given pair of annotators is calculated by iterating over every panel in a story, and trying every possible mapping from one annotator's outlines to the other's in each panel. The permutation of outline pairs for each panel that yields the highest IOU score, is stored as the inter-annotator mapping for that pair of annotators, and those pairs are considered "mapped' segments. All the IOU agreement scores for that panel are summed for use in an overall mean IOU score.

Naturally, one annotator may make more outlines than the other on a given page. If there is a mismatch in the number of outlines, an "empty" outline (with polygon area 0 and panel intersection 0) is added accordingly. Empty outlines always receive an IOU score of 0 when compared to all outlines from another annotator, hence penalizing the overall IOU score. Both *mapped-only* and *non-mapped-included* pair-wise IOU score distributions are calculated. The differences between mean pair-wise IOU scores is consequently a relative measure between stories.

Finally, additional qualitative data is collected to help interpret disagreements. The CAT includes a text area per page where annotators can write to express uncertainty regarding the animacy of identified entities. The reasons given by annotators can aid explanations of disagreement and guide the next experiment.

2.2 Results

Table 3 gives both the mean IOU scores for the distributions of annotator-pair scores, both mapped-only and unmapped-included outlines, per story. The results from previous work testing the annotation scheme for character using bounding box annotation (Edlin and Reiss, 2021) are also included for comparison, as the same stories were used except for story 4. Figure 3 shows the animacy distributions as boxplots; the median, 1st and 3rd quartiles, and min to max pairwise IOU scores per distribution are emphasised. Overall, the IOU threshold for overlapping outlines appears to be 0.7. The mean overlap IOU per story is more consistent compared to the results for character, indicating that polygon outlines are more reliable than bounding boxes.

[2] http://www.https://comicbookplus.com/

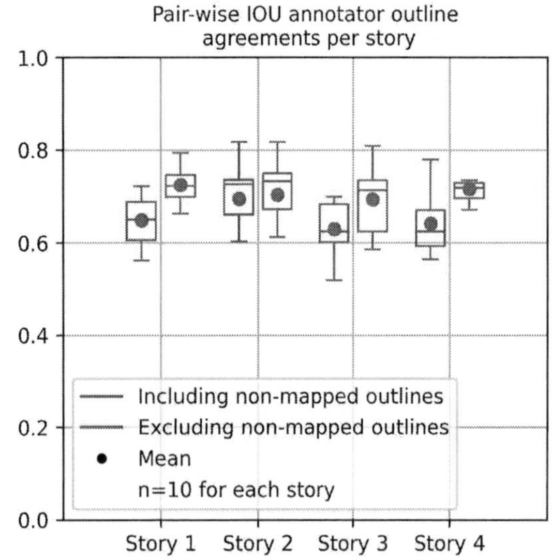

Figure 3: Boxplots showing both mapped-only and non-mapped-included distributions of IOU annotator pair agreements, per story.

Figure 4: Each panel shows an example of the most disagreed upon entity per story. Starting in the top-left and going clock-wise: story 1 features plant-men, story 2 has a man entering the fourth dimension, story 3 features a robot-plant, and story 4 shows a blob-like creature being shot and killed.

The difference between the two mean IOU scores per story provides a measure of agreement relative to the other stories. For the animacy results, Story 2 has the lowest difference between mean IOU scores, while Story 1 and 4 exhibit the greatest amount of disagreement. Disagreement between stories is due to both reader interpretation of entities as well as the number entity instances - a frequently appearing entity with uncertain animacy will pull the IOU score lower. Since reference labels for entities were not annotated as in previous work, the exact number of an individual entity's instances cannot be objectively verified. However, possible explanations for disagreement by taking instance frequency into account may be derived using annotator's written feedback.

Entities that are clearly human have negligible disagreement, as any disagreement can be explained as errors with using the CAT. Each story has a particular entity that elicits the most disagreement. Story 1 has high disagreement because it features "plant-men" being grown on mass as shown in Figure 4. Individual annotator's outline counts are between 64-112, which is the widest range of all stories; the high frequency of plant-men causes a double IOU penalty.

While the plant-men elicit disagreement on pages 1 and 2, they become unanimously agreed upon as animate by page 3-panel 4, and remain so the rest of the story. This panel appears to depict the plant-men moving on their own rather than planted in the ground. Annotator 5 states: "(It's) still unclear if the plant men are animate in section 1 and 2, but by section 4 and 5 it looks like they are displaying higher animal-like behavior (choosing to fight)." This suggests the their status changes due to new evidence of intentional movements, implying that intentional movement is more indicative of animacy than simply a human-like appearance.

Story 2 has the lowest disagreement. Annotators outline counts range from 43-47, suggesting fewer potential entity instances than in story 1. This story is about a man who enters the "fourth dimension" where his appearance changes into abstract shapes. Significant disagreement occurs in the very first panel on page 1 where the man is entering the fourth dimension for the first time, as shown in Figure 4. Some annotators outlined the whole entity, others outlined two separate parts divided by the plane, and others did not make any outlines. Several annotators expressed uncertainty about the fourth dimension. For example, annotator 1 states "... I'm not given enough information as to whether the in the fourth dimension, humans can communicate and move on their own volition".

While story 3 also appears to have fewer unique

entities than story 1 with a range of 48-58 individual annotator outline counts, disagreement occurs when a "robot-plant" is introduced on page 3. Annotators disagreed due to uncertainty as to whether it's movements are intentional. The agreement increased on page 4 as information about the robot plant's intentions are described in a speech by a human agent. Annotator 4 states "I thought the plant only displayed animate features when the text stated it was trying to water the men. Before that point, it was just growing as is usual." Unlike other stories where annotators only cited visual cues pointing to animacy status, in this case the text information was a significant factor in judging animacy status.

Finally, story 4 has a difference score similar to story 1, however fewer outlines were made overall with 35-44 range individual outline counts between annotators. This story is about a hunter on an alien planet. Two aliens are featured: one a blob-like creature, and the other dinosaur-like creature. The blob creature elicited more disagreement overall. However, both creatures were shown as being shot and killed, which elicited disagreement on whether these creatures remain animate while in the process of being shot. While the annotation scheme explicitly states that dead entities should not be outlined, some annotators continued to outline instances after the shooting depictions of shooting. This instruction to stop outlining killed entities therefore appears to be unintuitive.

2.3 Discussion

These findings point to several indicators of animacy, including: (a) being or having been shown to have been a human, (b) showing evidence of autonomous movement and speaking, (c) having the appearance of an animal, and (d) not having the appearance of a plant. Evidence of movement with intent appears to be a foundational facet of animacy, as the plant-men in story 1 and the robot-plant in story 4 gained higher agreement once they were considered to be moving on their own volition with clarified intentions.

These indicators could be interpreted as a coarse hierarchy that roughly reflects the one described by Zaenen et al. (2004). Humans are at the hierarchy's apex, with entities shown speaking in language just beneath. Entities with autonomous movements are next, however the threshold between human-like and animal-like animacy cannot be distinguished based on autonomous movement alone. For example, the human-like appearance of the plant-men in story 1 may suggest a higher level of animacy than the robot-plant in Story 4, even though they are both understood to be animate once they show intentional movements. Since animal-like refers to animals such as mammals, birds and reptiles, considering lower-animal level of consciousness may better describe certain cases where voluntary movement is not an animacy requirement. Lastly, the lower levels in the hierarchy include being a robot, followed by appearing as a plant. A dead entity would be at the bottom of the hierarchy if included.

Lastly, it appears that this method is successful in capturing a reader's updating mental model. This also suggests that animacy ambiguity in itself is a compelling narrative technique - some entities produced high disagreement in the beginning of the story only to increase in agreement as the story progresses. This uncertainty about an entity's animacy attentuates the ability of a reader to infer what comes next, which prompts the reader to continue on to resolve the tension and subsequently progresses the plot.

3 Experiment 2: introducing an animacy hierarchy

This experiment builds on the previous one by asking annotators to assign a hierarchical animacy type to pre-outlined entities on comic pages. Experiment 1 implemented animacy identification through a coarse binary choice - outlined areas contain an animate entity according to the annotators judgment, while everything outside the outline does not. While the results of this technique gives initial insight into animacy indicators, the nature of disagreements can be further parsed using a quantitative metric. A simple hierarchy of animacy status is devised to assess whether agreement can be achieved by offering annotators several options.

3.1 Methods

3.1.1 Annotation scheme and implementation

The new annotation scheme asks participants to judge the animacy status of a pre-outlined entity by selecting the best description from an animacy hierarchy list. The hierarchy broadly reflects potential animacy thresholds suggested

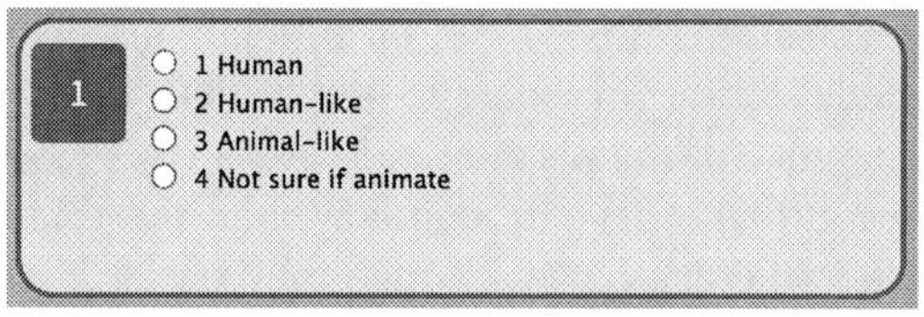

Figure 5: An example of animacy type choices as displayed in the CAT.

Example	Animacy type	Reason
Talking tree	Human-like	Speaks language through its own volition
Wolf	Animal-like	Displays animal-like behaviours
Zombie	Not sure if animate	Depends on the rules of the world established in the story - if the state of mind is unclear, it is best to put *not sure if animate*
A Sentient AI	Human-like	Speaks, thinks, or shows other higher-level behaviours
A Supercomputer	Not sure if animate	If an AI is not sentient, select the lowest animacy option of *not sure if animate*
Dragon	Animal-like	Displays animal-like behaviours

Table 4: Examples of entities, their animacy type, and the reason for the type assignment from the annotation scheme.

in experiment 1. *Human* is ascribed to clearly human entities. *human-like* refers to entities with sentience and intentions, primarily indicated through movement, speaking language, or showing other behaviours like deliberate humor or planning. Entities with sentience that cannot speak but show behaviours displayed by animals such as mammals, birds, reptiles, etc. are assigned *animal-like* animacy. Lastly, *not sure if animate* is chosen when there is uncertain, ambiguous, or no animacy detected. A pilot study was run that included an *inanimate* option at the bottom of the hierarchy, however this seemed to confuse annotators as an outline entity already suggests at least a slight potential for animacy. Overlapping outlines made by only one or two annotators out of five in experiment 1 are expected to be assigned *not sure if animate*.

The CAT is updated to deploy these tasks for remote annotation. Figure 5 shows an example form with animacy type choices. Each pre-made outline has a corresponding form, where the options are placed from top to bottom according to the highest-level animacy to lowest. Table 4 gives some examples entities of various animacy types.

Story no.	Age (mean/range)	Gender
1	39.8(21-62)	2F/3M
2	29.2(21-37)	1F/4M
3	31.2(23-39)	2F/3M
4	29.4(21-43)	3F/2M

F=female, M=male, NB=non-binary

Table 5: Participant demographics for experiment 2.

The same comics from experiment 1 are used to compare results. Outlines are placed where at least one annotator made an outline in the previous experiment. These are considered areas of potential animacy, as non-outlined areas indicate that all annotators agreed that there is no animate entities present.

3.1.2 Participants

Participants were again recruited from Prolific, with 5 unique participants allocated per story for a total of 20 annotators. The same criteria of English fluency and UK or US nationality were required, and each annotator was compensated £11/hour. An overview of participant demographics is given in Table 5.

3.1.3 Inter-annotator agreement metrics

Krippendorff's α (KA) is a standard inter-annotator reliability measure (Artstein and Poesio, 2008; Krippendorff, 2011). A KA score is between $[-1, 1]$; -1 indicates complete disagreement, 1 indicates complete agreement, and 0 indicates chance agreement. A score of 0.8 is considered a threshold for excellent agreement, while 0.68 is considered sufficient agreement (Artstein and Poesio, 2008, p. 591). Annotator's ratings are tested all-against-all to provide an overall KA score per story.

Ratings between annotators are weighted in the KA calculation according to the data measurement scale. The annotation scheme describes animacy types by name, as well as a numbered top to bottom hierarchy in the CAT itself. Therefore, KA scores for both ordinal and nominal weightings are calculated. The KA scores are calculated using the Krippendorf python package (Castro, 2017).

	All-against-all animacy KA scores	
Story no.	Nominal	Ordinal
1	0.441	0.541
2	0.551	0.751
3	0.388	0.558
4	0.72	0.787

Table 6: Results for Experiment 2, including both the all-against-all KA scores for the animacy hierarchy task and the mean pair-wise reference KA scores, per story.

3.2 Results

All-against-all KA scores per story are shown in Table 6. The nominal weighted scores consistently produced lower agreement than the ordinal weighted scores, with only story 4 reaching the threshold for adequate agreement. Both stories 2 and 4 reach adequate agreement with the ordinal scale weighting, while stories 1 and 3 only achieved middling agreement. Overall, adequate to high agreement was not universally achieved across all stories according to either scale. Nevertheless, these results support further development of an animacy hierarchy assignment using an ordinal-type ranking.

Stories 1 and 3 exhibit low agreement. As in experiment 1, story 1 elicits high disagreement due to the plant-men - two annotators primarily assigned them *human-like* animacy, while the other three assigned *not sure if animate.* Unlike the findings from experiment 1, only one annotator indicated a change in animacy status as the story progressed by updating the plant-men from *not sure if animate* to *human-like* on page 3. Story 3's low agreement is also again due to the robot-plant instances, where some annotators primarily categorized the robot-plant as *not sure if animate,* while others assigned *animal-like* animacy.

Similar to experiment 1, story 2 shows higher agreement than stories 1 and 3. Story 2 features the man entering the fourth dimension; this character is shown both as a normal human and then as a series of abstract shapes that can still walk and talk in the fourth dimension. Annotators mainly ascribed *human-like* animacy to instances where the man is fully in the fourth dimension, demonstrating a step down the hierarchy from *human* to *human-like.* Unlike the first experiment, disagreement actually occurred for another entity that first presents as a human-shaped shadow or a silhouette. Annotators assigned *human, human-like* and *animal-like* to this entity.

Finally, story 4 exhibits the highest agreement overall. Besides several instances of the blob and dinosaur-like the creatures, the story only appears to have humans which contributes to the high agreement. The blob-like alien again produced the most disagreement with annotators either choosing *not sure if animate* or *animal-like* animacy. The dinosaur-like alien was consistently assigned *animal-like* animacy.

3.3 Discussion

While providing a useful quantitative metric of disagreement, the hierarchy does not accurately capture judgments of animacy status for entities across these comics, as only two of the stories achieved adequate agreement using ordinal KA weightings. Examples of where this hierarchy fails can be seen in story 1 and story 3 which had the lowest scores. Both stories feature plant appearing entities - namely the plant-men from story 1 and the robot-plant from story 3. Since these entities caused significant disagreement in the previous experiment, the expectation in this experiment was for annotators assign them *not sure if animate.* However, if an annotator did detect animacy, then neither *human-like* nor *animal-like* animacy intuitively describes their status. An added lower-level category on the hierarchy that describes non-human and non-animal-like entities would be a beneficial addition.

The all-against-all KA scores were nonetheless consistently higher using ordinal weightings. Further development of an animacy type classification should therefore explicitly use an ordinal scale. Getting rid of category names to instead use a numbered scale may circumvent potential confusion due to the animacy category names themselves - naming a category *animal-like* may exclude some relevant entities like the blob-like creature from story 4, for instance. A numbered scale is also a less coarse and may more easily include lower levels of animacy without having to actually name them.

Finally, recall that the results from experiment 1 suggest that animacy ambiguity can be a purposely used narrative device. Capturing this type of ambiguity within the annotation scheme is therefore especially important for future work on narrative understanding. The *not sure if animate* category implemented in this experiment does not clearly achieve this. In future work, an ambiguity measure could be derived from disagreements themselves, or measured by developing an annotation scheme from the intentions of the author rather than the perspective of the reader.

4 Conclusion

Animate entities are an important component of defining characters and understanding broader narrative structures and affordances in comics. We explored methods of identifying animate entities visually through two rounds of annotation experiments: the first asked annotators to outline areas on comic pages with a polygon outlining tool, and the second attempted to quantify agreement by having annotators assign a hierarchical animacy category to each entity.

Results from the first experiment show that an outline-based agreement method, which imposes a binary concept of animacy, can qualitatively measure agreement between stories. In experiment 2, we develop a hierarchy of animacy types based on disagreements from the first experiment, with the results showing that a graded rather than categorical concept of animacy performs adequately for some stories. An ordinal scale may better capture edge cases where the line between human-like and animal-like behaviours; for instance, a crow shows human-like behaviours such as strategical planning. Additionally, both studies suggested that purposeful animacy ambiguity is a valuable narrative tool, and should be accounted for in future developments of the annotation scheme.

4.1 Future work

In future work we will refine the annotation scheme for implementation for corpus analyses. The resulting corpora, along with other annotations, can be used to derive narrative structures from lower-level units. The method from Experiment 1 for visual discourse referent annotation can be incorporated with linguistic reference annotation in the comic's text for multi-modal discourse processing. Additionally, both studies suggested that purposeful animacy ambiguity is a valuable narrative tool, and should be accounted for in future developments of the annotation scheme.

Limitations

Several limitations relate to the study setups. One shortcoming is the small number of comics used in the experiments. While this is adequate for initial exploration into animate entity identification, these results cannot be generalised - comics in particular have an incredible number of potential types of animate entities and beings, and four comic stories do not touch on most of them. Another limitation is the reliance on crowd-sourced recruitment and remote annotation. The researcher is not able to instruct the annotators in person and check their understanding of the annotation scheme. Although the annotation task are seemingly relatively simple at this point, word-of-mouth recruitment of annotators who are more familiar with annotation processes are likely a better choice in future work, especially as the annotation scheme develops to include more complicated concepts.

More significantly, the outlining method for identifying animate entities does not capture inanimate entities that become animate, as discussed in Section 1.1. An annotator using the scheme tested here would not outline the sofa in Figure 1, although the sofa should be included in an annotated corpus to capture an important update to the reader's mental model. While these experiments show that these updates are somewhat obtained through interpreting reader feedback about their outlines, the limitations in developing an annotation scheme solely from the reader's perspective are apparent. Developing a comparable annotation scheme from the creator's perspective may facilitate fuller analyses of narrative structures. Since a creator knows that the sofa and Kamala Kahn are linked through coreference, both would be outlined and given the same reference label. Integrating these two perspectives into one corpus could give insights into how creator's intentions to communicate larger narrative structures are expressed in lower-level configurations of image and text.

Acknowledgements

We offer a sincere thank you to all the annotators who took part in this study, and to the two anonymous reviewers who provided valuable and detailed feedback. This research was funded by the EPSRC and AHRC Centre for Doctoral Training in Media and Arts Technology (EP/L01632X/1).

References

Ron Artstein and Massimo Poesio. 2008. Inter-coder agreement for computational linguistics. *Computational Linguistics*, 34(4):555–596.

John A Bateman, Annika Beckmann, and Rocío Inés Varela. 2018. From empirical studies to visual narrative organization: Exploring page composition. In *Empirical Comics Research*, pages 127–153. Routledge.

Santiago Castro. 2017. Fast Krippendorff: Fast computation of Krippendorff's alpha agreement measure. https://github.com/pln-fing-udelar/fast-krippendorff.

Neil Cohn. 2013. *The Visual Language of Comics: Introduction to the Structure and Cognition of Sequential Images*. A&C Black.

Neil Cohn. 2020. Your brain on comics: A cognitive model of visual narrative comprehension. *Topics in cognitive science*, 12(1):352–386.

Lauren Edlin and Joshua Reiss. 2021. An empirically-based spatial segmentation and coreference annotation scheme for comics. In *Proceedings of the 14th International Symposium on Visual Information Communication and Interaction*, pages 1–8.

Labiba Jahan, Geeticka Chauhan, and Mark A Finlayson. 2018. A new approach to animacy detection. In *Proceedings of the 27th International Conference on Computational Linguistics*.

Labiba Jahan and Mark Finlayson. 2019. Character identification refined: A proposal. In *Proceedings of the First Workshop on Narrative Understanding*.

Klaus Krippendorff. 2011. Computing krippendorff's alpha-reliability.

David Kurlander, Tim Skelly, and David Salesin. 1996. Comic chat. In *Proceedings of the 23rd annual conference on Computer graphics and interactive techniques*, pages 225–236.

Joshua Moore, Christopher JC Burges, Erin Renshaw, and Wen-tau Yih. 2013. Animacy detection with voting models. In *Proceedings of the 2013 Conference on Empirical Methods in Natural Language Processing*, pages 55–60.

Ariel Shamir, Michael Rubinstein, and Tomer Levinboim. 2006. Generating comics from 3d interactive computer graphics. *IEEE computer graphics and Applications*, 26(3):53–61.

Ruck Thawonmas and Tomonori Shuda. 2008. Comic layout for automatic comic generation from game log. In *New Frontiers for Entertainment Computing*, pages 105–115. Springer.

Chiao-I Tseng and John A Bateman. 2018. Cohesion in comics and graphic novels: An empirical comparative approach to transmedia adaptation in city of glass. *Adaptation*, 11(2):122–143.

Chiao-I Tseng, Jochen Laubrock, and Jana Pflaeging. 2018. Character developments in comics and graphic novels: A systematic analytical scheme. In *Empirical Comics Research*, pages 154–175. Routledge.

Mihnea Tufis and Jean-Gabriel Ganascia. 2018. Crowdsourcing comics annotations. In *Empirical Comics Research*, pages 85–103. Routledge.

G. Willow Wilson, Wyatt Jacob, and Adrian Alphona. 2015. Ms.marvel: Generation y.

Xin Yang, Zongliang Ma, Letian Yu, Ying Cao, Baocai Yin, Xiaopeng Wei, Qiang Zhang, and Rynson WH Lau. 2021. Automatic comic generation with stylistic multi-page layouts and emotion-driven text balloon generation. *ACM Transactions on Multimedia Computing, Communications, and Applications (TOMM)*, 17(2):1–19.

Annie Zaenen, Jean Carletta, Gregory Garretson, Joan Bresnan, Andrew Koontz-Garboden, Tatiana Nikitina, M Catherine O'Connor, and Thomas Wasow. 2004. Animacy encoding in english: Why and how. In *Proceedings of the workshop on discourse annotation*, pages 118–125.

Mrs. Dalloway Said She Would Segment the Chapters Herself

Peiqi Sui[1,2], **Lin Wang**[2], **Sil Hamilton**[3], **Thorsten Ries**[1], **Kelvin Wong**[2], and **Stephen T. Wong**[2]
[1] University of Texas at Austin
[2] System Medicine and Bioengineering (SMAB), Houston Methodist Cancer Center
[3] McGill University
peiqisui@utexas.edu

Abstract

This paper proposes a sentiment-centric pipeline to perform unsupervised plot extraction on non-linear novels like Virginia Woolf's *Mrs. Dalloway*, a novel widely considered to be "plotless." Combining transformer-based sentiment analysis models with statistical testing, we model sentiment's rate-of-change and correspondingly segment the novel into emotionally self-contained units qualitatively evaluated to be meaningful surrogate pseudo-chapters. We validate our findings by evaluating our pipeline as a fully unsupervised text segmentation model, achieving a F-1 score of 0.643 (regional) and 0.214 (exact) in chapter break prediction on a validation set of linear novels with existing chapter structures. In addition, we observe notable differences between the distributions of predicted chapter lengths in linear and non-linear fictional narratives, with the latter exhibiting significantly greater variability. Our results hold significance for narrative researchers appraising methods for extracting plots from non-linear novels.

1 Introduction

What is the shape of a story? Narratologists have long been fascinated with reducing narratives to a compelling linear visual rhetoric: the narrative arc, a line chart that smoothly demonstrates the (emotional) rise and fall of the story (Freytag, 1895; Campbell, 1949; Propp, 1968). Recent scholarship has introduced emotive expressions and affect as a vital analytical tool for the construction of such narrative arcs (Kleres, 2011; Keen, 2011; Winkler et al., 2023). The digital humanities community has shown great interest in operationalizing this problem as a sentiment analysis task across various literary corpora (Jockers 2015; Underwood, 2015; Elkins, 2022). The success of this approach has recently been extended beyond the literary domain to encompass a wider range of inquiries driven by social science (Boyd et al., 2020; Chun 2021).

Meanwhile, existing methods for sentiment-based narrative arc extraction tend to underperform on what literary scholars call non-linear narratives (Richardson, 2000). We posit that literary works often assume varying degrees of clarity and straightforwardness when conveying a story, an explicative quality known as narrativity — computationally, it has been defined as a scalar measuring the success of a work in conveying a linear sequence of events as narrative discourse (Piper et al., 2021). While some novels may convey their story-worlds with relative transparency via chronological accounts of their fictional agents' actions, others may withhold it from the audience for artistic purposes (Pianzola, 2018). This non-linearity has been considered a hard problem for narratology, by both computational (Elkins and Chun, 2019; Bhyravajjula et. al, 2022) and traditional (Ryan, 2005) approaches. Virginia Woolf's 1925 novel *Mrs. Dalloway*, in particular, has been identified as an especially recalcitrant text to model with existing methods (Elkins, 2022), possibly due to its renowned stream-of-consciousness style.

This study takes on the challenging task of performing unsupervised plot extraction on *Mrs. Dalloway*, a novel widely held and celebrated by literary scholars to be essentially "plotless." We hypothesize that it is possible to excavate latent plot structures from nonlinear fiction if we use sentiment data to statistically model the notion of non-linearity itself. To avoid the pitfall of imposing

Proceedings of the The 5th Workshop on Narrative Understanding, pages 92–105
July 14, 2023 ©2023 Association for Computational Linguistics

linear narrative arcs onto non-linear narratives via smoothing-based de-noising techniques, we propose a sentiment-centric pipeline which instead aims to embrace the "noise" inherent to a non-linear and highly fragmented novel like *Mrs. Dalloway*. The goal of this pipeline is to capture the full expression of non-linearity in sentiment data. Leveraging the softmax probability distributions of pre-trained language models like BERT (Devlin et al., 2019) and ELECTRA (Clark et al., 2020), we perform a paired t-test that models sentiment's rate-of-change to identify breakpoints and correspondingly segment the novel into emotionally coherent parts. Our approach finds 19 such surrogate "chapters" in *Mrs. Dalloway*, which we then qualitatively evaluate to assess their literary and narratological coherence. To further verify the validity of our results, we quantitatively evaluate our pipeline on a linear fiction dataset to determine its ability to restore existing chapter structures, while also contributing a generative approach to the task of text segmentation in the literary domain.

Main contributions: 1) a segment-based approach to plot extraction, designed to address the challenge of modeling non-linear fiction 2) a sentiment-centric pipeline for fully unsupervised chapter segmentation 3) an attempt to consider literary theoretical claims as falsifiable hypotheses that could inform model design, in the hope for the greater inclusion of literary scholarship in the collaboration pipeline for NLP research.

2 Background and Related Work

2.1 Definitions

Our study will operate under the following narratological definitions:

- **Plot:** We define plot not as a fixed structure but a gradual process of structuration, a dynamic development that actualizes and amends itself as the narrative unfolds and constantly reshapes the experience of reading (Brooks, 1984; Phelan, 1989). The concept of structuration highlights the need to examine not just the general distribution of sentiment scores, but also as the relative rate of change between measured points of sentiment.
- **Linearity:** Colloquially, linear narratives often refer to storylines that are aligned with chronological order. In narratology, linearity is the side of plot that relates to causality (Forster, 1927), and linear narratives are the framing of fictional "action[s] as a chronological, cause-and-effect chain of events occurring within a given duration and a spatial field" (Bordwell, 1985:49). The metaphor of the "chain" necessitates something that comes before together with a subsequent, a sequence of events that becomes coherent for the audience through the clear cognition of time and a correspondence between the two. Linearity, therefore, is the plot made visible via having its causal sequences ordered in the plain sight of chronological time.
- **Sentiment:** We borrow our definition of sentiment from leading narrative theorist Patrick Hogan, who views emotion as the hallmark of non-linearity: "our emotion systems respond to perceptual fragments [...] these cluster into incidents that provoke emotional spikes in emotional experiences that are, like time, not smoothly continuous but jagged," (2011:66). In making this claim, Hogan draws a distinction between objective, universal clock time and our non-uniform experience of temporality. Just as objective time orders causal chains into a linear plot that makes sense to the audience, subjective narrative time is organized by emotional fluctuations into coherent units, which we hope to segment with sentiment analysis. In the context of our study, Hogan's argument implies that our sentiment analysis pipeline would be expected to extract a set of "jagged" distributions from non-linear novels, instead of a smooth line, to represent the non-linear narrative arc.

Hypothesis: Operationalizing Hogan's (2011) theory of affective narratology, which heavily emphasizes an underlying connection between plot, non-linearity, and sentiment, we propose a conception of plot as a continuous process of structuration with two components: the easily observable[1], time-dependent arm as a causal chain of events ordered in objective time, and the latent, time-independent arm as the fragmented, non-linear, yet internally coherent, narrative arc concealed in emotion. These two arms are not always present in all narratives. Rather, they are two ways for a plot to be expressed, and if they happen to coexist like in linear narratives, their structure tends to synchronize because they essentially describe different aspects of the same plot. This narratological unity they share enables the use of the observable arm as gold-standard ground truth to validate inferences made from the latent arm. Through a combination of qualitative and quantitative evaluations of our pipeline's output in Section 4, we aim to holistically validate our use of sentiment as a plausible approach to plot extraction.

2.2 Narrative Arc Construction with Sentiment Analysis

Prior research in this area has heavily relied on smoothing techniques to identify linear and human-readable patterns in the noisy sentiment data of long-form texts. Jockers' (2015) *Syuzhet* utilizes fast Fourier transform and discrete cosine transformation to extract sentiment arcs from its lexicon-based sentiment models. Gao et al. (2016) build on Jockers' work by employing a more complex model for smoothing with an adaptive filter. More recently, Chun (2021) proposes an ensemble approach that combines the outcomes of multiple sentiment models to mitigate model and dataset bias, while still requiring smoothing with simple moving average. To the best our knowledge, we are the first study to extract narrative arcs from sentiment data without any involvement of smoothing. For our intent and purposes, smoothing is problematic because it seeks to reduce non-linear narratives to a clean yet oversimplified line.

2.3 Text Segmentation in Fiction

Since our pipeline outputs a segmented narrative arc, it also contributes to the broader problem of text segmentation in the literary domain. Recent studies have fine-tuned pre-trained language models to perform chapter segmentation, and their methods tend to use classification-based, reducing the problem to the binary classification of each potential breakpoint candidate as a predicted chapter boundary or not. Pethe et al. (2020) fine-tune BERT's next sentence prediction model as a binary classifier for chapter break prediction, and use the inference's confidence score to rank all breakpoint candidates in each novel to select the top P as predicted chapter breaks, P being the number of ground truth chapters. Their approach outperforms all non-transformer baselines. Virameteekul (2022) further improves Pethe et al.'s performance by utilizing a XLNet and a CNN model instead of BERT.

Although our quantitative evaluations in Section 4.2 perform the same task as these existing approaches, we cannot use them as baselines due to significant differences in methods and experimental setting. This includes: 1) our pipeline is fully unsupervised, without any knowledge of P during inference 2) our sentiment models are not fine-tuned any chapter break training data, and 3) the paired t-test in our study could only infer segments on the multiples of the initial sequence length *alpha*, making it arithmetically impossible to locate most exact chapter breaks. Nonetheless, our study could be considered as a generative approach to text segmentation, an alternative to existing classification-based methods.

3 Methods

This section describes the experimental designs of our pipeline. It takes a text file of *Mrs. Dalloway* and outputs an unsmoothed narrative arc segmented into surrogate "chapters," as shown in Figure 1 below.

3.1 Literary Domain Fine-Tuning for Sentiment Analysis

For sentiment analysis, we fine-tune a pre-trained ELECTRA model on a Victorian fiction sentiment dataset (Kim, 2022), the only open-source fiction dataset we find with sentence-level sentiment labels. ELECTRA is selected over BERT because it reports better performance on benchmark sentiment analysis datasets (Clark et al, 2020). We also implement a popular BERT-based sentiment model obtained from HuggingFace fine-tuned on product reviews (nlptown, 2019) as a general-domain reference. Using an additional model allows us to troubleshoot the question of

[1] "Observable" here means both being visible on the page, i.e., chapter boundaries, and being causally cognizable, i.e., the chain-of-thought summaries of "what happened" ordered chronologically.

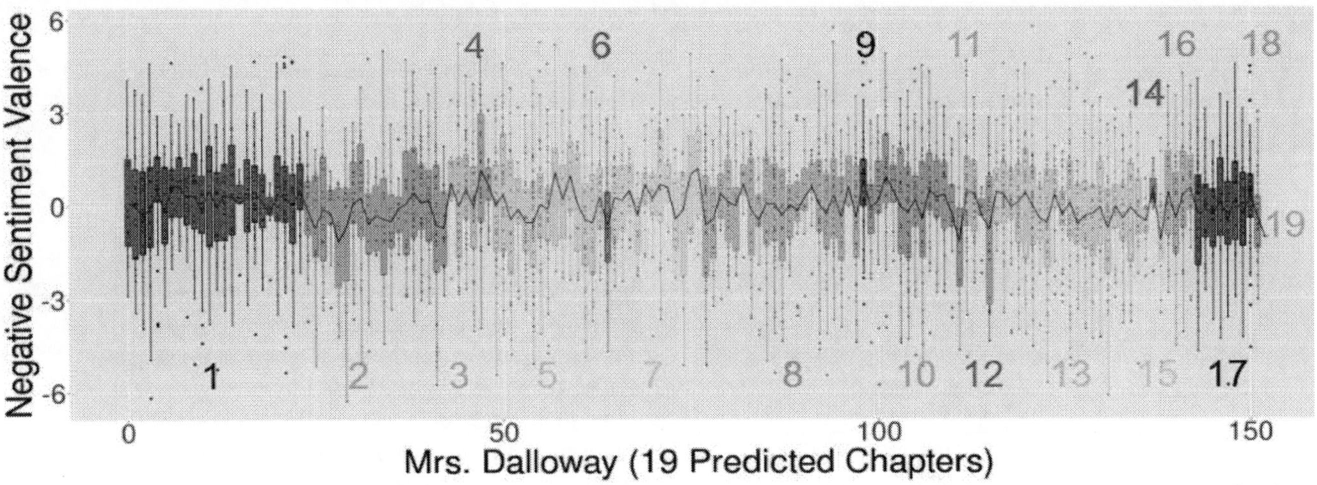

Figure 1. Segmented narrative arc the BERT model extracts from *Mrs. Dalloway*, with 19 predicted chapters (use of the same color does not indicate the continuation of the same chapter)

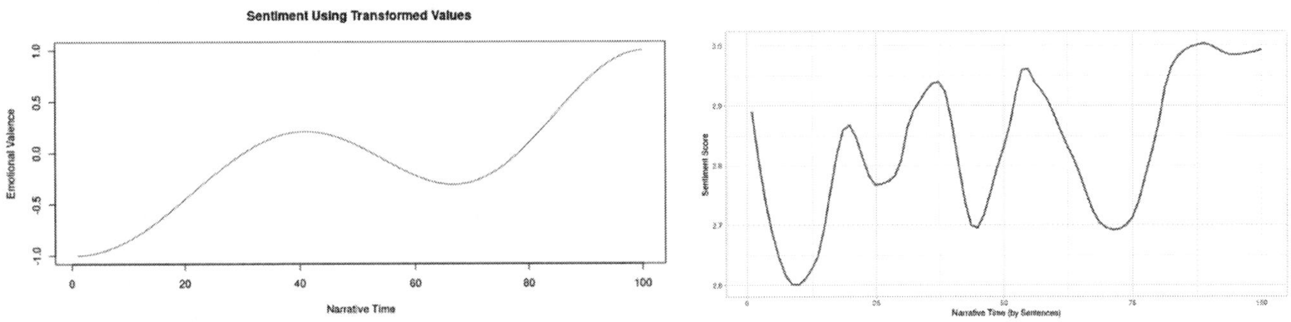

(a) (b)

Figure 2. *Mrs. Dalloway*'s sentiment visualized with existing methods: (a) fast Fourier transform from Jockers' *Syuzhet*, (b) Loess smoothing (span=0.3)

cross-domain consistency, as the performance of many NLP systems has been demonstrated to "drop precipitously" when applied to the literary domain (Bamman et al., 2019:2141). This is supported by our model evaluations, as the ELECTRA model's testing metrics on its hold-out test set (accuracy=0.49, ovr AUC=0.734) significantly outperforms that of the BERT model's inference on the same test set (accuracy=0.21, ovr AUC=0.613).

Inference: We run each sentence of *Mrs. Dalloway* (n=3626, no preprocessing) through the sentiment classifiers and generate a 5-dimensional probability distribution to represent the sentence's sentiment (details in Section 4.2). Despite the gap in testing performance, we pass the output of both models into our subsequent pipeline to further experiment with cross-domain consistency, since recent studies have demonstrated that there is no one-size-fit-all sentiment model for constructing narrative arcs (Elkins, 2022).

3.2 Breakpoint Analysis with Statistical Testing

When implemented on non-linear narratives like *Mrs. Dalloway*, past studies' use of smoothing (Section 2.2) often produces oversimplified and unconvincing results that lack explainability (Figure 2a & 2b). To address this shortcoming, we perform segment detection to extract a fully explainable narrative arc: any statistically significant movement on the sentiment arc could be traced back to the corresponding sentence where a breakpoint is identified, making it possible to explain model decision with close reading, the gold standard for evidentiary claims in literary studies (Felski, 2008).

Dimensionality Transformation: The default output of both the BERT and the ELECTRA model is a sentiment score on a 5-point Likert scale, a monolithic representation that often fails to capture the nuanced sentiment of literary texts. The neutral sentiment label, in particular, is

Input Sentence	ELECTRA Softmax	PCA (PC1, PC2)
"And then, thought Clarissa Dalloway, what a morning-fresh as if issued to children on a beach."	0.107, 0.453, 0.413, 0.002, 0.025	1.066, -1.942
"What a lark!"	0.118, 0.284, 0.0034, **0.595**, 0.178	-0.54, -0.457
"For it was the middle of June."	0.247, 0.131, 0.145, **0.367**, 0.111	3.899, 3.17

Table 1. Dimensionality transformation of sentiment data

responsible for many trivial zero values in narrative arc plotting whose presence does not necessarily correlate with actual emotional neutrality (Elkins, 2022). To avoid this pitfall and mitigate the issue of data oversimplification, we configure the sentiment models to directly output the 5-dimensional probability vector, instead of taking the argmax of the softmax probabilities of each sentence. This approach allows for a more holistic representation of ambiguous sentiment by transforming a discrete sentiment scale into a continuous one, as shown in Table 1. We also experiment with the unnormalized logits tensors prior to the softmax operation and observe similar outcomes in subsequent procedures.

To preprocess and denoise the 5-dimensional sentiment scores for segment detection, we utilize *principal component analysis* (PCA) to identify the two most significant emotional dimensions of any given distribution that are linearly independent from each other. PCA is an orthogonal linear transformation technique that renders the greatest variance of all projections of the data onto the first coordinate, then the second greatest variance on the second coordinate, and so on. This simplifies the dataset while maximizing data preservation, as PCA finds that the first two principal components could explain more than 99% of the variability in both the BERT and the ELECTRA model's sentiment predictions on *Mrs. Dalloway*[2]. We only keep these two dimensions, given that they contain the most substantial information regarding the data and contribute the highest variance. Since each pair of PC1 and PC2 can be traced back to their originating sentence, PCA allows for a more explainable interpretative framework than previous studies' use of smoothing and numerical filtering techniques.

Segment Detection: We design a statistical model that recurrently performs paired samples t-tests to trace sentiment's rate-of-change across a novel and predict potential locations for breakpoints. The t-test draws from sentence-level sentiment scores and groups them by paragraph. For one group of sentiment scores from passage *P1* with an average of *M1* and its next group *P2* with an average of *M2*, the null hypothesis $M1 = M2$ is assumed to be true unless the p-value is less than a critical value of 0.1, in which case the alternative hypothesis $M1 \neq M2$ would be established. Since a paired test would require the two groups *P1* and *P2* to have the same length, the model would also take one hyperparameter *alpha*, the number of paragraphs in each passage. To give the model a higher degree of freedom, we set *alpha*=5 for inference on *Mrs. Dalloway*, since the end of the fifth paragraph of the novel is qualitatively determined to be the earliest semantic focal point to break off the initial "chapter." From here on, the model treats each following *alpha* paragraphs as the *P2* and evaluates it against *P1*, concatenating them into a longer *P1* if the difference is not statistically significant, and marking a new chapter if it is while simultaneously making the paragraph in question the new *P1*.

Aside from our definition of plot as structuration, our decision to focus on the rate-of-change is also motivated by narratologist Tzvetan Todorov's equilibrium-disruption model (Todorov, 1971). Todorov posits that literary narratives typically 1) start out in a state of stability, 2) disrupted by an often unexpected event, and 3) iterate through multiple attempts to restore the initial equilibrium as new disruptions arise. This interplay between equilibrium and disequilibrium is often accompanied by rapid shifts in emotions, or fluctuations in sentiment scores that our pipeline captures as a non-linear analog of these movements. Our approach lends especially well to *Mrs. Dalloway*, as literary scholars have noted that such "interrupt[ions]" and "reinstate[ments]" occur recurrently in Woolf's fiction (Richardson, 2000: 686). These interruptions occur in a cyclic manner emblematic of the novel's non-linearity.

[2] This is also the case for all other novels we use for quantitative evaluations in Section 4.

4 Results and Discussion

To holistically evaluate the validity and limitations of our pipeline's output on *Mrs. Dalloway* shown in Figure 1, we follow the approach of Wang and Iyyer (2019) to present the outcomes for literary close reading alongside quantitative metrics.

4.1 Qualitative Evaluations

We perform a domain expert review of the predicted chapter divisions. Contrary to our expectations, the general domain BERT model returns more explainable results on *Mrs. Dalloway* when being compared against the ELECTRA model, extracting the boundaries of 19 reasonable segments that could be thought of as surrogate "chapters" (Table 6). This suggests that domain-specific fine-tuning with the Victorian fiction dataset could not be transferred to *Mrs. Dalloway*, a modernist and non-linear novel. By extension, different literary time periods could be considered as different domains, which is supported by the conclusion of an existing body of research in digital humanities (Underwood, 2013).

Our pipeline succeeds in capturing recurrent disruptions in fictional narratives. We observe that six of the sentences marking the beginning or ending of our predicted segments involve Dr. Holmes or Sir William Bradshaw, both of whom are particularly disruptive characters heavily involved in the suicide of Septimus, one of the novel's protagonists. Peter's conversation with Sally in "chapters" 17 and 18, for instance, represents how a thematically coherent whole could be interrupted by the appearance of the Bradshaws at Clarissa's party. Similarly, Bradshaw being sent for at the beginning of "chapter" 12 interrupts Septimus' last happy moment with Rezia paragraphs before his suicide. Moreover, we note that the first appearance of Holmes that ends "chapter" 7 opens the scene that formally initiates Septimus' radical downward spiral. While Woolf scholars have hypothesized the Bradshaws as the vital link between the Clarissa and Septimus storylines (Joyes, 2008), our findings take this a step further by dissecting the novel through its affective substratum to show his structural significance on an empirical level. We provide the detailed predicted chapters list in the appendix.

Datasets	Linear plot (ground truth segmentations)	Non-linear plot (predicted segmentations)
Linear fiction (9 novels, Section 4.2)	Gold-standard	Pipeline validation
Non-linear fiction (5 novels, Section 4.3)	Does not exist	Pipeline inference

Table 2. Schematic of the relations between linear vs non-linear datasets and the linear vs non-linear distinction in plot defined in Section 2.1.

4.2 Quantitative Evaluations

Data: For quantitative evaluation, we assemble two fictional datasets from Project Gutenberg (Gutenberg, n.d.): 1) 9 linear novels to vertically validate our pipeline's ability to accurately segment fictional narratives, 2) 4 additional non-linear novels to horizontally validate our findings in *Mrs. Dalloway*. For the purposes of quantitative testing, we define linear fiction as novels already divided into chapters by their authors. Conversely, non-linear fiction refers to novels published without existing chapter structures[3], usually out of aesthetic choices (Pianzola, 2018), accompanied by a greater degree of narrative fragmentation that makes them harder to model. Table 2 demonstrates the relation between these surface-level operational definitions and their conceptual counterparts defined in Section 2.1: by definition, non-linear novels do not have linear plot, while linear novels contain both, one observable (chapters) and one latent (sentiment). The non-linear narrative arc that our pipeline extracts is not mutually exclusive with linear narrative features like chapters — linear novels, too, are often embedded in latent emotional spaces, carrying a hidden sentiment arc that co-exists alongside the linear organization of plot through chapters.

The linear fiction dataset only contains Victorian novels, to maintain domain consistency with the ELECTRA model's fine-tuning set. We use Chapterize (Reeve, 2016) to extract from each novel's Gutenberg text file a list of paragraph indices that represent the locations of chapter breakpoints. All 9 lists are then manually curated to

[3] Some non-linear novels are segmented into sections or parts that are not labeled as chapters by the author. They are usually done out of editorial convenience, and do not have a chapter's commitment to thematic coherence and fictional causality. Therefore, we do not consider them as ground truth segmentations.

Novel	F1 (exact location)	*Alpha* (optimal initial chapter length)	F1 (rounded *alpha*)	Predicted chapters (actual chapters)
Adam Bede	0.197	14	0.691	54 (55)
Great Expectations	0.229	7	0.667	59 (59)
Little Dorrit	0.25	6	0.557	153 (70)
North and South	0.172	17	0.738	51 (52)
Lady Audley's Secret	0.217	10	0.633	79 (41)
Oliver Twist	0.29	4	0.641	135 (53)
The Woman in White	0.179	14	0.658	68 (51)
Vanity Fair	0.164	15	0.712	67 (67)
Pride and Prejudice	0.232	7	0.494	57 (61)
All	*0.214*	-	*0.643*	-

Table 4. The ELECTRA model's segmentation performance with tuned *alpha*

ensure that the annotations of chapter boundaries are correct, a step necessary due to the known header alignment issues in Project Gutenberg documents (Pethe et al., 2020). The curated output will be considered as the gold-standard ground truth labels for chapter segmentation.

Chapter Segmentation: The predicted chapter segmentation results from 4.1 could not be directly evaluated with quantitative metrics, due to the absence of author-assigned ground truth chapter segmentation labels in *Mrs. Dalloway*. To overcome this limitation, we opt for indirectly evaluating our results, by testing the ability of our pipeline to restore the existing chapter boundaries of linear novels. In doing so, we hope to validate our approach of extracting emotive plot itself, that it is indeed a form of plot, and generally of its linear counterpart.

We remove all chapter headers and related signals from the texts (the only input text preprocessing step in our study) and apply our pipeline to the linear fiction dataset. To match the inference with the format of the dataset's ground truth chapter segmentations for evaluation, we adjust the pipeline to output from each novel a list of paragraph indices where each predicted chapter begins.

We follow Pethe et al.'s use of F1[4] to report the performance of exact break prediction, with one key caveat: due to the nature of the paired samples t-test, the only potential breakpoint candidates would be the multiples of the hyperparameter *alpha*, which makes it arithmetically impossible for our pipeline to predict the exact location of most

Algorithm	F1 (exact location)	F1 (general area)
Random	0.037	0.101
Dummy	0.028	0.134
BERT	0.095	0.335
ELECTRA (ours)	**0.202**	**0.513**

Table 3. Segmentation performance when *alpha=5*

pipeline, we also compute a general area F1, where the locations of ground truth chapters are rounded up to the closest multiple of *alpha*.

Table 3 compares the performance of our pipeline when utilizing the ELECTRA and BERT sentiment models, with *alpha* set to 5 to remain consistent with the findings of Section 4.1. The literary domain ELECTRA model significantly outperforms the general domain BERT model. To further substantiate this result, we incorporate the following baselines into our evaluation:

- Random: *P* breakpoints are randomly selected from each novel, where *P* denotes the number of ground truth chapters.
- Dummy regressor: *P* breakpoints are randomly selected from all available multiples of *alpha* in each novel. This baseline is designed as an ablation of the use of sentiment analysis.

Since both baselines are randomly generated, we report their average F1 over 10 iterations. Even with the hint of *P* provided as supervision, the baselines' performance remains insignificant. This validates the complexity of the task and the effectiveness of our pipeline.

Table 4 reports the performance of the ELECTRA model on each novel when F1 is not

[4] Since our pipeline is not supervised with the correct number of chapters, it may not predict the same number of segments as the ground truth. This constraint does not meet the input data requirements for other commonly used metrics in text segmentation. Evaluative approaches that we are unable to appropriately utilize include sliding window-based methods, inter-annotator agreement measures, and geometric distances.

Dataset	Variance (ELECTRA)	Variance (BERT)	CV (ELECTRA)	CV (BERT)
Linear fiction	269.91	1025.49	92.11%	106.84%
Non-linear fiction	**744.83**	**1509.62**	109.16%	113.53%

(a) Sentiment models

Dataset	Variance (Random)	Variance (Dummy)	CV (Random)	CV (Dummy)
Linear fiction	3420.97	3875.62	89.06%	93.9%
Non-linear fiction	4157.5	5355.96	89.42%	94.3%

(b) Baselines (averaged iterations = 10)

Table 5. Predicted chapter lengths distribution

fixed. To explore *alpha* as a tunable hyperparameter, we experiment with *alpha* values ranging from 1 to 30, and use the exact location F1 to select the optimal value to compute the general area F1. The improvement provided by the optimal *alpha* is not significant, as the exact location F1 of most *alpha* values tend to be similar. A smaller *alpha* results in a larger number of predicted breaks, covering more ground truth breaks (true positives), while also predicting more breaks where one does not exist (false positives). Conversely, a larger *alpha* means fewer predicted breaks, fewer correct predictions, but also fewer mistakes. Nonetheless, the optimal *alpha* has a significant impact on the accuracy of predicting the number of chapters. The inference of 5 of the 9 optimal *alpha* falls within plus/minus 1 of the ground truth chapter count *P*, while all *alpha* values from 1 to 30 average a Manhattan difference of 53 from *P*.

Using the optimal *alpha*, the ELECTRA model achieves a general area F1-score of 0.643, indicating its ability to predict the location of most chapter boundaries within the margin of a few paragraphs, which is more than adequate given the room for ambiguity in literary works. Our quantitative findings validate the hypothesis put forward in Section 1 that the emotional patterns underlying fictional narratives often correspond with the linear arm of plot, evident in the number of breakpoints that sentiment analysis shares with the existing chapter segmentations of linear novels. This correspondence, in turn, supports the validity of using the sentiment-centric pipeline for inference on non-linear novels like *Mrs. Dalloway*, where the visualizations like Figure 1 serve as the surrogate of linear plot by making a novel's latent emotional space observable.

4.3 Towards Quantifying Non-Linearity in Fiction

Table 5a compares the distribution of predicted chapter lengths (counted by the paragraph) in the linear and non-linear fiction datasets, with *alpha* set again to 5 to maintain consistency with previous experiments. Notably, the lengths of counterparts. However, their coefficient of variation (CV), a metric measured against the mean, does not exhibit a significant difference. This suggests that non-linear novels have more variable chapter lengths compared to linear ones in terms of absolute variability, while the relative variability of the two groups is similar.

We validate this pattern with the baselines from Section 4.2. As Table 5b shows, the random and dummy baselines also produce similar CVs and different variances between linear and non-linear fiction, though the difference is less substantial than that of the sentiment models. This indicates that the difference in variance pertains to the two fictional corpora instead of methods for extraction. Furthermore, the fact that all 4 models produce similar CVs might undermine its effectiveness as a metric in this experiment.

One potential explanation for the discrepancy between variance and CV is that our pipeline identifies more outlier chapters in non-linear novels. The 1% longest chapters the ELECTRA model extracts from the non-linear set contain 7.8% of all paragraphs in the corpus, compared to 5.8% for the chapters in the 99th percentile in length obtained from the linear set. The length of "chapters" in non-linear novels is not constrained by the need to fit a linear plot, therefore containing more outliers that lead to greater variability and fragmentation.

This result further validates our findings in Section 4.1. The BERT model that outputs Figure 1 reports Var=1647.84 and μ=28.15 from the lengths its predicted chapters on *Mrs. Dalloway*, which are consistent with the averages of the non-linear fiction dataset (Var=1509.62, μ=34.97). This offers some support for the generalizability of the outcomes of Section 4.1 to other non-linear novels, if similar qualitative analysis is to be performed on them by domain experts.

5 Conclusion and Future Work

With a pipeline capable of excavating non-linear plot from both non-linear and linear novels, this study takes the first steps to 1) investigate the hypothesis proposed in Section 1, and 2) explore the positive impact literary theory could have on model design for narrative understanding. We demonstrate that it is possible to extract a narrative arc with coherent segments from non-linear narratives like *Mrs. Dalloway*, and the explainability of our approach affords actionable outcomes for literary studies—explainable results promote empirical theory testing. We validate our findings with both qualitative and quantitative evaluations, achieving a F1 0.643 (general area) and a 0.214 (exact) after hyperparameter tuning. In doing so, we also uncover some evidence for a potential correspondence between the linear (chronological, causal) and nonlinear (emotional) arms of plot in the linear fiction dataset. We further discover that the chapters we extract from non-linear fiction tend to vary more in length, which we understand as a corpus-level difference.

The qualitative analysis in Section 4.1 shows that the general domain BERT model produces more explainable results than the ELECTRA model fine-tuned on Victorian novels, while ELECTRA quantitatively outperforms BERT in Section 4.2. This is not so much a contradiction as a guidance for future research: perhaps the "literary domain" is not a monolith, but an umbrella term for a collection of domains that are significantly different from each other. Is the domain barrier between linear and non-linear fiction? If so, then ELECTRA could be considered as an "in-domain" model for experiments in 4.2 because the object of inference is linear fiction, while not for 4.1 since it concerns non-linearity. It is possible that if ELECTRA is fine-tuned on a non-linear fiction dataset with sentiment labels, it could further improve upon the findings of 4.1.

Aside from these questions, other potential directions for our future work include 1) designing more robust methods for quantifying non-linearity in fiction, which could be leveraged for a wide range of inquiries in digital humanities, 2) combining our sentiment-based pipeline with existing semantic-based approach to improve the performance of chapter segmentation, and 3) expanding this research to narratives beyond the literary domain, which is also a key interest of contemporary narratology. We also hope to open up the discussion of non-linearity in fictional narratives to event-centric and character-centric approaches to better understand the interplay between causal and emotional dimensions of plot.

6 Limitations

Due to various constraints, our experiments are only able to cover five non-linear novels and nine linear novels, listed in Table 7. This pales in comparison to the thousands of novels typically expected of large-scale studies in digital humanities, whose scale allows them to make generalizable claims regarding narratives or literary history (Piper et al., 2021). We hope to make up for this gap in our future work. One key challenge to scaling our dataset would be data availability. The use of non-linearity in fiction is predominantly a 20th century phenomenon, which suggests that many non-linear novels will not be in the public domain for some time to come.

In terms of experiment design, an important limitation of the quantitative evaluations in Section 4.2 is its assumption that a novel's chapter divides provided by its author could be thought of as a form of "gold standard" labels for model validation. This claim of authorial control and "authority" over the text has been thoroughly problematized in literary studies since the emergence of poststructuralism (Barthes, 1967; Foucault, 1969), while analogous suspicions have been raised in natural language generation against the assumed reliability of human evaluators (Clark et al., 2021). Unfortunately, the author's input is the only operationalizable criteria for ground truth available to us within the scope of this study.

Acknowledgement

We sincerely thank Fangyuan Xu, the workshop organizers, and the anonymous reviewers for their generous time, attention, and helpful feedback on this paper. Peiqi Sui, Lin Wang, Kelvin Wong, and Stephen T. Wong were supported by T. T. & W. F. Chao Foundation and the John S Dunn Research Foundation.

References

David Bamman, Sejal Popat, and Sheng Shen. 2019. An annotated dataset of literary entities. In *Proceedings of the 2019 Conference of the North American Chapter of the Association for Computational Linguistics (Volume 1: Long Papers)*, pages 2138–2144, Minneapolis, Minnesota. Association for Computational Linguistics.

Roland Barthes. 1967. The death of the author. *S/Z*. Hill and Wang.

David Bordwell. 2013. *Narration in the fiction film*. Routledge.

Ryan L. Boyd, Kate G. Blackburn, and James W. Pennebaker. 2020. The narrative arc: Revealing core narrative structures through text analysis. *Science Advances*, 6(32).

Peter Brooks. 1984. *Reading for the plot: Design and intention in narrative*. Harvard University Press.

Sriharsh Bhyravajjula, Ujwal Narayan, and Manish Shrivastava. 2022. Marcus: An event-centric nlp pipeline that generates character arcs from narratives. In *Proceedings of Text2Story: Fourth Workshop on Narrative Extraction from Texts held in conjunction with the 43rd European Conference on Information Retrieval (ECIR 2021)*, pages 67-74.

Joseph Campbell. 1949. *The hero with a thousand faces*. Princeton University Press.

Elizabeth Clark, Tal August, Sofia Serrano, Nikita Haduong, Suchin Gururangan, and Noah A. Smith. 2021. All that's 'human' is not gold: Evaluating human evaluation of generated text. In *Proceedings of the 59th Annual Meeting of the Association for Computational Linguistics and the 11th International Joint Conference on Natural Language Processing (Volume 1: Long Papers)*, pages 7282–7296, Online. Association for Computational Linguistics.

Kevin Clark, Minh-Thang Luong, Quoc V. Le, and Christopher D. Manning. 2019. ELECTRA: Pre-training text encoders as discriminators rather than generators. *arXiv preprint arXiv: 2003.10555*.

Jon Chun. 2021. SentimentArcs: A novel method for self-supervised sentiment analysis of time series shows SOTA transformers can struggle finding narrative arcs. *arXiv preprint arXiv: 2110.09454*.

Jacob Devlin, Ming-Wei Chang, Kenton Lee, and Kristina Toutanova. 2019. BERT: Pre-training of deep bidirectional transformers for language understanding. In *Proceedings of the 2019 Conference of the North American Chapter of the Association for Computational Linguistics: Human Language Technologies, Volume 1 (Long and Short Papers)*, pages 4171–4186, Minneapolis, Minnesota. Association for Computational Linguistics.

Katherine Elkins. 2022. *The shapes of stories: Sentiment analysis for narrative*. Cambridge University Press.

Katherine Elkins and Jon Chun. 2019. Can sentiment analysis reveal structure in a "plotless" novel?. *arXiv preprint arXiv:1910.01441*.

Michel Foucault. 1969. What is an Author. In *Language, Counter-memory, Practice: Selected Essays and Interviews by Michel Foucault*. Cornell University Press.

E. M. Forster. 1927. *Aspects of the novel*. London: E. Arnold.

Gustav Freytag. 1895. *Technique of the drama: An exposition of dramatic composition and art*. S. Griggs.

Jianbo Gao, Matthew L. Jockers, John Laudun, and Timothy Tangherlini. 2016. A multiscale theory for the dynamical evolution of sentiment in novels. In *2016 International Conference on Behavioral, Economic and Socio-cultural Computing (BESC)*, pages 1-4, Durham, North Carolina.

Project Gutenberg. n.d. www.gutenberg.org.

Patrick Colm Hogan. 2011. *Affective narratology: The emotional structure of stories*. University of Nebraska Press.

Matthew L. Jockers. 2015. Revealing sentiment and plot arcs with the syuzhet package. www.matthewjockers.net/2015/02/02/syuzhet.

Kaley Joyes. 2008. Failed witnessing in Virginia Woolf's Mrs. Dalloway. *Woolf Studies Annual*, 14: pp. 69–89.

Suzanne Keen. 2011. Introduction: Narrative and the emotions. *Poetics Today*: 32 (1): 1–53.

Hoyeol Kim. 2021. VictorianLit. https://github.com/elibooklover/VictorianLit.

Jochen Kleres. 2011. Emotions and narrative analysis: A methodological approach. *Journal for the theory of social behavior*, 41:182-202.

nlptown. 2020. Bert-base-multilingual-uncased-sentiment. https://huggingface.co/nlptown/bert-base-multilingual-uncased-sentiment.

Charuta Pethe, Allen Kim, and Steve Skiena. 2020. Chapter captor: Text segmentation in novels. In *Proceedings of the 2020 Conference on Empirical Methods in Natural Language Processing (EMNLP)*, pages 8373–8383, Online. Association for Computational Linguistics.

James Phelan. 1989. *Reading people, reading plots: Character, progression, and the interpretation of narrative*. University of Chicago Press.

Federico Pianzola. 2018. Looking at narrative as a complex system: The proteus principle. *Narrating complexity*, 101–122.

Andrew Piper, Richard Jean So, and David Bamman. 2021. Narrative theory for computational narrative understanding. In *Proceedings of the 2021 Conference on Empirical Methods in Natural Language Processing*, pages 298–311, Online and

Punta Cana, Dominican Republic. Association for Computational Linguistics.

Andrew Piper, Sunyam Bagga, Laura Monteiro, Andrew Yang, Marie Labrosse, and Yu Lu Liu. 2021. Detecting narrativity across long time scales. In *Proceedings of the 2021 Computational Humanities Research Conference*, pages 319-332.

Vladimir Iakovlevich Propp. 1968. *Morphology of the folktale*. University of Texas Press

Jonathan Reeve. 2016. Chapterize. https://github.com/JonathanReeve/chapterize.

Brian Richardson. 2000. Linearity and its discontents: Rethinking narrative form and ideological valence. College English, 62(6): 685–95.

Felski, Rita. 2008. *Uses of literature*. Wiley-Blackwell.

Marie-Laurie Ryan. 2005. On the theoretical foundations of transmedial narratology. *Narratology beyond literary criticism*, 6: 1–24.

Tzvetan Todorov. 1971. The 2 principles of narrative. *Diacritics*, 1(1): 37-44.

Ted Underwood. 2015. Free research question about plot. tedunderwood.com/2015/04/01/free-research-question-about-plot.

Ted Underwood. 2013. *Why literary periods mattered: Historical contrast and the prestige of English studies*. Stanford University Press.

Paveen Virameteekul. 2022. Paragraph-level attention based deep model for chapter segmentation." *PeerJ Computer Science*, 8:e1003.

Shufan Wang and Mohit Iyyer. 2019. Casting light on invisible cities: Computationally engaging with literary criticism. *arXiv preprint arXiv: 1904.08386*.

Julia R. Winkler, Markus Appel, Marie-Luise C.R. Schmidt, and Tobias Richter. 2023. The experience of emotional shifts in narrative persuasion. *Media psychology*, 26(2): 141-171

A Additional Tables

Chapter	Scene/Event	Starting Sentence(s)	Ending Sentence(s)	Chapter length (paragraphs)
1	Clarissa walking towards the flower shop; Septimus' back story; Clarissa returns home to prepare for the party	"Mrs. Dalloway said she would buy the flowers herself."	"'Star-gazing?' said Peter."	119
2	Clarissa lost in memories of Peter; Peter's surprise visit; Peter leaves, follows a young woman, falls asleep in Regent's Park, and dreams about woman figures	"It was like running one's face against a granite wall in the darkness! It was shocking; it was horrible!"	"So the elderly nurse knitted over the sleeping baby in Regent's Park. So Peter Walsh snored."	95
3	Peter links his dream to his memories of Clarissa	"He woke with extreme suddenness, saying to himself, 'The death of the soul.'"	"It was an extraordinary summer… Clarissa in bed with headaches."	19
4	Peter reminisces his parting with Clarissa	"The final scene, the terrible scene which he believed had mattered more than anything in the whole of his life…"	"...when the child ran full tilt into her, fell flat, and burst out crying."	9
5	Child runs towards Rezia in Regent's Park; Peter looks at the couple and thinks about Clarissa's marriage and his own; Septimus' romantic history	"That was comforting rather."	"Could she not read Shakespeare too? Was Shakespeare a difficult author? she asked."	75
6	Septimus' conditions and melancholia worsen	"One cannot bring children into a world like this."	"The verdict of human nature on such a wretch was death."	5
7	Dr. Holmes and Sir William Bradshaw's treatment of Septimus	"**Dr. Holmes** came again."	"But Rezia Warren Smith cried, walking down Harley Street, that she did not like that man."	64
8	Richard's lunch with Lady Bruton & Hugh, returns home, and a quick exchange with Clarissa; Clarissa laments on their distance in marriage, and thinks derogatively about Miss Kilman as Elizabeth leaves with her	"Shredding and slicing, dividing and subdividing, the clocks of Harley Street nibbled at the June day…"	"...upon the body of Miss Kilman standing still in the street for a moment to mutter, 'It is the flesh.'"	105
9	Miss Kilman resents Clarissa as well	"It was the flesh that she must control. Clarissa Dalloway had insulted her."	"...and she chose, in her abstraction, portentously, and the girl serving thought her mad."	8
10	Elizabeth starts to feel overwhelmed around Miss Kilman, and takes the omnibus home; Septimus and Lucrezia's moment of happiness in their apartment as a girl brings their evening papers	"Elizabeth rather wondered, as they did up the parcel, what Miss Kilman was thinking."	"He was very tired. He was very happy. He would sleep. He shut his eyes. But directly he saw nothing the sounds of the game became fainter and stranger and sounded like the cries of people…"	65

Table 6. Full list of predicted chapters (BERT) in *Mrs. Dalloway* (continues to next page). The corresponding narrative arc is displayed in Figure 1.

Chapter	Scene/Event	Starting Sentence(s)	Ending Sentence(s)	Chapter length (paragraphs)
11	Septimus fears the arrival of Holmes and Bradshaw	"He started up in terror."	"But this hat now. And then (it was getting late) **Sir William Bradshaw**."	9
12	Rezia shares a beautiful moment with Septimus before leaving; Holmes arrives the apartment; Septimus commits suicide	"She held her hands to her head, waiting for him to say…"	"'I'll give it you!' he cried, and flung himself vigorously, violently down on to Mrs. Filmer's area railings."	13
13	Guests arriving at the party	"'The coward!' cried **Dr. Holmes**, bursting the door open."	"She could not resist recalling what Charles Darwin had said about her little book on the orchids of Burma."	105
14	Clarissa talking to Lady Bruton about her lunch with Richard	"(Clarissa must speak to Lady Bruton.)"	"(Lady Bruton detested illness in the wives of politicians.)"	5
15	Peter's arrival at the party; Clarissa wants to talk but could not	"'And there's Peter Walsh!' said Lady Bruton"	"... she must go up to **Lady Bradshaw** and say . . ."	8
16	Clarissa hosting the party, then learns about Septimus' death and withdraws	"But **Lady Bradshaw** anticipated her."	"She must assemble. She must find Sally and Peter. And she came in from the little room."	29
17	Peter's conversation with Sally	"But where is Clarissa?' said Peter. He was sitting on the sofa with Sally."	"He made Sally laugh."	40
18	Peter and Sally looking at Elizabeth	"But **Sir William Bradshaw** stopped at the door to look at a picture."	"What is it that fills me with extraordinary excitement?"	5
19	"It is Clarissa, he said. For there she was."	"It is Clarissa, he said."	"For there she was."	2

Table 6 (continue). Full list of predicted chapters (BERT) in *Mrs. Dalloway* (continues from last page). The corresponding narrative arc is displayed in Figure 1.

Novel	Author	Type	Length (Paragraphs)
Mrs. Dalloway	Virginia Woolf	Non-linear	761
The Sound and the Fury	William Faulkner	Non-linear	3176
Swann's Way	Marcel Proust	Non-linear	1392
Good Morning, Midnight	Jean Rhys	Non-linear	1493
Ulysses	James Joyce	Non-linear	7444
Adam Bede	George Eliot	Linear	2563
Great Expectations	Charles Dickens	Linear	3898
Lady Audley's Secret	Elizabeth Braddon	Linear	3285
Little Dorrit	Charles Dickens	Linear	6610
North and South	Eliza Gaskell	Linear	3499
Oliver Twist	Charles Dickens	Linear	3900
Pride and Prejudice	Jane Austen	Linear	2081
The Woman in White	Wilkie Collins	Linear	4214
Vanity Fair	William Makepeace Thackeray	Linear	3432

Table 7. Full list of all novels used in this study

Composition and Deformance: Measuring Imageability with a Text-to-Image Model

Si Wu
Northeastern University
siwu@ccs.neu.edu

David A. Smith
Northeastern University
dasmith@ccs.neu.edu

Abstract

Although psycholinguists and psychologists have long studied the tendency of linguistic strings to evoke mental images in hearers or readers, most computational studies have applied this concept of imageability only to isolated words. Using recent developments in text-to-image generation models, such as DALL•E mini, we propose computational methods that use generated images to measure the imageability of both single English words and connected text. We sample text prompts for image generation from three corpora: human-generated image captions, news article sentences, and poem lines. We subject these prompts to different deformances to examine the model's ability to detect changes in imageability caused by compositional change. We find high correlation between the proposed computational measures of imageability and human judgments of individual words. We also find the proposed measures more consistently respond to changes in compositionality than baseline approaches. We discuss possible effects of model training and implications for the study of compositionality in text-to-image models.[1]

1 Introduction

> Did you ever read one of her Poems backward, because the plunge from the front overturned you? — Emily Dickinson (Samuels and McGann, 1999)

Imageability is the capacity of a linguistic string to elicit imagery. Humans can identify highly imageable words, such as "banana", "beach", "sunset", and words with low imageability, such as "criterion", "actuality", "gratitude"; however, it's difficult to measure imageability computationally. Psycholinguists and psychologists have conducted interviews with humans and released databases of the human imageability ratings, such as the Medical Research Council (MRC) Psycholinguistic Database, to help researchers in their fields, as well as other fields such as linguistics and computer science, to measure these intangible attributes of verbal content (Wilson, 1988). However, conducting these interviews is costly and laborious. Volunteers had to rate hundreds and thousands of words, thus expanding these psycholinguistics databases to the size of modern Natural Language Processing (NLP) corpora such as Corpus of Contemporary American English (COCA), which has more than 60k lemmas with word frequency and part of speech tags, is unrealistic.

Furthermore, these ratings are only on isolated words. To calculate a sentence's imageability, many applications have simply added the scores of its component words. Other work uses each word's concreteness level, which research has found highly correlated with imageability (Paivio et al., 1968; Ellis, 1991; Richardson, 1976). These methods, while they are able to roughly measure imageability, dismiss a fundamental property of a sentence: compositionality. Compositionality depends on word order as well as word choice. Sentences with the same component words but with different word order vary not only in their syntax and semantics, but also their intensity and construction of the imagery, e.g. the famous example: "the dog bit the man" vs. "the man bit the dog". Previous bag-of-word approaches such as Kao and Jurafsky (2015) would consider a sentence and its backward version as having the same imageability, but to human readers, the level of imageability has significantly altered.

In this paper, we investigate a new computational approach to measure imageability using text-to-image models such as DALL•E mini. We propose two methods to measure the imageability level of both individual words and connected text by generating images with a text-to-image model. We

[1] Our scripts are available at https://github.com/swsiwu/composition_and_deformance

Proceedings of the The 5th Workshop on Narrative Understanding, pages 106–117
July 14, 2023

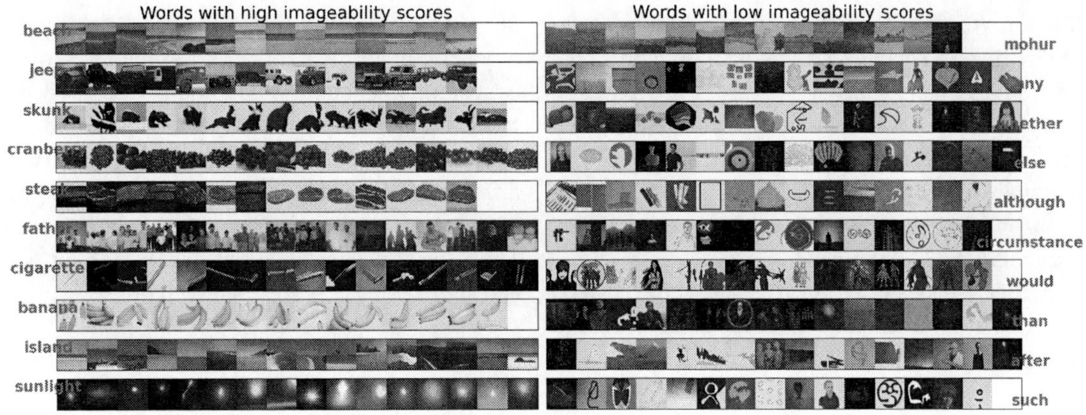

Figure 1: Generated images of words with high imageability ratings have more visual homogeneity comparing to the ones with low imageability ratings.

test our methods with both isolated words from the MRC database and connected text from poems, image captions, and news articles, and compare our result with previous bag-of-words methods such as Kao and Jurafsky (2015) and Hessel et al. (2018).

We propose, firstly, measuring the average CLIP score provided by DALL•E mini and, secondly, calculating the average pairwise cosine similarity between embeddings computed by a pretrained ResNet-18 model. We find that these methods are more highly correlated to human imageability judgments of individual words than other automatic techniques proposed by Hessel et al. (2018).

We further demonstrate the robustness of our proposed methods by subjecting connected text to various **deformances**. As suggested by the epigraph from Emily Dickinson, literary scholars design transformations of the original text to elicit more or less intense reactions from human readers (Samuels and McGann, 1999) and help them calibrate their interpretations of literary works. This approach is similar to how contrastive training might be used for models such as word2vec or BERT.

We compare our computational imageability measurements with human judgment collected from Amazon Mechanical Turk (AMT) and found that, on MRC isolated words, our methods have reasonable correlations with human judgment, but on connected text, the correlations vary among different types of connected text.

2 Related work

Paivio introduced the idea of imageability and defined imageability as "the ease/difficulty with which words arose a sensory experience" (Paivio et al., 1968; Dellantonio et al., 2014). Although imageability is associated with many modalities, some researchers have found that visual modality is its most prominent modality (Ellis, 1991; Richardson, 1976). Imageability is also highly correlated with concreteness (Paivio et al., 1968; Ellis, 1991; Richardson, 1976), and concreteness has also been found to be most related to visual modality (Brysbaert et al., 2014). However, some researchers have found their relation to be more complex: words with high imageability and concreteness "evoke sensations connected to the perception of the objects they denote", words with high imageability and low concreteness "evoke sensations connected to affective arousal" (Dellantonio et al., 2014). An example for the latter is "anger", which is highly imageable since most of us have the experience of being angry, but "anger" itself is an abstract word. Since imageability and concreteness are highly correlated, in this paper, we will compare some works using concreteness to measure word imageability, but we agree that these two attributes should ideally be disentangled (Richardson, 1976; Boles, 1983).

The imageability rating of an isolated word in psycholinguistics research is usually derived from interviewing human subjects: asking them how imageable a word or a concept is on a 7-point Likert scale (Wilson, 1988; Toglia and Battig, 1978; Gilhooly and Logie, 1980; Coltheart, 1981). Due to the cost of this procedure, the most popular dataset, MRC Psycholinguistics Database, combines three different sources and, even so, has a limited vocabulary size of 9240.

Others have attempted to expand MRC imageability ratings using synonyms and hyponyms identified in WordNet (Liu et al., 2014); Schock et al. (2012) made a small expansion of 3000 words but only on disyllabic words.

Concreteness ratings in the MRC database were obtained in the same way as imageability ratings, although recently Brysbaert et al. (2014), using Amazon Mechanical Turk, was able to expand the vocabulary to 37,058 words.

A concrete idea is assumed to have more shared representation than an abstract idea. Hessel et al. (2018) estimate the concreteness of a word in a database by measuring how clustered a word's associated images according to the image embeddings provided by ResNet-18. Kastner et al. (2020) estimate imageability using more explicit visual features, such as color distributions, local and global gradient descriptions, and high-level features, such as image theme, content, and composition. However, this approach is supervised and requires a large amount of data to train.

The above works are all on isolated words. Our paper aims to measure a sentence's imageability beyond bag-of-words methods, where the latter is insensitive to compositional change and imagery loss/gain. We will compare both to the work of Kao and Jurafsky (2015), who measure imageability with bag-of-words models, and of Hessel et al. (2018), who estimate word concreteness in an unsupervised manner. We will demonstrate our methods' advantage via correlation with single-word human judgments from MRC (Table 2). For connected text, we will inspect the measurement change with respect to human expectation (Table 4, Fig 4).

3 Datasets

3.1 Connected text datasets

Data	imag	concrete
Poems	323.477	0.537
Captions	383.270	2.659
News	317.478	2.049

Table 1: Sentence-level average imageability and concreteness scores for different connected text corpora.

The **Poetry dataset** consists of 355 English poems written by different types of poets: imagists, contemporary poets, contemporary amateur poets, and 19th-century poets. They were collected by Kao and Jurafsky (2015) from different poetry websites and publications: *Des Imagistes* (1914), *Some Imagist Poets* (1915), Contemporary American Poetry (Poulin and Waters, 2006), Amateur Writing (website), and Famous Poets and Poems (website). In their paper, they use various linguistic and psycholinguistic attributes as features for identifying different poets and poem types. In this paper, however, we do not focus on poem-level classification. The dataset was provided by the authors of Kao and Jurafsky (2015) for research purposes.

Conceptual 12M (CC12M)[2] (Changpinyo et al., 2021) is a dataset of 12 million image-caption pairs, designed for vision-and-language pre-training. We randomly sampled 5000 captions from the dataset. In the 12M captions, real names are replaced with `<PERSON>`, and some captions contain hashtags. We only use captions with no `<PERSON>` or #.

Cornell Newsroom Dataset[3] (Grusky et al., 2018) is a summarization dataset of 1.3 million articles from 38 major English-language news publications. We extract sentences using nltk "sent_tokenize", then randomly sample 5000 sentences of 10–30 words from the training set original news articles.

3.2 Psycholinguistics databases

MRC Psycholinguistics Database contains 150,837 words and their linguistic and psycholinguistic attributes including imageability, concreteness, familiarity, age of acquisition, and Brown word frequency (Wilson, 1988). It was originally published by Coltheart (1981) and made machine-usable by Wilson. The later version also added new entries and made corrections to the previous one. Out of 150,837 words, only 9240 entries have imageability ratings, and there are only 4828 unique words with imageability ratings. The imageability ratings range between 100 and 700. Duplicated imageability word entries are all agreeing on the imageability rating but vary in other attributes, such as different word types (noun, adjective, verb, etc.) and having "N/A" or empty entries. This is possibly because the database was a concatenation of 3 different databases. We will denote this imageability rating as $imageability$ in tables and figures.

Brysbaert et al. Concreteness Human Ratings

[2]Available to download at `https://github.com/google-research-datasets/conceptual-12m`

[3]Available to download after accepting the data licensing terms `https://lil.nlp.cornell.edu/newsroom/download/index.html`

contains 37,058 English words and 2896 two-word expressions that were crowd-sourced from over 4000 participants on AMT. All lemmas in the dataset were known by at least 85% of the participants. Concreteness is defined as the ability to have immediate experience through senses or actions and is more experience-based, as opposed to abstractness, which can't be experienced through senses or actions. It's also more language-based. Raters were asked to rate a word on a 5-point scale, where 5 is the most concrete and 1 is more abstract. The Brysbaert ratings are also highly correlated with the MRC Psycholinguistics Database's concreteness ratings, with $r = 0.919$. In the following experiments and analysis, we will denote this concreteness rating as $concreteness$.

4 Methods

4.1 Model

We use DALL•E mini (Dayma et al., 2021)[4] as our text-to-image model. DALL•E mini is developed by developers and researchers as an open-source alternative to the original DALL•E developed by OpenAI. It's trained with 15 million webcrawled images and 0.4 billion parameters comparing to the original DALL•E, which is a 12-billion parameter autoregressive transformer trained on 250 million image-text pairs. The image outputs of DALL•E model are ranked by their Contrastive Language-Image Pre-training (CLIP) scores, a neural network that learns to correlate image and text (Radford et al., 2021). Like similarity scores, CLIP score has the range of $[0, 1]$; DALL•E mini adjusts this to a percentage in $[0, 100]$.

Specifically, we are using DALL•E mini version "mini-1:v0". One of the hyperparameters for generation is temperature. Temperature acts as a threshold for the quality of the sampled images. We use a temperature of 0.85 to ensure that the sampled images are highly correlated (high CLIP score) while allowing mild visual diversity. When we did a grid search over this parameter on a small set of poems, it did not have a noticeable effect on the average CLIP scores. Lastly, a higher conditioning scale (cond_scale) will result in a better match to prompt but low diversity, and we decided to use a cond_scale of 3 (out of 10) informed by a report written by a DALL•E mini developer Dayma (2022).

[4]https://github.com/borisdayma/dalle-mini

We use 4 Tesla V100 SXM2 GPUs for this paper. For each connected text corpus and each deformance, it takes about 24 hours to generate images. For MRC vocabulary, it takes about 24 hours as well. We will release the code we use for this paper in this GitHub repository[5].

4.2 Measurements

A human can evaluate and "feel" how imageable a text is. For example, "mom is angry at me" is not as imageable as "mom's eyes are throwing knives at me". A good computational measurement should be able to quantify and estimate the magnitude of imageability, and when the original text is subject to a compositional change (deformance), it should manifest the direction of change in imageability.

To first examine the text-to-image model's ability to measure the magnitude of imageability, we will first test on isolated words from MRC and benchmark our methods against the MRC human imageability ratings as well as comparing to other bag-of-words measurements in section 4.3. Then in section 5, we will test on different connected text. We will alter the original text's composition and imageability with deformances, and by doing so, we'd like to observe both the magnitude and direction of change using our methods and previous bag-of-words methods. In some deformances, bag-of-words methods will fall short since they don't consider word order and word choice, while our methods will demonstrate both magnitude and direction of imageability change.

We will also briefly mention how word frequency is unrelated to imageability in section 4.4.

4.3 Measuring isolated word's imageability

For the isolated word experiments, our vocabulary is all the words in MRC Psycholinguistics Database that have imageability human ratings. For each word, we will have the MRC imageability rating ($imageability$) and the concreteness rating ($concreteness$) from Brysbaert et al. (2014). Then we use DALL•E mini to generate a maximum of 16 images for each word to obtain 3 other measurements:

- The concreteness score introduced by Hessel et al. (2018), where each image will only have one label which is the word we used to generate that image, and each word will have a

[5]https://github.com/swsiwu/composition_and_deformance

maximum of 16 images associated with that word. We will say Hessel et al. when we refer to this score.

- **Average CLIP score**: our first proposed method. Each image has a CLIP score provided by DALL•E mini when it was generated. We average all generated images' CLIP scores for the target word to produce the average CLIP score. We will denote it as $\underline{aveCLIP}$ in tables and figures.

- **Average pairwise image embedding cosine similarity**: our second proposed method. For each generated image, we obtain its image embedding with ResNet-18, then compute the average pairwise cosine similarity score between all images for the target word. We will denote this score as $\underline{imgSim}$ in tables and figures. Mathematically, let M be the set of image embeddings, $M = \{\mathbf{m_1}, \mathbf{m_2}, \mathbf{m_3}, ...\}$, $n = |M|$, N be the unique pairs in M, and $k = |N| = {}_nC_2$.

$$imgSim = \frac{1}{k} \sum_{(m_x, m_y) \in N} \frac{\mathbf{m_x} \cdot \mathbf{m_y}}{||\mathbf{m_x}||||\mathbf{m_y}||}$$

  This is to be distinguished from Hessel et al.'s method, which calculates the average size of the mutually neighboring images associated with a word and then normalizes it by a random distribution of the image data (Hessel et al., 2018).

We visualize these MRC word imageability ratings and their corresponding $aveCLIP$ and $imgSim$ in Figure 2, where they are colored by $aveCLIP$. The figure shows that words with very high average CLIP scores tend to have high imageability human ratings and high average image embedding similarity. In Figure 3, we plot $aveCLIP$ vs. $imgSim$ on the MRC words, and it shows a positive linear correlation between them.

4.4 The case of familiarity of MRC vocabulary

We use word frequency to measure familiarity. Word frequency counts are from Brown Corpus for 3979 out of 4828 MRC words. In table 2, we show the Pearson Correlation coefficients between all other measurements and MRC imageability ratings. The Brysbaert et al. (2014) concreteness ratings and MRC imageability ratings are highly correlated with $r = 0.780$, then followed $aveCLIP$ ($r = 0.537$) and $imgSim$ ($r = 0.429$). Word frequency is irrelevant to imageability ratings as it shows a negative and minuscule linear correlation.

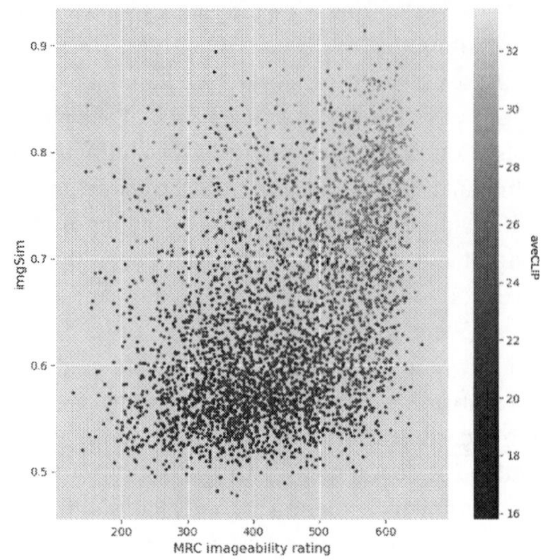

Figure 2: X-axis is MRC imageability human rating. Y-axis is $imgSim$, and each dot is a word colored by its $aveCLIP$.

Type	L.C. to imageability ratings
word freq	-0.072
concreteness	0.780
Hessel et al.	0.415
aveCLIP	**0.537**
imgSim	0.429

Table 2: Linear correlations to MRC imageability ratings.

5 Connected text and compositionality

5.1 Preprocessing

For connected text, the prompt input is each individual caption, news sentence, with the exception that for poems we use every 2 lines (no overlaps) as a single prompt. We use 2 poem lines to ensure enough visual and semantic content for DALL•E mini to generate meaningful images. These two lines are combined with a space character since the majority of the poem lines end with a punctuation mark.

5.2 Measuring Imageability

We use the same imageability measurements as the single-word experiments, with these specifications:

Deformance	Description	Example
Original	The original poem lines.	“The people pass through the dust On bicycles, in carts, in motor-cars;"
Backward	Preserving punctuations and their locations but reversing the word order for each line.	"Dust the through pass people the Bicycles on, carts in, motor-cars in;"
Permuted	Splitting the original sentence by space characters, then randomizing the word order.	"The pass people through dust the bicycles, in carts, On motor-cars; in"
Just nouns	Keeping only nouns and removing other words and punctuation.	"people dust bicycles carts motor-cars"
Replaced nouns	Replacing nouns that can be found in the MRC database with another word with the same imageability ratings. Plural nouns that can't be found in the database are ignored.	"The ox pass through the murder On bicycles, in carts, in motor-cars;"

Table 3: Description of different deformances and their examples.

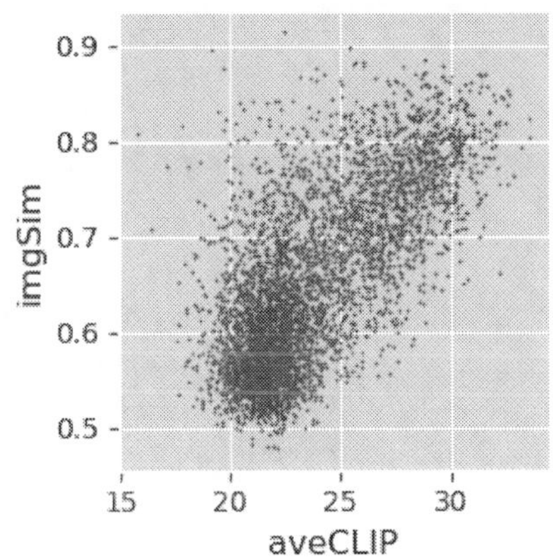

Figure 3: Average CLIP score vs. average pairwise image embedding cosine similarity. Each dot is a MRC word.

- Imageability rating: the imageability score for a connected text is the sum of all words' imageability human ratings found in the MRC database divided by the number of words found in the database, as did in Kao and Jurafsky (2015).

- Concreteness rating: the sum of all words' concreteness ratings found in the Brysbaert et al. (2014) database divided by the total number of words in the prompt.

- Concreteness score by Hessel et al. (2018): their method was designed to estimate single word concreteness scores. To get sentence-level concreteness scores, we use the sum of the concreteness scores of all words in a sentence divided by the total number of words. Notice that the same word will have a different concreteness score under a different deformance because a word concreteness score is estimated from all its associated images, and the images are generated using DALL•E mini with deformed sentences as prompt. Also notice that a word concreteness score is not only estimated from one sentence, but all sentences that contain this word under the same type of deformance. We modify their tokenizer so that all punctuation is omitted for a cleaner output.

- Average CLIP score: we average each prompt's generated image CLIP scores, then divide it by the total number of images.

- Average pairwise image embedding cosine similarity: we calculate the average pairwise image embedding cosine similarity among the images given a prompt.

5.3 Deformances

The above measurements are repeated for each deformance, and we evaluate the percent change for each measurement. We use percent change instead of difference since these scores are on different scales. A good measurement should show the change in imagery caused by the change of

Different imageability measurements' average pairwise percent change compared to the original text +: more imageable, -: less imageable						
Text	**Deformance**	**imag**	**concreteness**	**Hessel et al.**	**aveCLIP**	**imgSim**
Kao & Jurafsky Poems	Backward	0	0	3.842	-0.817	0.046
	Permuted	0	0	490.159	-0.110	-0.182
	Just nouns	24.478	9.644	141.191	1.566	1.253
	Replaced nouns	0	0.285	41.403	-0.002	0.130
Conceptual 12M	Backward	0	0	-4.444	-1.830	-0.886
	Permuted	0	0	111.336	-1.465	-9.398
	Just nouns	31.848	16.693	60.494	-0.657	0.049
	Replaced nouns	0	-1.128	8.046	-3.963	-3.270
Cornell Newsroom	Backward	0	0	2.001	-0.757	-0.426
	Permuted	0	0	280.888	-0.899	-0.934
	Just nouns	33.243	3.288	163.973	1.829	-0.149
	Replaced nouns	0	-0.433	176.456	0.020	-0.718

Table 4: Comparing different methods percent change between the original and the corresponding deformed text under different deformances.

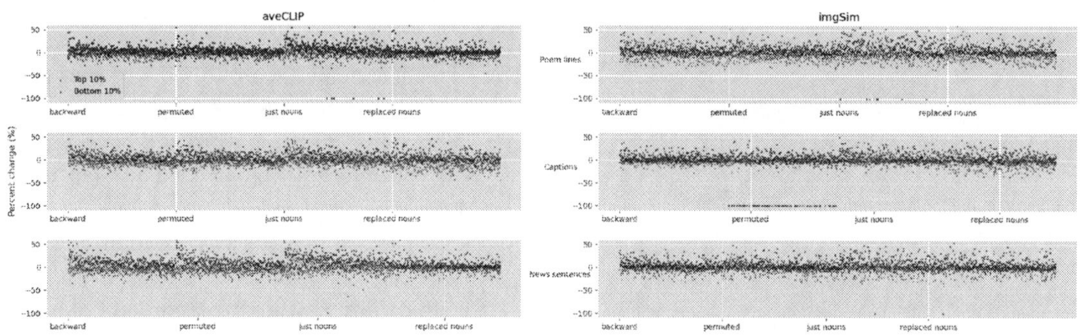

Figure 4: Percent change between lines with the top 10% and bottom 10% {aveCLIP, imgSim} scores and their associated deformed text.

composition. The traditional bag-of-words methods as displayed in Table 4 cannot display this change if the component words remain the same; Methods using DALL•E-generated images such as $aveCLIP$, $imgSim$, and Hessel et al. are able to detect changes in both word order and word choice. Hessel et al.'s method, however, does not always correctly show the direction of imagery change.

As defined by Samuels and McGann (1999), a deformance is designed to change text composition by altering its word order and/or word choice. A deformance disturbs the linguistic structure of a sentence, hence it changes not only the surface of the sentence: syntax, word order, and composition of the sentence, but also the underlying information of the sentence: semantics and pragmatics. We perform 4 different types of deformances on each connected text to examine the model's ability to measure compositional change compared to the bag-of-words methods. The deformances are backward, permuted, just nouns, and replaced nouns, and we provide an example and the elaborated description for each deformance in Table 3.

The backward and just nouns deformances appear in Samuels and McGann (1999) *Deformance and Interpretation*, in which they analyze different poetry reading practices. The backward deformance alters the word order: even though having the same set of words, it becomes less intelligible. Permuted is similar to backward: the dependency structure is disturbed, and it becomes chaotic nonsense. Just nouns strips off everything but nouns that are more likely to be imageable, but since there's no linguistic structure between them, the sentence is less specific in its imagery. Unlike backward and permuted, replaced nouns preserves the sentence structure and bag-of-words imageability ratings but alters the imagery via syntax. Backward, permuted, and replaced nouns are experiments where imageability scores remain the same in the bag-of-words approach, but other methods will manifest the change in imagery.

For replaced nouns, we ignore plural nouns not in the MRC vocabulary. Nouns in both just nouns and replaced nouns deformances are identified by the NLTK tagger.

By construction, all these deformances except just nouns cause no change in bag-of-words imageability and concreteness measures. We would expect that applying backward and permuted deformances to a text would make them less imageable, since the word order becomes less comprehensible, and that is precisely what we see with the $aveCLIP$ and (with one exception) the $imgSim$ measures. In comparison, the Hessel et al. (2018) metric mostly rates the output of those deformances as far more imageable.

6 Human judgment

We recruit workers on Amazon Mechanical Turk (AMT) to rate the imageability of randomly sampled MRC words, poem lines, captions, and news sentences. Workers were informed that they would be participating in a psycholinguistics and natural language processing research study before they accepted the task. For MRC vocabulary, we sample 400 words in total, and for each connected text corpus, we sample 120 sentences for each deformance. We recruit 300 workers in total: the first 100 workers rated 4 MRC words and 6 poem lines each, and the second 100 workers rated 6 captions each, and the rest of the workers rated 6 news sentences. Each worker is only allowed to participate in the entire research once. In total, we recruit 300 workers, and workers are paid \$0.50 for answering 6 or 10 questions. Every participating worker has HIT approval rates for all Requesters' HITs greater than 95% and number of HITs approved greater than 100, and we require their location to be in the US or Canada. For poems, we mistakenly use two lines of deformed text as one single prompt for workers to rate, and we counter that mistake by averaging the $aveCLIP$, $imgSim$ from the two lines. Table 5 shows the linear correlations between our measurements and the AMT human judgment. We find that while MRC words and captions have relatively high, positive correlations, the linear correlations between poem lines and news sentences are insignificant. We suspect the AMT rating is noisy given that each instance is only judged by one rater. The distribution of human judgments in the appendix also shows interesting variations in rating behavior across corpora.

Type	aveCLIP	imgSim
MRC words	0.350	0.316
Poem lines	-0.014	-0.127
Captions	0.185	0.137
News sentences	0.017	0.058

Table 5: Linear correlations between {aveCLIP, imgSim} and human judgment for different corpora across different deformances.

7 Discussion

Acquiring human imageability judgments is costly and laborious, which makes expanding existing imageability databases difficult. We propose two computational methods that utilize an open-source text-to-image model to estimate isolated words and connected text imageability. Both of our methods require only the input text, and the estimated imageability is calculated based on the properties of the generated images: average CLIP scores and average pairwise image embedding cosine similarity. On isolated words, our proposed methods $aveCLIP$ and $imgSim$ outperform previous unsupervised method proposed by Hessel et al. (2018): $aveCLIP$ has a linear correlation of 0.537 to MRC human judgment, followed by $imgSim$ 0.429, and Hessel et al. 0.415. Our proposed methods $aveCLIP$ and $imgSim$ also achieve relatively high linear correlations of 0.350 and 0.316 respectively with AMT human judgment, despite the noisiness of collecting that data.

For connected text, we test our methods on three different corpora: poem lines, captions, and news sentences. Unlike isolated words, sentences' meaning is compositional and depends on word choice and word order. A good sentence imageability method, therefore, should detect the change in imageability caused by compositional change. The biggest downfall of previous bag-of-words methods is that when a sentence is subject to a deformance such as permutation, imageability is unchanged, which is contradictory to human expectation. With a text-to-image model, our methods are able to take the entire sentence as one entity, preserving its composition. We test our methods against a noisy AMT human judgment (Table 5) and obtained vastly different performances on different styles of connected text. We further inspect the performance of these methods by examining the percent change between different deformances and the original text (Table 4). Our methods overall follow human expectation: the imageability level goes down when the original sentence is under a deformance, although we expect our methods to manifest more significant change. In comparison, the direction of change with the method of Hessel et al. doesn't follow our expectation. Although their method can take DALL•E mini generated images as input images, which allows it to learn compositionality from images generated from deformed prompts, it ultimately calculates each sentence's score as a sum of all words in that sentence. Each word's concreteness score is estimated from multiple sentences of the same deformance that contain that word. We know that a word's meaning varies in different sentences, thus this method loses a word's contextual meaning and can not precisely understand compositionality of a sentence.

The language of these three different corpora is very different. Overall, image captions have the highest average imageability rating as well as Brysbaert et al. concreteness rating, with poems being the second most imageable, and news sentences being the second most concrete. Since image captions' language is usually concise, and it possibly has higher noun density, it's reasonable to see overall the highest impact from deformances under $aveCLIP$ and $imgSim$. All three corpora experience negative impact from permutation under both $aveCLIP$ and $imgSim$, which we assume to be the strongest deformance since it completely randomizes the word order of a sentence. When $aveCLIP$ and $imgSim$ have opposite signs, we notice that a higher absolute value from one measurement also tends to result in a lower absolute value of the other measurement if their signs are different, thus we use Fig 4 to explore the percent change distribution between two measurements. In Fig 4, we look at the original lines with the highest and lowest 10% $aveCLIP$ and $imgSim$ and inspect the percent change between them and their different deformances (Fig 4): the lines with the highest scores consistently decrease their scores after deformances, and vice versa. While the lines with top scores follow our intuition, the increase in lines with low scores reverses the mean: given the lowest score is 0, there isn't much room for the imageability score to fall further.

The performance difference between different connected text also makes us wonder if the training data of the text-to-image model has an effect on the performance. The performance on captions is more contrastive in Table 4, while one of DALL•E mini's training datasets is also Conceptual 12M.

Future work should consider further ways of measuring imageability computationally. As more text-to-image models become available and hopefully more transparent with their training process, we hope researchers will be able to compare different models' performance.

Limitations

Since DALL•E mini is trained on English-language material, and since our input text is English only, our proposed methods will only be able to measure the imageability of English isolated words and connected text.

The text-to-image model we use, DALL•E mini, requires GPUs or TPUs to generate images. While we used 4 GPUs (see section 4 for more details) to obtain the results in this paper, we were able to use a single GPU to successfully run the same experiments with longer runtime.

7.1 AMT experiments

We didn't ask the AMT workers what device they were on. Some workers provided feedback via email saying that on mobile phones, the AMT interface didn't show the complete description of the task before they accepted it. Although during the task, detailed instruction was provided, and workers had access to both the brief and long versions of the instruction at any time during the task. It's unclear how the interface will affect the workers' performance and if it would significantly bias their judgment of text imageability.

We were only collecting a single human judgment for each text input. In retrospect, collecting several human ratings per text input and using the average would have reduced noise.

7.2 Other text-to-image models

Stable diffusion: using HuggingFace Stable Diffusion release, we generated images using every 2 poem lines as described in section 5.1. The number of generated images per prompt was significantly less than 16, and most prompts generated images that were labeled as harmful even when the prompt didn't have suggestive content. Given this behavior, we decided not to use Stable Diffusion, but we'd like to see future development of Stable Diffusion that allows it to generate abundant and safe images given a prompt.

Ethics concerns

Potential risks: DALL•E mini has potential risks of generating offensive images and is vulnerable to other misuses. The poetry corpus we use contains language that might cause DALL•E mini to generate suggestive images. We are concerned about the ethical issues raised by DALL•E mini and similar models and hope further study of DALL•E mini will develop guidelines for responsible use.

Acknowledgements

Si Wu was supported by a grant from the Andrew W. Mellon Foundation's Scholarly Communications and Information Technology program. Any views, findings, conclusions, or recommendations expressed do not necessarily reflect those of the Mellon Foundation. We would like to thank Justine Kao and Dan Jurafsky for providing us with their dataset, and we appreciate all the feedback from anonymous reviewers.

References

David B. Boles. 1983. Dissociated imageability, concreteness, and familiarity in lateralized word recognition. *Memory & Cognition*, 11:511–519.

Marc Brysbaert, Amy Beth Warriner, and Victor Kuperman. 2014. Concreteness ratings for 40 thousand generally known english word lemmas. *Behavior Research Methods*, 46:904–911.

Soravit Changpinyo, Piyush Sharma, Nan Ding, and Radu Soricut. 2021. Conceptual 12M: Pushing web-scale image-text pre-training to recognize long-tail visual concepts. In *CVPR*.

Max Coltheart. 1981. The mrc psycholinguistic database. *The Quarterly Journal of Experimental Psychology Section A*, 33(4):497–505.

Boris Dayma. 2022. Dalle-mega - effect of conditioning scale. Available at https://wandb.ai/dalle-mini/dalle-mini/reports/DALLE-Mega-Effect-of-conditioning-scale–VmlldzoxOTc2NjA0.

Boris Dayma, Suraj Patil, Pedro Cuenca, Khalid Saifullah, Tanishq Abraham, Phúc Lê Khc, Luke Melas, and Ritobrata Ghosh. 2021. Dall·e mini.

Sara Dellantonio, Remo Job, and Claudio Mulatti. 2014. Imageability: now you see it again (albeit in a different form). *Frontiers in Psychology*, 5.

Nick Ellis. 1991. Chapter 21 word meaning and the links between the verbal system and modalities of perception and imagery or in verbal memory the eyes see vividly, but ears only faintly hear, fingers barely feel and the nose doesn't know. In Robert H. Logie and Michel Denis, editors, *Mental Images in Human Cognition*, volume 80 of *Advances in Psychology*, pages 313–329. North-Holland.

Ken J Gilhooly and Robert H Logie. 1980. Age-of-acquisition, imagery, concreteness, familiarity, and ambiguity measures for 1,944 words. *Behavior research methods & instrumentation*, 12(4):395–427.

Max Grusky, Mor Naaman, and Yoav Artzi. 2018. Newsroom: A dataset of 1.3 million summaries with diverse extractive strategies. In *Proceedings of the 2018 Conference of the North American Chapter of the Association for Computational Linguistics: Human Language Technologies*.

Jack Hessel, David Mimno, and Lillian Lee. 2018. Quantifying the visual concreteness of words and topics in multimodal datasets. In *Proceedings of the 2018 Conference of the North American Chapter of the Association for Computational Linguistics: Human Language Technologies, Volume 1 (Long Papers)*, pages 2194–2205, New Orleans, Louisiana. Association for Computational Linguistics.

Justine T. Kao and Dan Jurafsky. 2015. A computational analysis of poetic style: Imagism and its influence on modern professional and amateur poetry. In *Linguistic Issues in Language Technology, Volume 12, 2015 - Literature Lifts up Computational Linguistics*. CSLI Publications.

Marc A. Kastner, Ichiro Ide, Frank Nack, Yasutomo Kawanishi, Takatsugu Hirayama, Daisuke Deguchi, and Hiroshi Murase. 2020. Estimating the imageability of words by mining visual characteristics from crawled image data. *Multimedia Tools and Applications*, 79:18167–18199.

Ting Liu, Kit Cho, G. Aaron Broadwell, Samira Shaikh, Tomek Strzalkowski, John Lien, Sarah Taylor, Laurie Feldman, Boris Yamrom, Nick Webb, Umit Boz, Ignacio Cases, and Ching-sheng Lin. 2014. Automatic expansion of the MRC psycholinguistic database imageability ratings. In *Proceedings of the Ninth International Conference on Language Resources and Evaluation (LREC'14)*, pages 2800–2805, Reykjavik, Iceland. European Language Resources Association (ELRA).

Allan Paivio, John C Yuille, and Stephen A Madigan. 1968. Concreteness, imagery, and meaningfulness values for 925 nouns. *Journal of experimental psychology*, 76(1p2):1.

Alec Radford, Jong Wook Kim, Chris Hallacy, Aditya Ramesh, Gabriel Goh, Sandhini Agarwal, Girish Sastry, Amanda Askell, Pamela Mishkin, Jack Clark, Gretchen Krueger, and Ilya Sutskever. 2021. Learning transferable visual models from natural language supervision. In *ICML*.

John T. E. Richardson. 1976. Imageability and concreteness. *Bulletin of the psychonomic society*, 7:429–431.

Lisa Samuels and Jerome McGann. 1999. Deformance and interpretation. *New Literary History*, 30(1):25–56.

Jocelyn Schock, Michael J Cortese, and Maya M Khanna. 2012. Imageability estimates for 3,000 disyllabic words. *Behavior Research Methods*, 44:374–379.

Michael P Toglia and William F Battig. 1978. *Handbook of semantic word norms*. Lawrence Erlbaum.

Michael Wilson. 1988. Mrc psycholinguistic database: Machine-usable dictionary, version 2.00. *Behavior Research Methods, Instruments, & Computers*, 20:6–10.

A A sample of the original poem and its deformed text's generated images (Figure 5)

B AMT instruction details

The header: "Please rate the ease or difficulty with which the word/sentence arouses imagery. If an image quickly forms in your mind when reading, give the text a high rating. Only 1 HIT allowed per user."

The short instruction: "Please rate each item from one (low) to seven (high) according to the ease or difficulty with which the item arouses imagery. Any item which, in your estimation, arouses a mental image (i.e., a mental picture, or sound, or other sensory experience) very quickly and easily should be given a high imagery rating; any word/sentence that arouses a mental image with difficulty or not at all should be given a low imagery rating. Please do not go back to refer to your previous ratings."

C A sample screenshot of the AMT interface (Figure 6)

D The AMT human rating distributions (Figure 10)

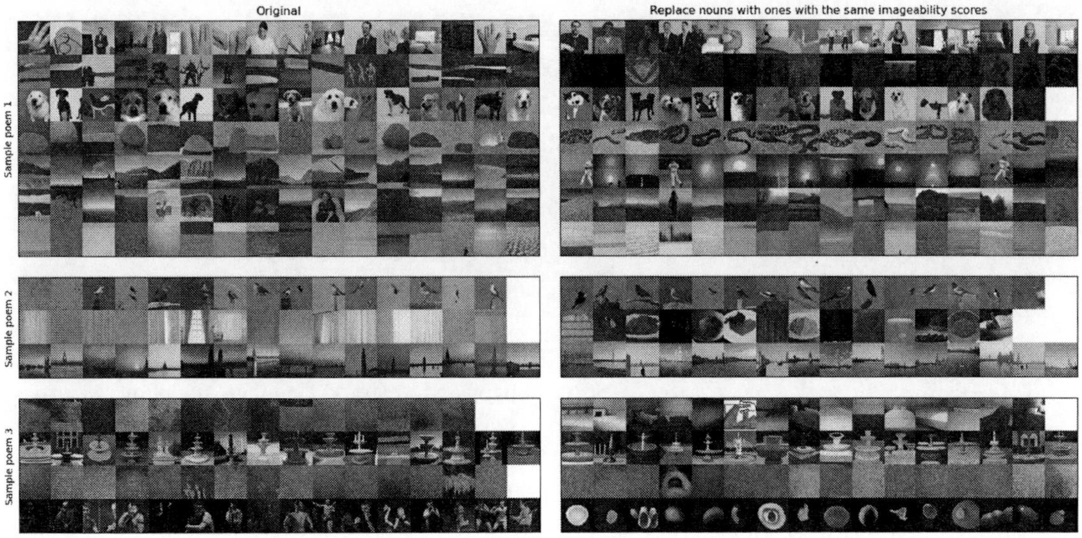

Figure 5: The original poem vs. its replaced noun version. Displaying only the changed lines.

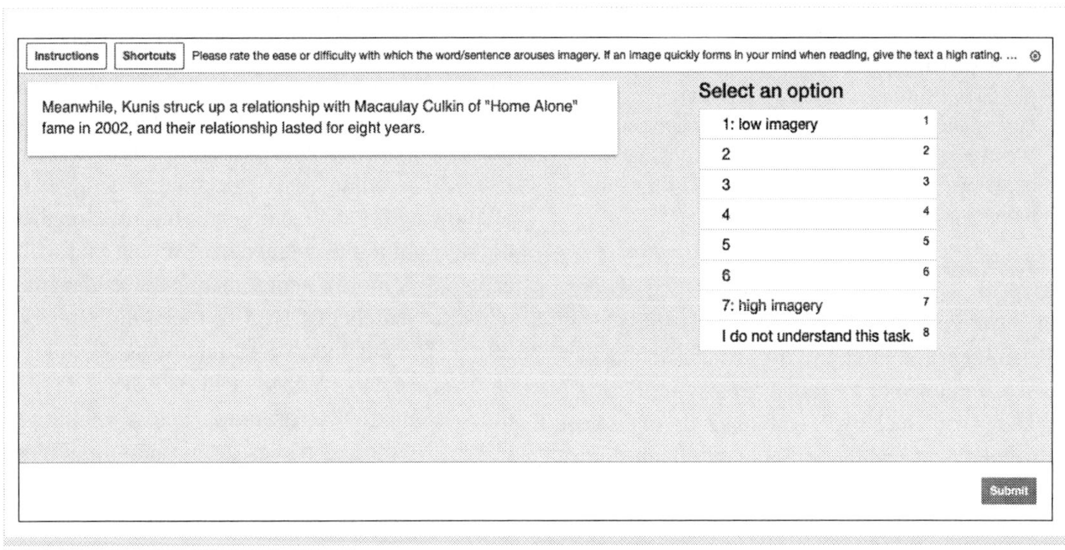

Figure 6: A screenshot of the AMT interface that the workers used to participate in our research. The example device was a laptop.

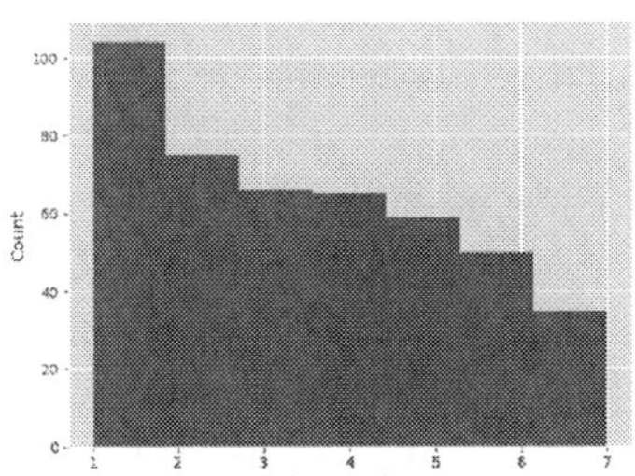

Figure 7: Poem lines

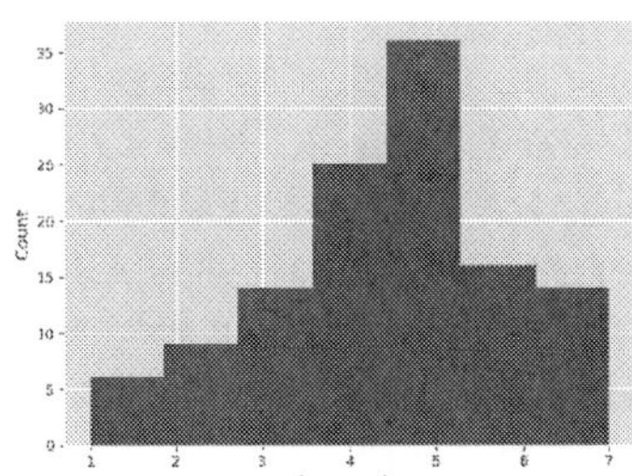

Figure 8: Captions

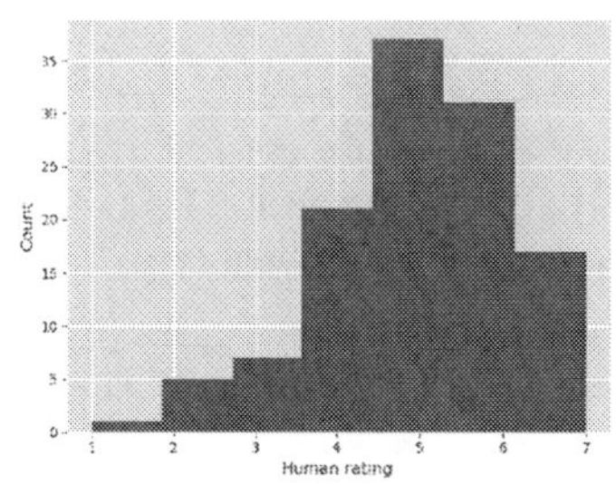

Figure 9: News sentences

Figure 10: AMT human rating distributions for different connected text corpora.

Narrative Cloze as a Training Objective: Towards Modeling Stories Using Narrative Chain Embeddings

Hans Ole Hatzel
Language Technology Group
Universität Hamburg, Germany
hans.ole.hatzel@uni-hamburg.de

Chris Biemann
Language Technology Group
Universität Hamburg, Germany
chris.biemann@uni-hamburg.de

Abstract

We present a novel approach to modeling narratives using narrative chain embeddings. A new dataset of narrative chains extracted from German news texts is presented. With neural methods, we produce models for both German and English that achieve state-of-the-art performance on the Multiple Choice Narrative Cloze task. Subsequently, we perform an extrinsic evaluation of the embeddings our models produce and show that they perform rather poorly in identifying narratively similar texts. We explore some of the reasons for this underperformance and discuss the upsides of our approach. We provide an outlook on alternative ways to model narratives, as well as techniques for evaluating such models.

1 Introduction

The narrative cloze task was originally introduced by Chambers and Jurafsky (2008) and is the task of, given a sequence of narrative triples, predicting a masked triple. Such triples are made up of subject, verb, and object, and the triples in one chain share a common participant, referred to as the protagonist. Their subsequent work (Chambers and Jurafsky, 2009) improved upon the results from the original paper and formulated the task slightly differently, expanding it to schemas with multiple participants. Granroth-Wilding and Clark (2016) extract additional information and introduce evaluation metrics. An excerpt from one of their automatically extracted chains goes as follows: (A, plead, [with, B]), (_, heartbroken, A), (A, die, _), where A and B are entities, and each triple represents a verb with its arguments.

One of the early motivations for the narrative cloze task was modeling narrative contexts and inferring narrative schemas (Chambers and Jurafsky, 2009). We aim to adapt the semantic modeling performed as part of the task to identify documents that share similar narrative schemas rather than explicitly inferring such schemas. That is to say: analogously to masked language modeling, we use narrative cloze as a training objective to train narrative understanding, rather than language understanding. The motivation being that abstract story similarities may be found, eventually enabling computational comparisons of stories rather than texts. Such an approach could, for example, be useful in digital humanities with researchers already experimenting with word embeddings to identify and compare adaptations of the same story (Glass, 2022). Our approach to modeling narratives constitutes a continuous and embedding-based approach to schemas like Propp's model of Russian folklore (Propp, 1968). The chain-based approach has the upside of allowing for abstracting over information that is not relevant to the actual narrative, but that will be captured by more recent semantic embedding methods like SentenceBERT (Reimers and Gurevych, 2019). The method's potential downside, however, as discussed by Wilner et al. (2021) is that too much contextual information is lost, making the task of predicting triples ambiguous or impossible. Through the use of contextual embeddings and an optional additional re-contextualization process, they improve on existing narrative cloze results by using additional information. Our ultimate goal of this work is to enable embedding-based computational narrative similarity comparisons of texts, a task we see as closely related but not identical to the popular narrative generation field (see e.g. Gervás, 2021).

The three key contributions of this work are **(1)** a dataset of German narrative chains and **(2)** the application of narrative embeddings to a down-stream task in the form of replicating human narrative similarity judgments, as well as **(3)** state-of-the-art models on English and German for narrative chains without external information from contextual embeddings.

Proceedings of the The 5th Workshop on Narrative Understanding, pages 118–127
July 14, 2023 ©2023 Association for Computational Linguistics

2 Background

To evaluate the capability of our embeddings in recognizing similar narratives, we rely on comparisons to human annotations. Conceptual work on text similarity (Bär et al., 2011) pointed out that text similarity is not inherently well defined by showing that, without further instructions, some annotators focus strictly on content, whereas others additionally take the text's structure into account. Accordingly, our task calls for a dataset that explicitly annotates narrative schema similarity. Chen et al. (2022a) introduced such a dataset in the form of a multilingual news similarity dataset containing the similarity of news article pairs along seven dimensions. According to their annotation code book (Chen et al., 2022b), dimensions are to be rated independently of each other, with the *narrative* dimensions focusing on similarity in narrative schemas as defined by Chambers and Jurafsky (2009); the dataset thus contains human ratings of schema similarity.

Since its inception, the narrative cloze task has seen work in different directions. Chambers (2017) has criticized newer approaches to the task as deviating from its original formulation, focusing on extracted events in text order rather than manually annotated ones; they emphasize that the automated approach is much more aligned with the capabilities of language models. Wilner et al. (2021) approach the narrative cloze task but reformulate it to use contextual embeddings instead of verb lemmas. While this approach yields much higher accuracies and can help disambiguate events, we feel that in the light of modeling narrative disjointly from the surface form, such contextual embeddings would potentially hamper the model's performance in any downstream application.

In the narrative cloze task, the model is asked to predict a masked triple describing an event. In practice, this is a four-tuple of the subject, verb, indirect object, and object in more recent implementations like the one by (Granroth-Wilding and Clark, 2016). Evaluation has, as suggested by Granroth-Wilding and Clark (2016), in the recent past been performed in a MCNC (multiple choice narrative cloze) setup where the model is asked to pick the most fitting triple for a corresponding masked triple in a chain given exactly 5 options that are randomly sampled from the entire corpus. This evaluation setup was introduced to enable more interpretable results and pays tribute to the fact that, in most cases, the exact triple is ambiguous not just by virtue of synonymous verb lemmas but also due to contextual ambiguity.

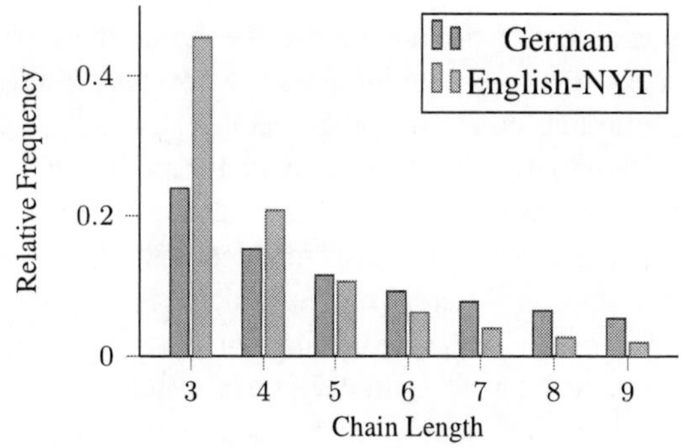

Figure 1: Relative distribution of chain lengths our German dataset compared to the English NYT dataset

The work by Granroth-Wilding and Clark (2016) discusses multiple models, with the best score being achieved by a model that calculates the compatibility of a given candidate triple by averaging across its compatibility (as scored by a neural model) with all other elements of the chain.

3 Datasets

We use the Gigaword dataset with the preprocessing pipeline presented by Granroth-Wilding and Clark (2016). In addition, we build a German dataset based on scraped German news data. The data is extracted using a German coreference resolution system by Schröder et al. (2021) and dependency parsing from SpaCy (Honnibal et al., 2020). We produce a dataset of around 1.8×10^6 German narrative chains; we filter out any chains shorter than three at dataset creation time. Compared to the approximately 5.7×10^6 chains with a length of at least three in the Gigaword-derived dataset, this is a relatively small collection but still allows us to explore the adaption to a different language.

While we rely on the intrinsic MCNC evaluation for comparison to existing work, for assessing the use for narrative modeling, we need a downstream evaluation, and only limited data is available for this purpose. The multilingual news-similarity SemEval dataset (Chen et al., 2022a) is, at first sight, a great fit; the pairs of articles making up the dataset are each annotated with regard to their similarity along seven specific dimensions, with each being dimension scored on a scale of 1–4. The dataset's *narrative* dimension is, however, highly (ρ=.88) correlated with its *overall* dimensions, meaning that when articles are narratively similar, they are likely to also be similar in a general sense. It may seem that, due to this alignment in similarity, no differentiation needs to be made for modeling the two dimensions, but we believe this difference is crucial in identifying texts that deal with the same narrative in different circumstances. This difference may also be interesting for other domains, especially narrative literary texts, where the correlation may, in practice, not be as high. In these texts, two scenes telling a similar narrative may not share any concrete entities; for example, the circumstances of two arguments between multiple characters may be entirely different with different surroundings and differently named characters, yet share some conceptual similarity. As the *overall* dimension can be modeled well using existing text similarity models, however, it seems unlikely that our approach based on narrative chains will be able to outperform existing models for the news domain. Still, we employ the dataset as a testbed for extrinsic evaluation for the narrative cloze task.

We make all our extracted chains, the ones from the NYT dataset, our German dataset, and the SemEval dataset, available for download to enable further research. [1]

4 Experimental Setup

To enable some comparison with prior work, we replicate the testing setup by Granroth-Wilding and Clark (2016) wherever possible. In this section, we discuss the specifics of the task and provide an embedding baseline for our downstream evaluation.

4.1 Task Details

Various evaluation details for the MCNC are not clearly defined; subsequently, we discuss the parameters we chose as well as their impact on the evaluation.

Minimum Chain Length: Chambers and Jurafsky (2008) only consider chains of a length of at least five triples. While Granroth-Wilding and Clark (2016) do not explicitly discuss this parameter but seem to also apply a limit, the exact value is not known to us; in the implementation, a default value of 9 is present. A minimum length limit seems reasonable as (a) predicting lemmas in chains of length one is largely up to chance, and (b) an actual story is likely told with multiple events. In line with (a), we found the choice for this evaluation parameter to have a fairly large impact on our results; for example, using the minimum chain lengths 9, 5, and 3 resulted in the accuracy dropping from 50.21 to 49.08 and 48.48 respectively for a variant of our static embedding model on the dev set. Choosing a specific value is, to some degree, an arbitrary decision; for comparability, we adopt the choice of a minimum chain length of 9 in our experiments.

Minimum Lemma Count: With this parameter, verb lemmas below a certain absolute count are removed from the training and evaluation data. Due to the long-tail nature of verb lemma count distributions, many verbs occur very infrequently in the input. In preliminary experiments, we found this to have some impact on the results; it is not clear which threshold was chosen in previous work. We do not employ this filtering step and instead use all verb lemmas that occur in the dataset.

Maximum Lemma Count: In previous work, "stop events" have been used to refer to the process of excluding verbs that occur too often. Rather than picking a specific threshold in terms of count, Granroth-Wilding and Clark (2016) used the top ten most frequent verbs. We found this filtering criterion helpful for model convergence (otherwise, the very frequent lemmas would dominate others). While "see" or "go" are not stop words in the traditional sense (i.e., they do carry semantic information in a text), in the context of our chains, in the news domain, they could conceivably occur in any chain at any point and do not bear any information content.

Chain vs. Schema-based: Evaluation can either be performed on the basis of entire narrative schemas, i.e., multiple chains that share common participants or on the individual chain. In this work, we operate on individual chains making the multiple choice task, at least in theory, harder than in full-schema scenarios.

Mention Surface Forms: Including the surface form of entities means including the concrete form of each entity mention in the triple. Consider the short chain (A, gives, B) (B, write, C) and compare it with a version including surface forms (A: source, give, B: reporter) (B: reporter, write, C: article). Here predicting the second verb is difficult with no entity surface forms given, but once entity information is present, the task becomes manageable. In an open prediction task without multiple choices, the solution only becomes relatively un-

[1] https://ltdata1.informatik.uni-hamburg.de/narrative-chains/

ambiguous when the surface form "article" is also given.

Candidate Triples: Another important parameter is the makeup of the triples the model is asked to choose from in the MCNC evaluation. In terms of candidate triple selection, Granroth-Wilding and Clark (2016) randomly sample from all triples in the dataset, as setup which we follow. The second aspect is whether the whole triple is presented as a candidate solution, which is largely the case in prior work, although Wilner et al. (2021) also consider a verb only variant. It is clear that with actual full text for the events (i.e., the mention's surface forms), the prediction is trivial in many cases, as entity names are usually unique within the five presented choices. For this reason, we only mask the verb in our experiments (except for when explicitly stated in the case of the T5 model, see below), sampling four random verb lemmas from the dataset as the distractors in the MCNC task.

4.2 Downstream Evaluation and Baseline

We perform the extrinsic evaluation on narrative similarity (using the dataset by Chen et al., 2022a) by means of embedding similarity. To align with their evaluation and following a substantial number of submitted systems in their shared task, we embed each document independently and compute the cosine similarities.

Model	Dataset	Overall	Dimension Narrative	Entity
All Verbs	EN	49.40	**50.02**	50.58
All Words	EN	43.12	43.37	44.10
Chain Verbs	EN	19.99	19.21	14.03
Chain Mean	EN	12.65	11.09	6.63
Transformer[2]	EN	81.78	**78.16**	83.76
Chain Verbs	DE	44.81	**48.49**	41.07
Chain Mean	DE	24.56	19.12	17.91

Table 1: Correlation of cosine distance of fastText embeddings with the dimensions *overall* and *narrative* on the English evaluation split of Chen et al. (2022a), with a sentence transformer model provided as a comparison.

As a weak baseline for comparing narratives, we introduce a word embedding-based comparison. For simplicity, we only consider those pairs where both articles are written in our model's language (either English or German). On the English and German sections of the news similarity evaluation

Embeddings	MCNC
FastText-German	**31.23**
Muse-German	25.04
BPEmb	30.19

Table 2: Comparing embedding sources on the German dev set. No mention surface forms are used.

data, we compute fastText (Bojanowski et al., 2017) embeddings of all words, all verbs, and then of all the verbs included in the narrative chains. The best results were achieved using a word-level best-match approach, following BertScore's (Zhang et al., 2020) token similarity matching. For comparison, we also provide a method where this matching is done on the mean of the verb embeddings of individual chains and, therefore, a chain best match approach. Table 1 shows that these approaches lack far behind a sentence encoder baseline and that while a focus on verbs helps, especially concerning the *narrative* dimension, the limitation of only including the verbs that are part of narrative chains as extracted by Granroth-Wilding and Clark (2016) pipeline severely impacts the results. We can observe that, for the German evaluation split, the results are generally much better than for the English data. We attribute this to the improved extraction pipeline. Note that we discard all pairs where either document has no extracted chains; unlike in the German training dataset, even chains of a length below three are retained. Taking only the verb embeddings clearly outperforms the variant that considers all words; we do not even see a clear effect concerning the narrative dimension being represented better by this setup. Given these initial results, it seems possible that the "all verbs" embedding baseline will not be outperformed. Nevertheless, it remains interesting to see if the narrative cloze task can prioritize the narrative dimension over others.

5 Model Setup and Architecture

We present a neural model that, using static word embeddings as input features, performs state-of-the-art narrative cloze prediction.[3] To provide an additional point of comparison, we build a baseline based on modern techniques, specifically the T5 (Raffel et al., 2020) architecture and training setup.

[2]We use all-mpnet-base-v2 from Reimers and Gurevych (2019).

[3]Implementation: `https://github.com/uhh-lt/narrative-chain-embeddings`

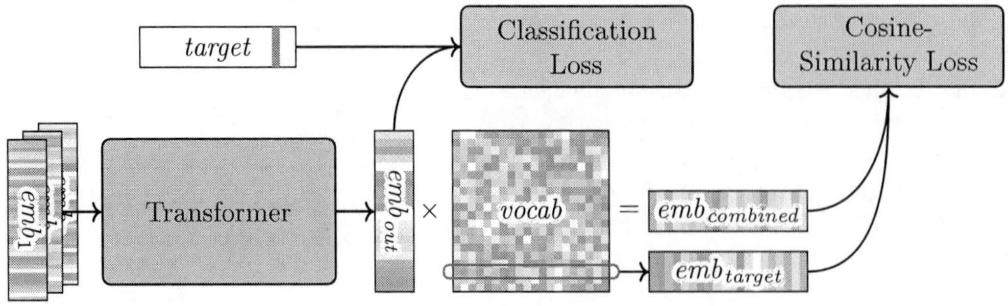

Figure 2: In our model architecture, we improve training using a linear combination of embeddings in the output vocabulary.

5.1 Static Embedding Approach

We model narrative sequences using a fixed-sized context of surrounding triples. Our model is a transformer that makes use of static embeddings of individual words as the input (cf. Fig 2), unlike Granroth-Wilding and Clark (2016), we do not train static embeddings based just on verbs but instead rely on existing embeddings trained on entire texts. We take a twofold approach to entity representation, allowing both word embeddings of entity surface forms as well as identity one-hot-encodings that remain consistent inside of a specific chain. These entity representations are concatenated with the verb lemma's embedding to form our model's input embedding for each triple. The training objective, inspired by masked-language-modeling, has the model predict one verb lemma at a time. Due to the long tail distribution of verb lemmas, we need a fairly large but manageable output vocabulary of $\approx$7500 words for the English Gigaword-based dataset.

Our model approaches the task as a classification task at inference time, in that the output is a probability distribution across the vocabulary. To improve convergence, we train on a cosine distance objective; the loss function is a cosine-similarity-based embedding loss, comparing the output-distribution-weighted average of the classes' word embeddings with the gold class's corresponding word embedding. The more straightforward approach of using a cross-entropy classification loss did not produce adequate results. During training, we do not update any parameters in the system creating the embeddings. We expect that the embedding loss allows us to learn better from ambiguous training examples, as the embeddings of semantically similar verbs will also have a smaller cosine distance. For extrinsic evaluation, we use the emb_{out} embedding, the output state of the transformer.

In terms of embedding sources, Table 2 shows a minimal difference between BPEmb (Heinzerling and Strube, 2018) and FastText for German, making BPEmb an interesting choice and possibly enabling cross-lingual knowledge transfer.

For all presented training runs on the static embedding approach, we use the same set of manually optimized hyperparameters: a dropout chance of 0.2, a learning rate of 1×10^{-3} , and the one cycle learning rate scheduler (Smith and Topin, 2019). The scheduler increases the learning rate for the first 30 epochs, slowly decreasing it afterwards. In practice, early stopping finished most runs shortly before or after reaching the maximum learning rate.

5.2 Langauge Model Approach

For comparison, we employ a state-of-the-art language model in the form of T5, converting chains into textual representations of the form `(subj, verb lemma, iobj, obj)`, where subject, object, and indirect object each come with a unique identifier and the mention's surface form. We use the tiny variant of T5 with randomly initialized weights with a custom tokenizer trained on our dataset. Our implementation is based on an existing training script, meaning the masking is not limited to verbs but instead to random tokens in the input.

For the MCNC task, we align the inference with T5's denoising training objective by masking a single event and comparing the likelihood of all multiple-choice options as generated outputs. Embeddings are created by using the last encoder state of the T5 model.

Setup	MCNC
Full Model	**52.00**
+ classification loss	48.29
+ classification loss - embedding loss	25.04
- mention surface forms	50.21
- mention surface forms - FastText + BPEmb	49.78

Table 3: Ablation study for our model on the English dev set with our static embedding approach, + and - indicate added and removed model options, respectively.

Dataset	Entity String	Model	MCNC-Accuracy
Ours (German)	✗	Ours	30.66
Gigaword-Verb	✓	Ours	**50.89**
	✗	Ours	49.06
	✗	T5-based	28.01
Gigaword-Triple	✓	T5-based	**92.33**
	✓	G&C (2016)	49.57
Gigaword-Context	✗[4]	W,W&G (2021)	92.22

Table 4: MCNC results on the Gigaword NYT and our own dataset show that our models outperform previous approaches in the same setup.

6 Results

In Table 3, we report the impact of different parameters on our model. In terms of embeddings, FastText slightly outperforms BPEmb by .43 percentage points but does not provide any multilingual capabilities. Additionally, the impact of mentions' surface forms is only 1.79 percentage points, making it potentially viable to exclude them, thereby increasing the model's focus on the narrative over the mentioned entities. For the choice of loss functions, it is clear that the embedding loss performs much better than the classification-based loss on its own by a large margin of 26.96 percentage points; even the combination of both performs appreciably worse than the embedding loss on its own.

We did not find success with reusing weights, from our BPEmb setup, from one language in the other but did not experiment with multi-task learning to handle both languages at once.

Table 4 shows that our model outperforms previous approaches in the MCNC setting with a minimum chain length of nine, outperforming approaches in the same setup by more than 1.8 percentage points. Further, it shows that the inclusion of entity surface forms enables the T5 model to perform incredibly well at over 92% accuracy, making it ostensibly outperform the best models by Wilner et al. (2021), which uses contextual representations. Their evaluation setup may, however, differ in terms of minimum chain length, making this comparison an unclear one. It is to be noted that the Gigword-Triple models are asked to predict the entire triple of arguments rather than just the verb lemma, as is the case for the other models. As supported by the much worse performance of the T5 model without access to entity strings (a drop by over 60 percentage points), we strongly suspect that the T5 model is only looking for compatible mentions and will often only find one such option in the five choices presented. We manually confirmed that this strategy works in the majority of cases. The performance compared to that of the Granroth-Wilding and Clark (2016) model can be explained by the fact that this model only compares pairs of triples, averaging across their coherence scores, and can thus not look for mention compatibility globally in the entire chain. Overall, removing entity surface forms leads the T5 model to underperform drastically, whereas our static-embedding-based model only suffers a minor performance penalty. As previously discussed, we suspect this setup may lead to more meaningful narrative modeling.

[4]While the model does not explicitly use the mention's surface forms, they are captured by the verb's contextual embedding.

Model	Dimension		
	Overall	Narrative	Entity
Ours (no surface forms)	11.06	16.68	10.82
+ shuffle	11.33	**17.18**	10.65
- entities	8.76	11.83	7.26
Ours German	25.78	23.64	21.64
+ shuffle	25.71	**23.94**	21.55
- entities	26.74	23.66	21.73
English T5 model	13.17	**9.95**	10.13
+ entity surface forms	5.69	2.53	6.05

Table 5: The extrinsic evaluation on the news similarity dataset is evaluated using Pearson correlation of embedding distances with human judgments.

As a downstream evaluation of our embeddings, in Table 5, we use them to predict the narrative similarity as annotated by humans in the multilingual news similarity dataset (Chen et al., 2022a). Our results clearly show that narrative chains fail to be a good model of narrative, with our results on static embeddings indicating that the loss of context is, at least in part, at fault. Table 5 further supports our explanation of T5's overperformance; rather than focusing on semantic aspects of the chain, T5 appears to focus on matching mention surface forms, which is reflected in its very low performance on the extrinsic evaluation.

After qualitative analysis, we suspected that our model might only be a topic model of sorts that considers the domain of verbs rather than any sequential nature of them. This is supported by the fact that it is overall still comparable in MCNC performance with the coherence based Granroth-Wilding and Clark (2016) model. Further news articles often do not tell happenings in their chronological order while our extraction pipelines rely on text order, meaning that the order does not necessarily follow logical sequences of actions. We test this hypothesis of no sequential understanding in Table 5 by shuffling the triple sequence. We find that both models perform slightly better with shuffling on this specific data (although only by a margin of up to 0.5 percentage points), proving that there is, in fact, no reliance on ordering information. Interestingly, removing entities (meaning identity information in the form of one-hot encoding rather than surface forms in case) has a much larger impact of ≈ 5 percentage points on the results for the English dataset. This is in line with our findings in manual prediction experiments on the MCNC task, where we found a good strategy to be the compatibility of actions of a given entity (e.g., someone who "raises" may also "announce" or "purchase" but probably will not "live"). The effect of entities having a large effect on the results is, however, not seen in the German data, indicating that it may take a different approach to narrative modeling. Overall the German model exhibits better performance, which may be attributed to the different extraction pipelines, which already produced better results in Table 1; in fact, the German model is the only one that outperforms one of its baselines, the "Chain Mean" variant by a margin of ≈ 4 percentage points on the narrative dimension. This is surprising, given that it performed much worse than the other variants on the MCNC, casting doubt on the usefulness of narrative cloze evaluation, at least in this specific setup.

6.1 Silhouette Scores

To further inspect the model, we analyze the produced embeddings in terms of their cluster-

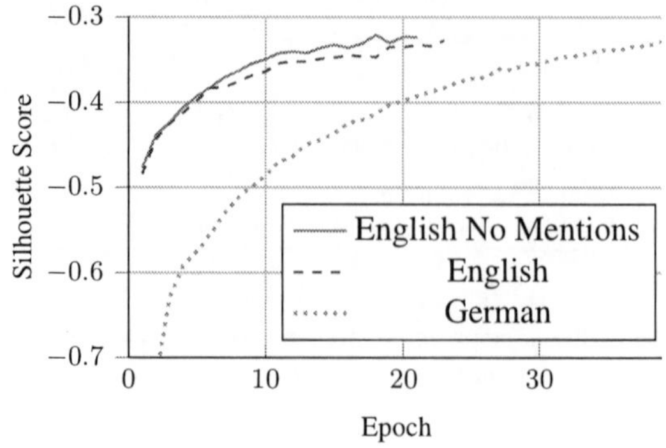

Figure 3: Silhouette scores of three models keep improving throughout training, indicating that verb lemmas are increasingly separated throughout the training process.

ing. Specifically, we make use of the silhouette score (Rousseeuw, 1987), a cluster evaluation metric, to assess how well-separated individual verb lemmas are. The embeddings are created by masking an individual lemma and taking the corresponding predicted output representation. The silhouette score can take values from -1 to 1, where each of the extremes means the data points are perfectly mixed and perfectly separated. To be clear, we do not expect a perfect performance from either method here, as polysemous verbs mean that the same lemma should not always receive the same embedding while (due to synonyms) different lemmas may take the same embedding form; a comparison across models may, however, provide additional insights.

Figure 3 illustrates that, in all runs, the silhouette scores steadily improve. For the German dataset, it is expected that convergence takes more epochs due to the smaller training set, but it is surprising that the silhouette score ends up at -0.33, equivalent to both English runs at -0.33 and -0.32, despite the much worse performance of the models on the MCNC task. This result further supports the idea that the narrative cloze task, in its current form, may not be a perfect approximation of narrative modeling capabilities.

6.2 Qualitative Exploration

For insights into the model's performance, we manually assess its output. First, we ask the English model (without mention surface forms) to predict the lemma in a triple of two participants. The model outputs the following lemmas: "join", "win", and "support". Interestingly, this is not in line with the most common lemmas ("think", "play", and "call", after filtering stop-lemmas), which may be explained by short chains having different content than longer ones.

The chain (A, kill, B), (C, catch, A), (D, _, A), where the underscore denotes a masked lemma, results in the following top three lemmas predicted in descending order of probability: "hit", "find", "face". If we add the information that we are in a judicial context by adding (D, sentence, A) to the end of the chain, we get the following list of lemmas instead: "shoot", "kill", "catch". While these lemmas are more compatible with the domain, it seems unlikely that the same entity sentencing the subject would also shoot or kill them, indicating that the identity information of entities does not have a large effect.

We test if the ordering can, in extreme cases, affect the outcome using the following chain: (A, hug, B), (A, insult, B), (A, _, B). In this chain, changing the order of "hug" and "insult" leads to the lemmas "kiss" and "hit" changing their order in terms of model score, with "hit" receiving the higher score when "insult" comes directly before it. This reversal indicates that some ordering information is present in the model even though it is not conducive to narrative embeddings (as evidenced by the results in Table 5). We observe the same behavior in the German model using a translation of the above chain.

The examples illustrate the natural ambiguity created by removing most contextual information, an effect that likely places an upper limit on MCNC performance. The fact that ordering information is used to check the compatibility is a promising sign that some narrative understanding may be present in our model that goes beyond the best-performing approach by Granroth-Wilding and Clark (2016), which does not take order into account.

7 Conclusion

In this work, we presented models with state-of-the-art MCNC performance in two different setups and on German and English datasets. We produced vector embeddings as narrative representations and performed extrinsic evaluations of our narrative cloze models using the comparison to human narrative similarity ratings. In a qualitative review of our model outputs, we illustrated that the model captures sequential information. The performance of our embeddings indicates that narrative-cloze may not be a perfect fit for narrative similarity modeling; on the other hand, we were able to, in some scenarios, produce embeddings that model narrative similarity better than overall similarity, placing emphasis on the desired aspects of a text. In almost all cases, our models were also able to place less emphasis on entities than plain word embedding and especially sentence encoder models did. Overall, it can be concluded that limiting the model's access to information can help create embeddings that represent a specific aspect of the text.

It is also clear that in the current state, in almost all setups, our chain embeddings are outperformed even by static verb embeddings. We see two major roadblocks to applying this approach to the computational modeling of narratives. The first is the limited evaluation data: while the SemEval dataset by Chen et al. (2022a) is a step in the right direction, it fails to clearly demonstrate the need for narrative modeling as, in the news domain, dimensions are strongly correlated. A dataset on another domain is needed; this is something we seek to address in upcoming work.

The second is the actual quality of predictions. In preliminary annotation experiments, we were unable to perform on par with the predictions system. While further analysis is required, we suspect that this is attributable to the fact that the chains provide too little information.

8 Future Work

As we see the limited information as a crucial shortcoming of narrative chains, we will conduct further research in the direction of Wilner et al. (2021), using contextual embeddings and trying to explicitly remove information on the actors (e.g., by renaming them). In our opinion, the approach of narrative cloze in its original form is no longer a promising approach for building semantic representations of narratives. Avenues to improving the performance on the narrative cloze task still exist and go beyond improving the extraction process or the representation of individual events. An example of this may be exploiting the knowledge of pre-trained large language models, which we did not find success in preliminary experiments.

If the semantic modeling by means of extracted narrative chains was to be successful in the future, we suspect that a much-improved event representation would be needed. It may, however, be more promising to pursue alternative ways of modeling narratives, perhaps through the use of supervised narrative similarity data. Any supervised training on the text level will, however, need to deal with the effect that other similarity markers, such as common entity names, already are a strong indicator of narrative similarity. Such markers are not present during inference on unrelated texts sharing similar narratives.

Acknowledgements

This work was supported by the DFG through the project "Evaluating Events in Narrative Theory (EvENT)" (grant BI 1544/11-1) as part of the priority program "Computational Literary Studies (CLS)" (SPP 2207).

References

Daniel Bär, Torsten Zesch, and Iryna Gurevych. 2011. A Reflective View on Text Similarity. In *Proceedings of the International Conference Recent Advances in Natural Language Processing 2011*, pages 515–520, Hissar, Bulgaria. Association for Computational Linguistics.

Piotr Bojanowski, Edouard Grave, Armand Joulin, and Tomas Mikolov. 2017. Enriching word vectors with subword information. *Transactions of the Association for Computational Linguistics*, 5:135–146.

Nathanael Chambers. 2017. Behind the Scenes of an Evolving Event Cloze Test. In *Proceedings of the 2nd Workshop on Linking Models of Lexical, Sentential and Discourse-level Semantics*, pages 41–45, Valencia, Spain. Association for Computational Linguistics.

Nathanael Chambers and Dan Jurafsky. 2008. Unsupervised Learning of Narrative Event Chains. In *Proceedings of ACL-08: HLT*, pages 789–797, Columbus, Ohio, USA. Association for Computational Linguistics.

Nathanael Chambers and Dan Jurafsky. 2009. Unsupervised learning of narrative schemas and their participants. In *Proceedings of the Joint Conference of the 47th Annual Meeting of the ACL and the 4th International Joint Conference on Natural Language Processing of the AFNLP: Volume 2 - ACL-IJCNLP '09*, volume 2, pages 602–610, Suntec, Singapore. Association for Computational Linguistics.

Xi Chen, Ali Zeynali, Chico Camargo, Fabian Flöck, Devin Gaffney, Przemyslaw Grabowicz, Scott Hale, David Jurgens, and Mattia Samory. 2022a. SemEval-2022 Task 8: Multilingual news article similarity. In *Proceedings of the 16th International Workshop on Semantic Evaluation (SemEval-2022)*, pages 1094–1106, Seattle, Washington, USA. Association for Computational Linguistics.

Xi Chen, Ali Zeynali, Chico Q. Camargo, Fabian Flöck, Devin Gaffney, Przemyslaw A. Grabowicz, Scott A. Hale, David Jurgens, and Mattia Samory. 2022b. SemEval-2022 Task 8: Multilingual news article similarity: Codebook for text similarity annotations. URL: `https://zenodo.org/record/6507872`.

Pablo Gervás. 2021. Computational Models of Narrative Creativity. In Penousal Machado, Juan Romero, and Gary Greenfield, editors, *Artificial Intelligence and the Arts: Computational Creativity, Artistic Behavior, and Tools for Creatives*, pages 209–255. Springer International Publishing, Cham.

Grant Glass. 2022. An Adaptive Methodology: Machine Learning and Literary Adaptation. In *Digital Humanities. 2022 Combined Abstracts*, pages 210–212, Tokyo, Japan.

Mark Granroth-Wilding and Stephen Clark. 2016. What happens next? Event prediction using a compositional neural network model. In *Proceedings of the AAAI Conference on Artificial Intelligence*, pages 2727–2733, Phoenix, Arizona, USA.

Benjamin Heinzerling and Michael Strube. 2018. BPEmb: Tokenization-free pre-trained subword embeddings in 275 languages. In *Proceedings of the Eleventh International Conference on Language Resources and Evaluation (LREC 2018)*, pages 2989–2993, Miyazaki, Japan. European Language Resources Association (ELRA).

Matthew Honnibal, Ines Montani, Sofie Van Landeghem, and Adriane Boyd. 2020. spaCy: Industrial-strength Natural Language Processing in Python. Software Release, URL: `https://zenodo.org/record/7970450`.

Vladimir Iakovlevich Propp. 1968. *Morphology of the Folktale*, volume 9. University of Texas Press.

Colin Raffel, Noam Shazeer, Adam Roberts, Katherine Lee, Sharan Narang, Michael Matena, Yanqi Zhou, Wei Li, and Peter J. Liu. 2020. Exploring the limits of transfer learning with a unified text-to-text transformer. *The Journal of Machine Learning Research*, 21(1):140:5485–140:5551.

Nils Reimers and Iryna Gurevych. 2019. Sentence-BERT: Sentence embeddings using Siamese BERT-networks. In *Proceedings of the 2019 Conference on Empirical Methods in Natural Language Processing and the 9th International Joint Conference on Natural Language Processing (EMNLP-IJCNLP)*, pages 3982–3992, Hong Kong, China. Association for Computational Linguistics.

Peter J. Rousseeuw. 1987. Silhouettes: A graphical aid to the interpretation and validation of cluster analysis. *Journal of Computational and Applied Mathematics*, 20:53–65.

Fynn Schröder, Hans Ole Hatzel, and Chris Biemann. 2021. Neural End-to-end Coreference Resolution for German in Different Domains. In *Proceedings of the 17th Conference on Natural Language Processing (KONVENS 2021)*, pages 170–181, Düsseldorf, Germany. KONVENS 2021 Organizers.

Leslie N. Smith and Nicholay Topin. 2019. Super-convergence: very fast training of neural networks using large learning rates. In *Artificial Intelligence and Machine Learning for Multi-Domain Operations Applications*, volume 11006, Baltimore, Maryland, USA. International Society for Optics and Photonics, SPIE.

Sean Wilner, Daniel Woolridge, and Madeleine Glick. 2021. Narrative Embedding: Re-Contextualization Through Attention. In *Proceedings of the 2021 Conference on Empirical Methods in Natural Language Processing*, pages 1393–1405, Online and Punta Cana, Dominican Republic. Association for Computational Linguistics.

Tianyi Zhang, Varsha Kishore, Felix Wu, Kilian Q. Weinberger, and Yoav Artzi. 2020. BERTScore: Evaluating Text Generation with BERT. In *Eighth International Conference on Learning Representations*.

Author Index

Association for Computational Linguistics
209 N. Eighth Street
Stroudsburg, Pennsylvania 18360

ISBN 978-1-7138-8238-1

9 781713 882381